WONDERS OF THE PEAK DISTRICT

EXPLORING THE BRITISH ISLES

WONDERS OF THE PEAK DISTRICT

Published by The Reader's Digest Association Limited

LONDON • NEW YORK • SYDNEY • MONTREAL

ABOUT THIS BOOK

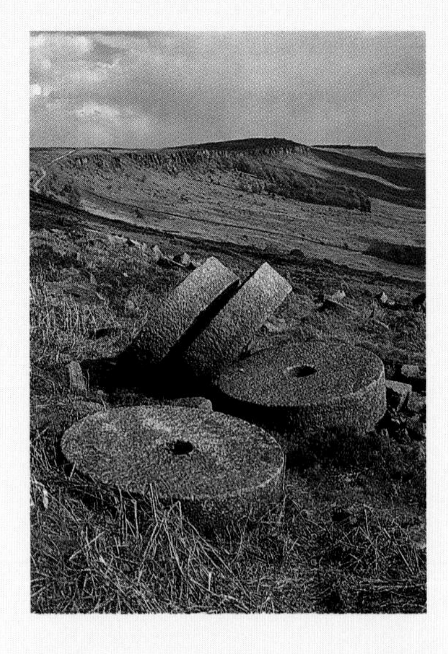

THE PEAK DISTRICT is a place of such rare beauty that in 1949 the heart of the region was designated Britain's first national park. Magnificent countryside—encompassing wooded valleys, meandering streams, gritstone crags and heather-covered moors—is bordered on all sides by bustling cities; indeed, it was the diversity of the Peak District that appealed to travel writer John Kahn, who introduces this book. Since the 16th century authors have argued over the pick of the Peaks; Kahn joins the debate by presenting his selection of the area's wonders—its abundant wildlife and amazing geology, its lavish architecture and fascinating industrial heritage.

The introduction is followed by the reminiscences of local author Roger Redfern, who shares his memories of life in the Peaks in a bygone age. A lifelong resident, Redfern conducts the reader through his world, and in his role as narrator of local stories and teacher of the region's history—industrial, natural and otherwise—he paints a vivid portrait of his beloved home country.

Wonders of the Peak District concludes with a 'Highlights' section, which will help those readers inspired to visit the Peaks to discover the delights of this fascinating region for themselves.

WONDERS OF THE PEAK DISTRICT was edited and designed by The Reader's Digest Association Limited, 11 Westferry Circus, Canary Wharf, London E14 4HE

Peakland Days Condensed from the original full-length versions of *Peakland Days* and *South Pennine Country* by Roger Redfern, first published by Robert Hale & Co, 1970 and 1979 respectively.

CONTRIBUTORS

Series Editor Steve Savage
Volume Editor Charlotte Rundall
Assistant Editor/Researcher Miriam Sharland
Associate Editors David Blomfield, Hugo de Klee
Copy Editors Morag Lyall, Barbara Roby
Editorial and Picture Research Assistant Kate Michell
Art Editor Karen Stewart
Designer Carl Meek
Picture Researcher Helen Ashford
Additional material and research by Anthony Burton, Nigel Foster, James Harpur, Lindsay Hunt, John Kahn, Tim Locke, Roly Smith
Cartography Anthony Sidwell (page 9), Malcolm Porter (pages 150–51)
Index Brian Amos

FRONT COVER *A commanding view of the moors can be had from the Salt Cellar outcrop on Derwent Edge.*
BACK COVER (TOP) *The Emperor Fountain is one of the most eye-catching features on the Chatsworth Estate.*
BACK COVER (BOTTOM) *A brave caver emerges from the murky depths of Blue John Cavern.*
TITLE PAGE *Kinder Downfall is a dramatic sight—and a challenge to ice climbers—when frozen in winter.*

THIS PAGE *Abandoned millstones, symbols of a once-thriving local industry, lie on Stanage Edge.*
PAGES 6–7 *From Mam Tor a pathway entices walkers to seek ever-changing viewpoints.*
PAGES 24–5 *The village of Taddington in Derbyshire nestles at the head of the dale that takes its name.*
PAGES 148–9 *Schoolchildren gaze awestruck at the geological wonders of Poole's Cavern in Buxton.*

CONTENTS

EXPLORING
THE PEAK DISTRICT

with John Kahn

EXPLORING

THE PEAK DISTRICT

with John Kahn

WITH THE RUINS of Peveril Castle glowering down from the hilltop above, I strolled out of Castleton town centre into spectacular Cave Dale. It was the last day of my recent trip to the Peak District, and the walk would make a fine lingering farewell. A long, curving hike round to the aptly named Windy Knoll, a last stiff climb, and I was on the top of Mam Tor, stepping over the Iron Age earthworks and striding along the grassy ridge. Battered by the wind but enraptured by the views radiating in all directions, I had the chance to look back on a memorable week of travels.

To get to Castleton that morning, I'd hopped on the free shuttle bus from Edale station, and to get there I'd earlier caught the local train from my base at Hathersage. The Hope Valley railway line runs between Sheffield and Manchester, and is a blessing for visitors wishing to avoid the weekend traffic congestion. It was the railways that, in a sense, created the Peak District—gave it the status, that is, that it still enjoys in the public imagination: a refuge from the harsh and squalid life of industrial cities; a haven of calm in the tempestuous modern world. For over a century now, the trains have been granting working men and women the great escape they crave at weekends—away from the cramped backstreets into the sunny and airy expanses of nature. If the 'heart of England' lies somewhat farther south, the Peak District could reasonably claim to be its lungs.

Not that the region was lacking industries of its own. It teemed with mills and mines and quarries. But they remained fairly unobtrusive, being well spaced out, or just well hidden, and the impression persisted of an unspoilt land, a kind of Eden. Relative to the factory towns and potteries roaring and groaning on its borders, no doubt it was.

And it still is, though the contrast is nothing like as stark as it used to be. On the one hand, Manchester and Sheffield are for most of their residents vastly pleasanter places to live in today than they were 100 years ago; and on the other, the Peak District is a vastly busier place than it used to be, with tourism now virtually a heavy industry there, and cars—endless cars—having long ago overtaken the trains as the weekenders' preferred mode of transport.

Yet the magical feel of the place persists. Your cares seem to fall away, and all the wrong turnings that life has taken seem never to have happened.

A NAME TO CONJURE WITH

Part of the exhilarating character of the region derives from its location. Some 20 million people, it is estimated—more than a third of Britain's population—live within an hour's drive of it. On a map it looks like a redoubt under siege, gallantly defying the encircling encampments on its margins: not just Sheffield and Manchester, but Oldham and Barnsley and Huddersfield too in the north, and Nottingham, Derby and Stoke-on-Trent on the southern flank.

In keeping with its debonair disposition, the Peak District has no clearly defined borders. The Peak District National Park (which does have precise borders) makes no claim to cover the Peak District as a whole. Nor does Derbyshire: although its northern and central reaches certainly embrace most of the Peak District, five neighbouring counties or metropolitan authorities have a share as well.

A first-time visitor might expect the Peak District to abound in peaks, and be puzzled at the shortage of them. The highest summit in the region has the suggestive name of Kinder Low, and stands at a very modest 2,088 feet. Certainly there are plenty of hilltops, and soaring cliffs, and craggy 'edges', and prominent rock outcrops, but very little in the way of Alp-like pinnacles of the kind that the word 'peak' usually suggests: just a few tapering rock pillars, such as Ilam Rock and Pickering Tor in Dove Dale; and a total of exactly four sharp-pointed hills, including Shutlingsloe, a miniature Matterhorn out in the west of the region near Wildboarclough.

The scarcity of Peak District peaks is not quite as paradoxical as it sounds. The 'Peak' of the Peak District seems to derive from the name of a tribe inhabiting the Castleton area in Anglo-Saxon times, the 'Pecsaetnas' or 'Peaksattans' (the 'peak' element possibly meaning 'hill'), whose territory became known as 'Peakland' and eventually 'the Peak'.

At all events, peaks are conspicuously missing in the Peak District, but they are hardly missed. There are glories and wonders enough.

To enumerate these wonders is to join a long-established tradition. The 'Seven Wonders of the Peak' seems to have been the idea of Michael Drayton, a poet contemporary with Shakespeare. In a verse portrait of England, he nominated three caverns, two wells or springs, a forest, and 'Sandy Hill'—the very same mountain, Mam Tor, that I was traversing on my final walk. Ben Jonson, the playwright, also assessed the candidates. The philosopher Thomas Hobbes endorsed most of Drayton's choices, the main adjustment being to replace the Peak Forest with Chatsworth House, the home of the Cavendish family (who were, by pure coincidence of course, Hobbes's patrons).

In due course, Daniel Defoe mocked most of the wonders previously nominated, and in effect dismissed the entire debate. He had a point, though not, to my mind, in the way he imagined. To identify seven sites as the wonders of the Peak District is just too neat, and bound to provoke a dispute anyway. Above all, it does the region such an injustice. As if its wondrous sites number no more than seven!

ABOVE *A reconstruction of the 7th-century Benty Grange Helmet, which might have belonged to a local king.*

RIGHT *A miniature of Michael Drayton, whose poem* Poly-Olbion *celebrates the 'Seven Wonders of the Peak'.*

The trick, it occurs to me, is to avoid being so specific and take a much wider-ranging view: to choose seven broad themes or topics, rather than seven individual highlights, as the region's seven wonders. Here's my choice, then.

WONDROUS PANORAMAS

The first of these wonders has to be the landscape in general, which is far more varied than it is often given credit for. Fair-sized lakes—artificial reservoirs for the most part, but tending to blend convincingly into their surroundings—notably the three linked reservoirs in Derwent Dale in the north (where the Dambusters raid was rehearsed during the Second World War, and where the film version of it was later shot). Valued woodlands, in the Bakewell vicinity for example. Sensational gorges with sheer, soaring limestone cliffs, such as those in Chee Dale and outside Matlock. Dizzying mountain passes, such as Snake Pass and the Winnats. On the northern moors, cloughs—austere steep-sided valleys—and groughs—deep trenches or drainage gullies winding through the peat bogs. A startling hidden chasm, in the form of Lud's Church, a secret meeting place for religious dissenters in the 14th and 15th centuries, and reputedly one of Robin Hood's occasional hiding places. And a splendid waterfall, after good rains, in the form of Kinder Downfall.

These are all embellishments or variations on the landscape's general pattern: two ancient, interlocking plateaus, both lifted high in places by geological pressure, and both carved by rivers or glacial water in varying degrees—the Dark Peak in the north, east and west; and the White Peak in the centre and south. Marking the boundary between them is a broken curtain of eroded cliffs draped over the edge of the Dark Peak, often descending into deep shale valleys.

ABOVE *Kinder Downfall, where the water is often blown back up the rocks by the wind.*

The Dark Peak is a wide, upland arc of gritstone, like an inverted horseshoe; in the White Peak, lying within this arc and to its south, the bedrock consists of limestone, gentler in tone and colour.

Typifying the White Peak are the lush valleys and sunny hillsides of the delightful Derbyshire dales—Dove Dale, Miller's Dale, Lathkill Dale—and their leafy villages, quiet pathways, rippling streams and occasional stunning limestone cliffs.

Typifying the Dark Peak are flat, often boggy, tracts of moorland, with those forbidding rock valances sliding down at its perimeters—Curbar Edge, Stanage Edge, Derwent Edge... Beloved of rock climbers, this fractured escarpment is equally alluring to sightseers. The view of it, from below, is as dramatic in its way as the view from it, down over the miles of rolling countryside beneath.

The gritstone of the Dark Peak is a hard, coarse sandstone, formerly used for making grindstones or millstones. Traces of that old industry still litter various hillsides. Take a walk on Stanage Edge, near Hathersage, for instance, and you will find many half-completed or near-completed millstones lying forlorn, like giant fossilised chariot wheels, among the rocks from which they were being chiselled.

The most prolific carvers of the gritstone are, of course, the wind, ice and rain, and their works are widely exhibited, on the most popular cliff tops and the remotest moors alike—eerie, corrugated obelisks twisting up from the ground, looking like colossal fungi, or the handiwork of some mad modern sculptor: Eagle Stone on Froggatt Edge; the Salt Cellar on Derwent Edge; the Boxing Gloves on Kinder Scout; and the Kissing Stones on Bleaklow.

As for the limestone of the White Peak, it often erodes in the reverse way, to create craters, clefts—and caverns.

LEFT *Curbar Edge, composed of hard gritstone, proves irresistible to climbers, who enjoy one of the finest views in the Peak.*

OPPOSITE *The limestone crags of Bunster Hill, seen here from the top of Thorpe Cloud, are typical of the rock formations of Dove Dale.*

AN OTHERWORLDLY UNDERWORLD

The second of my seven Peak District wonders, then, is its set of 'show caves'. The White Peak's limestone sheet—laid down about 330 million years ago in a shallow tropical sea—has been rasped by subterranean streams and gnawed at by the dilute carbonic acid in rainwater. Over the millennia, it has in some places taken on the texture of a Swiss cheese. The region is a paradise for potholers, but most visitors will content themselves with the show caves—the more accessible, commercially developed cave complexes.

ABOVE *In the Poached Egg Chamber at Poole's Cavern, iron oxide has stained stalagmites a yellowy-orange colour.*

A disproportionate number of them lie in the vicinity of Castleton. Each has its unique characteristics. Peak Cavern, for instance, burrowing beneath Peveril Castle, has a gaping vestibule, one of the widest cave mouths in Europe. In Speedwell Cavern you glide by boat along a flooded mining tunnel to an awesome cathedral-like chamber and its supposedly bottomless lake. The Treak Cliff Cavern, with its dazzling array of stalactites and stalagmites, has for 250 years been the haunt of miners, chipping away at seams of the brittle mineral Blue John, a rare and colourful form of fluorspar. The term 'Blue John' is a corruption of the epithet given it by French importers, '*bleu et jaune*', meaning 'blue and yellow'.

My own favourite show cave, however, lies well to the south of these, in Buxton. Poole's Cavern acquired its name in the 15th century, in honour of a legendary outlaw called Poole, who adopted it as his hide-out. Not that he was by any means its first occupant. Prehistoric tribesmen used it as a shelter for 3,000 years. And the Romans probably used it as a place of worship. The guided tour of today is a very different affair from the version that visitors (such as Drayton and Hobbes) would have enjoyed in previous centuries. No more crawling or slithering from chamber to chamber, no more guttering candles to illuminate (and cover with soot) the cave's breathtaking natural treasures. The path has been smoothed, and electric lighting installed. At one stage, you can gaze 500 feet along the main river passage, the longest vista in any British show cave. Nothing can prepare you for the diversity of the cave's calcite adornments. Some are stained purple-grey by manganese in the water, and some orange by iron oxide. As for their range of shapes, consider the formations' names: Elephant's Head and Frozen Waterfall, for instance; or the Font and the Flitch of Bacon, a stalagmite and stalactite respectively, each over six feet in length.

In its remoter recesses the cave is home to a colony of bats—three different species of them, in fact. You're unlikely to see these nocturnal tenants, however, as they tend to appear when human visitors are safely above ground.

WILDLIFE IN THE PEAKS

The rich diversity of fauna and flora is the third of my Peak District wonders. Though most of the other Peakland mammals are just as elusive as the bats—the foxes and badgers, shrews and stoats, wood mice, water voles and even the hares—the bird life and plant life are on open display, and a never-ending treat to observe.

ABOVE *In spring, delicate wood anemones carpet the woodland floor.*

The White Peak's primeval forests of oak, ash and alder, on the tops, sides and bottoms of the dales respectively, with their wolves and bears and beavers, were extensively cleared in the Bronze Age, making way for grasslands and heath lands, and, later on, farmland. But the ash and alder woods are still present to some extent, especially in the Derbyshire Dales National Nature Reserve, made up of Lathkill Dale and five other limestone dales. Time your visit to the ash woods right, and a glorious scene of lilies of the valley, perhaps, or wood anemones, yellow archangel or wood sorrel, will be spread out in your honour. The bird population, whether full-time or migrant, is prized by amateur naturalists. It includes various species of warbler, owl, flycatcher and woodpecker, and a community of Britain's smallest bird, the goldcrest.

BELOW *The diminutive goldcrest breeds successfully in the Peak.*

Out of the woods, on the grassy slopes, among the Jacob's ladder, bloody cranesbill and early purple orchids, and the medley of grasshoppers and butterflies, you might spot wheatears and meadow pipits. On the rivers, moorhens build their nests and little grebes dive for fish and snails. Herons and kingfishers pay seasonal visits to these waters, and two particularly charming habitués parade along the banks: the mischievous grey wagtail, and the one and only diving songbird, the dipper. The rivers and streams are celebrated for their fish—in particular the brown trout—thanks mainly to one enthusiast, the 17th-century author Izaak Walton. In one of the best-known books ever written on fishing, *The Compleat Angler*, he evokes the joys of the sport, as experienced over the years in Dove Dale.

BELOW *Birdwatchers may spot skylarks or merlins on Bleaklow.*

The Dark Peak presents, as always, a stark contrast. On some moors, the wondrous feature is the *lack* of wildlife. The boggy reaches of Bleaklow Moor are sometimes referred to as England's sole desert, where even the common moorland vegetation—sphagnum moss, cotton grass, heathers, bilberry and bog asphodel—struggles to maintain a foothold. But birdwatchers love these uplands, at least the drier parts of them. Red and black grouse flourish contentedly, heedless of the coming shooting season. A merlin swoops on a hapless skylark. Golden plovers, redshanks and curlews assemble in the early summer. And in August, prior to emigrating, flocks of ring ouzels can be seen gorging on rowan berries.

Some ramblers have been surprised on their walks by an unexpected encounter. I can remember the very moment, twenty years ago, when a companion of mine returned from a solitary hike near The Roaches (a spellbinding line of crags north of Leek) and announced, 'I could swear I've just seen... a wallaby.' Our disbelief—his own almost as much as mine—was soon laid to rest, when our enquiries revealed that the area did indeed accommodate a small community of red-necked wallabies, descendants of a pioneering group that had escaped from a local private menagerie during the Second World War.

NATIONAL PARK, NATIONAL TREASURE

However broadly you draw the Peak District's boundaries, the lion's share of it lies within the 555 square miles of the Peak District National Park—and it is this institution, a kind of joint venture between nature and human endeavour, that I've chosen as the fourth of the Peak District's seven wonders. The park's own

ABOVE *The boundaries of the Peak District National Park are marked by millstones, reminders of a small-scale local industry from another age.*

boundaries are carefully drawn (presumably to avoid conflict with pre-existing industrial and urban interests) to skirt many of the region's quarries and almost all of its towns, such as Ashbourne, Leek, Matlock and Glossop, not to mention Sheffield, Huddersfield, Oldham and so on. At one point, the boundary line takes a singularly contrived looping diversion in order to exclude Whaley Bridge and Buxton from its domain. The largest town within the National Park is Bakewell, and it is by no means a large town.

The national parks of England and Wales number eleven in all now (with a twelfth on the way), and cover some 10 per cent of the land area. Each national park has three broad roles: to conserve the regional landscape, wildlife and culture; to look after the inhabitants' interests; and to provide for the education and enjoyment of visitors. The parks don't actually own or manage the land (or not much of it—only 4 per cent, in the case of the Peak District National Park) as they do in the United States and elsewhere. Instead, they exercise certain legal powers, regulating industrial development, negotiating rights of way with landowners, enforcing environmental standards, and so on. And they run a ranger service, to help build stiles, for instance, or restore footpaths, or rescue the lame and strayed. The network of walking trails overseen by the Peak District National Park amounts to some 1,500 miles of footpath.

ABOVE *One of the jobs of a Peak District National Park Ranger is to keep footpaths, stiles and fences in good repair.*

What makes the Peak District National Park so special is a threefold distinction. One, it is easily the most popular of the eleven national parks in England and Wales (and reputedly the second most popular in the world—runner-up to that of Mount Fuji in Japan), recording some 22 million visits a year from sightseers and holidaymakers. Two, it was the first of the eleven to be established, in April 1951—a well-deserved honour, in view of the region's historic role: ramblers' protests at being excluded from the Dark Peak grouse moors, culminating in the 'Kinder trespass' of 1932, had given the right-to-roam campaign the impetus and publicity that eventually led to the requisite legislation. Three, it has a unique record for securing right of access. Thanks to carefully negotiated agreements, some 81 square miles of privately owned land, especially grouse moors, is now open to ramblers (with some exceptions—during the shooting season, for example). That's more access land than is mustered by all the other ten national parks put together.

ARCHITECTURAL WONDERS

My choice for the fifth of the Peak District's wonders goes to its collection of great houses. As if to pay tribute to the beauty of their surroundings, many of the region's great and good, or at least rich and noble, have in the past built themselves magnificent residences, their descendants often maintaining them down the centuries to the present day. On the southern periphery of the region, for example, lie Kedleston Hall, built in the 1760s to a classical Robert Adam design, and Alton Towers, the huge former home of the Earls of Shrewsbury, now largely in ruins (though its gardens are more gorgeous than ever) and overshadowed by the adjoining leisure park with its ice shows and roller coasters. On the western periphery lies Lyme Park, originally Tudor but converted in the 18th century into a majestic Palladian mansion (recognisable to millions now as Mr Darcy's home in the BBC adaptation of *Pride and Prejudice*). And on the eastern periphery lie Bolsover Castle, a bulky 17th-century baroque fantasia, again largely in ruins,

ABOVE *Haddon Hall, one of the best-preserved medieval houses in England, sits in beautiful wooded grounds.*

but with a well-restored keep, and Hardwick Hall, an unusually light and airy Elizabethan manor, 'more glass than wall', as the saying goes, and boasting a renowned collection of antique tapestries and embroidery.

Pride of place goes to two more centrally positioned houses, Haddon Hall and Chatsworth House. Parts of Haddon Hall date back to medieval times—the 14th-century wood-panelled banqueting hall, for instance—and even though extended and altered repeatedly through to the Elizabethan era, its feeling of unity remained. And remains still: thanks to generations of benign neglect, it escaped the 'improvements' so often imposed on old buildings by meddlesome voguish architects in the 18th and 19th centuries. Instead it became a popular 'Gothic' attraction for poets and painters, and was even the setting of an opera written by Sir Arthur Sullivan. Finally, in the 1920s, it was beautifully restored by the ninth Duke of Rutland.

As for Chatsworth, when Thomas Hobbes championed its inclusion among the Peak District's seven specific wonders, it was an Elizabethan manor house, built by the same redoubtable Bess of Hardwick who would subsequently build Hardwick Hall. But several generations later, towards the end of the 17th century, the first Duke of Devonshire replaced it with an ambitious building that was partly of his own design. That building is essentially the stately home of today, though many changes and additions have been made to both house and estate since.

Today's Chatsworth ranks among the very grandest of English country houses, alongside Blenheim Palace and Castle Howard. The honey-coloured western façade; the sumptuous Staterooms and carvings; the ornate Library; the Sculpture Gallery; and outside, the famous stone bridge, the Cascade, and the Emperor Fountain... but a description cannot do justice to the place, let alone a list: only a visit will do.

Sites of architectural interest extend beyond the region's country estates, of course. There are several prehistoric monuments, the most notable being Arbor Low, the 'horizontal Stonehenge': a Bronze Age stone circle in the hills near Youlgreave, with the massive stones lying prone rather than perched upright. There are some noted churches, especially the 14th-century Church of St John the Baptist in Tideswell, known as the Cathedral of the Peak. There are the imposing ruins of Peveril Castle, towering above Castleton.

The spa town of Buxton features several architectural triumphs: the famous Georgian Crescent, the Edwardian Opera House, and the immense dome, added in 1880, of the Devonshire Royal Hospital. At the time of its construction it was the

ABOVE *St Ann's Well in Buxton, famous for its restorative waters, was one of the original 'Seven Wonders of the Peak'.*

LEFT *This aerial view of Buxton shows the Crescent, which rivals Bath's for splendour, and the huge hospital dome.*

biggest unsupported dome in the world, with a span of 154 feet, surpassing those of the Duomo in Florence, the Pantheon and St Peter's in Rome, and the Capitol in Washington DC.

Two other monumental structures, particular favourites of mine, hint at the sixth of the Peak District's seven wonders. First, the stone viaduct straddling the River Wye at the head of Monsal Dale—a pre-eminent example of Victorian civil engineering, designed to carry the Buxton to Bakewell railway track. (No longer in use, the line has now been converted to a ramblers' trail.) At the time of its construction, the critic John Ruskin cursed the way it 'desecrated' the beautiful valley, but to modern eyes, or mine at any rate, its graceful proportions add to rather than detract from the charm of the scenery. Second, Cromford Mill in the Derwent Valley—a fortress-like complex of workshops and warehouses, unsentimental yet somehow amiable in design. It is now being redeveloped, partly as a museum to its own history. Built over 200 years ago, it claims to be the world's first real factory of the modern age, with its automated cotton-spinning mill drawing on waterpower to drive the machinery and applying basic mass production techniques. Sir Richard Arkwright, who built it (and others nearby), is justly hailed as one of the fathers of the Industrial Revolution.

PIONEERING INDUSTRY

ABOVE *Lead-mining tools carved on Wirksworth's Moot Hall recall the town's industrial past.*

BELOW *In days gone by, steam trains puffed through the gorges of the High Peak Railway.*

My sixth Peak District wonder, then, is the region's industrial heritage. It is inscribed in the names of several of the outlying towns and villages: New Mills, Milltown, Coal Aston, Ironville. But most of its hallmarks can be found more centrally, concentrated in the vicinity of Cromford.

The town of Wirksworth, for example, has been a lead-mining site since Roman times, and more recently a quarrying and silk-processing town. This proud industrial history is vividly recounted in an exhibition in the town's Heritage Centre, based, appropriately enough, in a former silk mill. Or you can arrange a guided tour of the Good Luck Mine—just a couple of miles outside Cromford, along the road called Via Gellia (not, as you might suppose, a Roman road, but a more recent one, named after a local landowning family, the Gells)—and venture underground into a real 19th-century lead mine, one of several mining museums in the region. (It is from Via Gellia, by the way, that the trade name Viyella derives, since the fabric used to be manufactured at a textile mill there.)

For industries such as these to prosper in the early days, one further industry was crucial: the transport industry. Canals and railway lines, tunnels and viaducts were duly constructed, slowly and ingeniously, through the unobliging terrain. Some of these survive almost unchanged today; others now consist only of tantalising remnants. Either way, the Peak District offers handsome rewards to the enthusiast—not least Roger Redfern, the author of the text that follows, who writes with relish about these early engineering masterworks.

Back near Cromford village, you can get a first-hand impression of them yourself. You can amble along the Cromford Canal to see the Leawood Pumphouse, containing a beam engine dating from 1849, now restored to working order, which was used to replenish the canal by pumping water from the River Derwent. Built at much the same time, and also serving the canal, was the extraordinary High Peak Railway line, its gradient rising to one in nine along one stretch. You can still make your way along it, but on foot, bicycle or horseback rather than in a train carriage: again, like the line running over the Monsal Dale viaduct, it has been converted into a ramblers' trail.

Not that railway buffs are overlooked. On the contrary. The region is a kind of marshalling yard for them, providing numerous museums and steam train centres, whether at Buxton, or near Cromford itself, or at Cheddleton and Butterley on the outskirts of the region. Between Matlock and Rowsley a four-and-a-half-mile section of the Midland Railway has been restored to run old trains as a tourist attraction. As you jolt along, you will feel as if you are travelling back in time. Fortunately, you can always pretend that the tear in your eye is caused by the smoke from the locomotive.

PEAK TRADITIONS

From industrial heritage to cultural heritage—the last of my seven wonders of the Peak District. The wonder could be that this cultural heritage survives at all, bearing in mind how greatly the region's inhabitants are outnumbered, for much of the year, by tourists. The tourism that the region attracts, however, is not generally of the amusement-arcade and theme-park variety (at least, not within the borders of the National Park, where most such excesses would be forestalled by the planning authorities), but much more placid and respectful. Writers and artists today can still draw inspiration from the region, as they did in the past—Arnold Bennett, Lord Byron and D. H. Lawrence; Joseph Wright of Derby, L. S. Lowry and J. M. W. Turner—so little has it changed in its essentials. It's as if most visitors realise the risk: their fondness for the place would prove self-defeating if their visits disrupted things and thereby altered its character.

In the event, tourism arguably sustains rather than undermines the traditional way of life. If it weren't for taking in bed-and-breakfast guests during the summer, many farmers might fail to make ends meet, and have to leave the land. Local cheeses, Bakewell puddings, Ashbourne gingerbread—who knows if they would still be made if the tourists didn't keep up the demand for them?

But even though tourism does have such a key role in the local economy, the region's inhabitants seem to carry on with their lives unaffected by those passing through. Unlike so many 'victims' of tourism elsewhere, they seem the opposite of envious; if anything, they seem to pity the tourists, who are excluded from this Arcadia for most of the year. They pursue their own interests and conduct their traditional festivals and customs with confidence and pride.

BELOW *The tastes of the Peak District—Bakewell pudding, Hartington Stilton and Ashbourne gingerbread.*

Here are some of the ceremonies you might chance upon during a visit. There's Garland Day in Castleton—a fancy-dress pageant held on or around Oak Apple Day (May 29) each year, possibly pagan in origin, but officially to commemorate the Restoration of Charles II. There's the Plague Sunday remembrance service in Eyam, held on the last Sunday every August, in tribute to the village's heroic

ABOVE *Townsfolk wrestle for the ball in the Ashbourne Shrovetide Football match—a game that knows no bounds.*

quarantine during the Great Plague of 1665–6. There's the Wirksworth Clypping on the first or second Sunday in September—a symbolic embracing of the church by the congregants circling its walls. There's the Boxing Day raft race at Matlock, the fell race known as the Dovedale Dash, and the notorious Shrovetide Football match near Ashbourne, held on Shrove Tuesday and Ash Wednesday—an anything-goes game, with hundreds of players on each side, and the goalposts set three miles apart.

The most prominent local custom is that of well dressing. More than two dozen towns and villages in the region—from Buxton to Bakewell, from Tideswell to Tissington—celebrate the tradition at some point between May and September each year, and for a week the local well or spring flaunts a colourful tableau—a still-life or a biblical scene, perhaps—made up of a mosaic of petals, leaves, twigs, seeds, even berries or alder cones.

For most of the participants, as well as onlookers, the inspirational value of the ceremony seems to lie less in religious stirrings than in the quiet feeling of continuity evoked: the sense of maintaining, from the distant past and into the distant future, the deep attachment between a community and the wonder-filled land in which it lives.

A FRAGILE SYMBOL

From my vantage point on top of Mam Tor, I could look towards the Dark Peak escarpment one way and the White Peak dales another. The views swept down over Castleton and through the Hope Valley; along the ridge to Rushup Edge or to Lose Hill and Win Hill; across the Vale of Edale to the amphitheatre of Grindsbrook Clough and on to the Kinder Scout skyline. Even the sight of the enormous Hope Valley cement works failed to break the spell: the smoke billowing from its chimney seemed to be effortlessly absorbed by the crystalline air, and the factory itself, like the flaw in a Chinese vase, was somehow assimilated into the exquisite surroundings. Manchester and Sheffield could be a thousand miles off, though according to the map they're barely twenty miles to the west and east as the crow flies, and just a short train ride away.

Mam Tor itself, with its alternating layers of grit and shale, is geologically unstable, so much so that it is nicknamed the Shivering Mountain. Landslides have been recorded as far back as Elizabethan times, and they remain as serious a risk as ever. Much of the scarring on its Castleton flank has occurred well within living memory. The mountain's fragility has sometimes been regarded as a symbol or

ABOVE *The crumbling face of Mam Tor, the mountain that dominates the head of the Hope Valley.*

omen, intimating how fragile the region as a whole is, and how vulnerable its seven wonders are to the ravages of time and human folly. But with 'sustainable tourism' established now, and visitors and residents alike so conservation-minded, Peakland's prospects look very good, and with luck its wonders will never cease.

INTRODUCING *PEAKLAND DAYS*

Roger Redfern has lived in or on the edge of the Peak District all his life. His portrait of the region, then, is not just a loving and heartfelt one, but an expert one too. It ranges widely in time and subject matter. More often than not, his expeditions are to the lesser-known corners of the region, off the beaten track plied by most guidebooks. His sharp observations mingle with reminiscences of his childhood and with historical anecdotes, whether about railways or reservoirs or Robin Hood. And he creates a kaleidoscope of country-life cameos—on farming folklore, the shapes of fields, or rare breeds. With his enthusiasm and his distinctive tone of voice, combining innocence and experience, he makes a most genial chaperone.

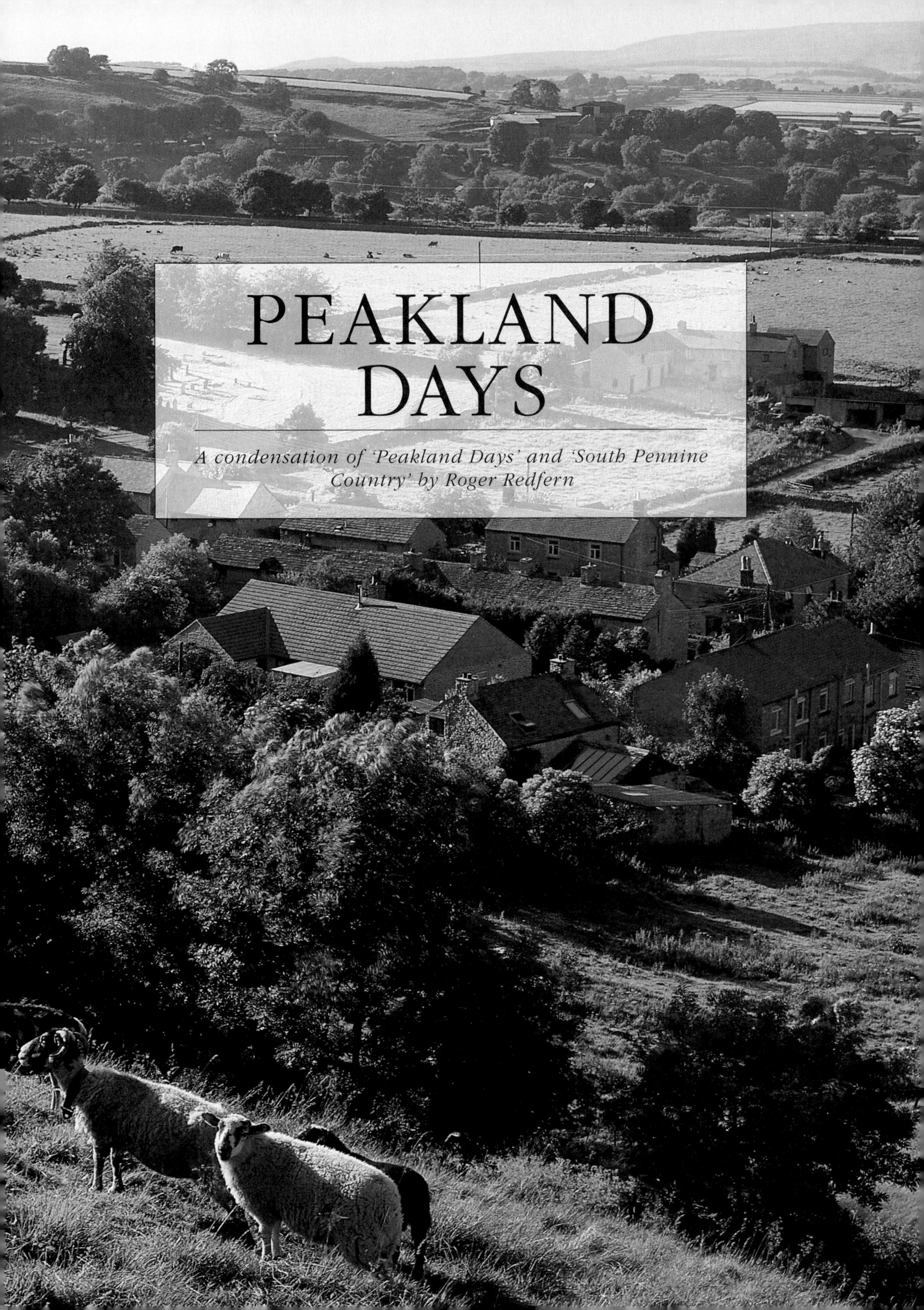

PEAKLAND DAYS

A condensation of 'Peakland Days' and 'South Pennine Country' by Roger Redfern

CHAPTER ONE

FROM EAST TO WEST

ABOVE *The author, Roger Redfern, is a Peaklander born and bred and has recorded his love of the region in several books.*

FROM THE CALDER VALLEY in the north to the upper vale of Trent in the south, the southern Pennines extend as a tract of upland with so much variety and so many stories to tell that one book might do little more than scratch the surface. The northern part is hemmed in between the textile districts of Lancashire and West Yorkshire, outliers of which climb the slopes and are logically part of these hills. Farther south the uplands reach to the edge of the Cheshire Plain and the industrial lowlands of the Derbyshire coalfield. The width of the region varies greatly but is, at its widest, about thirty-five miles between east and west.

A large chunk of the South Pennines lies within the boundaries of the Peak District National Park, but there are many fine parts of the region lying outside this National Park, all the better because they are rarely visited: quiet paradises far from roads, car parks and scenic viewpoints; unassuming country thick still with the associations of working natives and their lifestyles, far removed from the lives of modern suburbanites not many miles distant. With this in mind, instead of simply scratching the surface I have attempted to be selective, to go deeper here and there, giving the reader an impression of life and scenery in that particular place.

The traveller here, as anywhere else, cannot hope to know a place and its particular character completely unless he uses his legs and gets to grips with the country. So the subject of this first chapter is a ninety-mile ramble which took three of us from the heart of Sherwood Forest to the heights of eastern Cheshire.

At 10.30am on a bright July morning we set off along a wide ride leading northwards. We were at the heart of ancient Sherwood, a sea of conifers isolating the massive oaks that are the true natives of the district. We passed the Major Oak and entered the Dukeries by Thoresby, Clumber Park and the vast estate of Welbeck. And so, in thirteen and a quarter miles, we came under gathering cloud to Welbeck Bar and passed from Nottinghamshire into Derbyshire.

Up we went through Hodthorpe with its southerly view of colliery and cornfields which sweep away towards the ocean of woodland edging Welbeck Park. Then into

ABOVE *Pale limestone escarpments stand out across the south of the Peak District National Park. This area is known as White Peak after the pale colour of its limestone rock.*

the red brick of Whitwell—actually only eastern Whitwell is like that, for at the centre of the settlement there is a dramatic change in character. Ancient Whitwell is as lovely as any village in Derbyshire, built largely of mellow magnesian limestone and pantiles, and in complete contrast to the urban eastern half. Two buildings impress themselves on the observer. The first one is the old parish church of St Lawrence, notable for its Norman tower and the chancel erected between 1300 and 1350. The other building—close to the church on its northern side—is Whitwell Manor House, which overlooks the graveyard. It gives the impression of great size and complex design, possessing fine mullioned windows looking to the west.

And it was towards the west that we continued, out across Whitwell Common, as the clouds began to break and sunlight spilled all about us. On Bondhay Common the grass and corn were brightly illumined, displaying all the gorgeous colours of high summer and backed by the dark horizon of Whitwell Wood.

ARISTOCRATIC HOUSES

The glorious turrets of Barlborough Hall shone white ahead as we gained Pebley Cottages beside the disused colliery. Crossing the wide, grassy sweep of Barlborough's ancient park, we looked fruitlessly for the herd of deer, and gasped at the northern vista of sunlit lake and the far lands of corn and coal towards Kiveton. We came up towards the great avenue of limes and glimpsed the front of the 16th-century hall, its many windows glinting in the late sun. A short sprint across the drive brought us to that sudden and exhilarating westward revelation of the free, wide land of the southern Pennines, for we were at the crest of the magnesian limestone escarpment.

Sadly, though, all the golden light and freedom of westward space and far, blue hills was tainted by an unpleasant roar, for we had come into sight of the M1 motorway, and what a sad prospect: all that noise and those poor occupants of fast-moving vehicles, imprisoned where they sat.

A farm track went beneath the motorway, and so it was only a matter of minutes before we emerged onto the wide fields that fall down by Spinkhill. At 6pm we sat in the tea-time sunshine on the wall bordering the Catholic Church of the Immaculate Conception, the dark stone seeming unusual after all those limestone miles. The present church was erected in 1846, but there was a place of worship here from about 1600. The copper dome of Mount St Mary's College shone green beyond the tall spire, and a west wind refreshed us as we contemplated the golden corn lands which sweep down towards the Rother Valley.

The crossing of Whitwell Common had made us footsore, and it was a change to go downhill the short distance to Renishaw. Then we were ascending by the wooded way through the parkland of Renishaw Hall. The turrets and chimney-stacks of this famous house of romantic and literary association came into view

RENISHAW'S SINGULAR SIBLINGS

EDITH, OSBERT and Sacheverell Sitwell, celebrated intellectual trio of the interwar years, were born into a landed Derbyshire family to an eccentric father and a gambling mother. From an early age they formed a fiercely independent unit and were also intensely dependent on each other. In adulthood their modernity, sharp wit and striking looks made them key figures on the London arts scene.

While the Sitwells all wrote prolifically, their work has received mixed responses from critics over the years. Some say Dame Edith was the only one to have any literary ability, but others maintain that none of them did, and that they were merely famous for being famous. On the whole, though, Edith's poetry is well-regarded; Sir Osbert's autobiographies, if not his novels, are highly acclaimed; and 'Sachie' was a respected art historian.

One arena in which Edith and Osbert excelled was self-promotion. Edith, who loved to adorn herself in exotic robes and jewellery, was one of the most painted and photographed women of the 20th century. She and Osbert endlessly courted publicity, deriding any artists, writers or musicians they disliked, and responding vocally to any criticism of the threesome. The Sitwells will also be remembered, however, for promoting others as much as themselves: as patrons they supported many young talents, such as the composer William Walton and the poet Dylan Thomas.

Today's generation of Sitwells leads a more low-key life, preferring to reveal only the gardens of Renishaw Hall, the family estate, to the public gaze.

ABOVE AND LEFT *Edith Sitwell* (above) *was photographed by Horst P. Horst in 1948. All three siblings maintained a great attachment to the family home, Renishaw Hall* (left).

over the grassy slope as we crossed above the lakes, making westwards. How refreshing to tired legs and sore feet was that melancholy view down to the lake, framed on the far shore by a drift of pink rosebay willowherb.

At 7pm we began the 300-foot ascent through fields to the Handleys. Distantly to the south rose Hardwick Hall, sending us on our way across those endless barley fields. Behind us beautiful Bolsover Castle, of pale magnesian limestone, atop its tree-lined ridge and barely scarred by the nearby industrialisation, was fully lit by the western sun.

ABOVE *Bolsover Castle, now partly in ruins, commands a sweeping view of the town and the surrounding countryside from its hilltop position.*

In 1633 William, Earl of Newcastle, entertained King Charles I and Queen Henrietta Maria at Bolsover Castle. The hospitality extended to the royal visitors was the most lavish to have taken place in this country at any time: the cost of the formal dinner alone ran to £4,000! Ben Jonson was engaged to provide 'such speeches and scenes as he could best devise', the result being the masque *Love's Welcome.* A decade later Newcastle was commander-in-chief of Royalist forces in the North and Midlands. He placed Colonel Mushchamp as governor of the garrison at Bolsover Castle. By August 1644 the castle had been taken by the Parliamentary forces without any great struggle. Some of it was pulled down, but William's brother Sir Charles Cavendish was able to repurchase it and preserve many of its treasures.

Close by Bolsover stands Sutton Scarsdale Hall. Though now a ruin, it is, according to no less an authority than Sir Nikolaus Pevsner, the great architectural historian, 'easily the grandest mansion of its date in the county [of Derbyshire]'. The first great period of the history of the Manor of Sutton began in 1415, when it passed by way of marriage to the ancient Leake family. But there is a tradition that an earlier Sir Nicholas Leake left Sutton for the Holy Land as a crusader and was taken prisoner by the Turks where he languished many long years. As time passed he became ill and prayed that he be given the chance to see once more 'his fair domains at Sutton'. Upon waking next morning he found himself in the porch of the parish church of St Mary at Sutton. He was turned away from the doors of the hall, for everyone believed him to be a worthless beggar on account of his wretched appearance. Remembering that he possessed half the gold ring broken and shared by his wife and himself before he left for the East, he sent his half via a servant, and his wife immediately recognised it. They were happily reunited and he lived as master at Sutton Scarsdale Hall for many years afterwards. After his death his will was found

RIGHT *In the 17th century Sutton Scarsdale Hall was Derbyshire's grandest mansion. Today, although a roofless ruin, the stone hall, with its giant fluted pilasters, is still one of Britain's most important architectural treasures.*

ABOVE *In 1966 the parish of Sutton revived for just one year the local tradition of distributing loaves to the poor on St Nicholas's Day. This village custom died out in the 18th century, but locals are trying to revive it.*

to contain instructions that eight bushels of wheat be baked into large loaves and distributed on St Nicholas's Day ever afterwards to the needy of Duckmanton, Sutton and Temple Normanton.

The Sir Francis Leake (Lord Deincourt) who upheld the King during the Civil War, and so temporarily forfeited the estate at Sutton, is recorded as becoming so 'mortified after the horrid murder of his rightful sovereign' that he clothed himself in sackcloth, had his grave dug and lay down in it every Friday right up to his death on April 9, 1655.

The Earls of Scarsdale followed as lords of the manor later in the same century, and early in the 18th century work began on completely rebuilding the old hall. The original was not demolished but subjected to metamorphosis by building around it. This was the work of Smith of Warwick, in a building programme covering a period of four years between 1724 and 1728. The hall's major architectural feature is provided by the giant fluted pilasters on each front of the two-storeyed stone building. The north front contained the principal entrance and the finest rooms, once renowned for their fabulous decorations. Some of these were removed to the Philadelphia Museum in the United States, where they are still to be seen, giving an impression of what the interior of this noble house must have been like. A fantastic amount of money was spent on these modifications, the plaster work being executed by the outstanding Italian experts of the period, Vossali and Artari. As work on the house was completed, the three lakes in the park to the north of the mansion were made and several of the estate farms were improved. Nicholas, Earl of Scarsdale, the instigator of all this noble improvement, died eight years later owing so much money that the estate was sold.

For ninety-five years (1824–1919) Sutton Scarsdale Hall was the home of the famous Arkwrights. The inventor and industrialist Sir Richard Arkwright never lived at Sutton; his descendant Robert was the first member of the family to make his home here. After 1919 the property was owned by a consortium, whose only interest was to make capital out of the great house. It remained empty, the grounds invaded by willowherb and nettle, the plaster and fireplaces torn out and sold and much fine stonework removed.

Some years ago the consortium decided to demolish the entire building, but fortuitously, three days before work was to begin, the late Sir Osbert Sitwell of Renishaw Hall came with friends to visit ancient St Mary's Church and, meeting the sexton in the graveyard, learned of the forthcoming demolition. In the nick of time he bought the estate and so saved the hall. And so this wonderful ruin stands above the shallow dale where the River Doe Lea drains, across the fields from the nobler ruin of Bolsover Castle.

The north side of the parish church tower supports several outbuildings of the hall. J. Charles Cox suggested, in his *Churches of Derbyshire* (published in 1876), that a section of the graveyard was taken over at the time of the rebuilding of the hall because access to the church from both northern and eastern sides is

A TALE OF RAGS TO RICHES

BORN IN PRESTON in 1732, the 13th child of a tailor, Richard Arkwright was one of the great inventors and entrepreneurs of the Industrial Revolution. His successful water-powered spinning machine revolutionised the manufacture of cotton, turning it from a cottage industry to a mechanised one.

Although Arkwright began his working life as an itinerant barber and wig-maker, by the 1760s he was applying his ingenuity to making a machine that would spin cotton. In 1769 he and his partners patented the 'water frame'—a machine that used a system of rollers and was powered by large millwheels turned by running water. In 1771 Arkwright opened his first cotton mill at Cromford, a few miles south of Matlock. Spurred on by his success, Arkwright built a second mill at Cromford in 1776, and a third one, Masson Mill, several years later. He also opened factories at Ashbourne, Bakewell and other parts of the Peak as well as farther afield, in Lancashire and Scotland. By 1782 he had a huge workforce of 5,000 people and had amassed a personal fortune of £200,000.

In 1786 this 'bag-cheeked, pot-bellied' Lancastrian was given a knighthood—an honour he would enjoy for only six more years until his death. Although his sons carried on the family business, by the 1840s the cotton industry in Derbyshire was in decline: steam power was replacing waterpower, and Lancashire towns, profiting from their proximity to the transatlantic port of Liverpool, had become the undisputed kings of cotton.

RIGHT *Richard Arkwright patented his water frame in 1769 and put his invention to use at his mill in Cromford.*

RIGHT *Sir Richard Arkwright, painted by Wright of Derby. Arkwright was an early pioneer of the Industrial Revolution.*

ABOVE *Arkwright chose Cromford as the site of his first mill because of its 'remarkable fine Stream of Water'.*

NATURE'S NIGHTLIFE

ABOVE *Blackberries make a juicy snack for the common dormouse, which feeds at night to avoid predators.*

LEFT *A barn owl returns to its nest in a farm building, carrying a mouse in its beak with which to feed its owlets.*

BELOW *The hedgehog, a nocturnal feeder, roams abroad at night searching out slugs, snails and worms with its sensitive snout.*

WHEN THE LIGHT OF DAY begins to fade, and humans move inside, dancing swarms of gnats and midges—and the bats and birds that actively seek these insects out—begin to appear. They are part of the wildlife night shift which rests during the day and emerges after dark to eat—or be eaten.

Some animals lead a nocturnal existence because the darkness protects them from predators. Others prefer the cool evening air to the heat of day. Hedgehogs, with their prickly coat and ability to roll up into a tight ball, have little to fear from any but the most determined foe; they feed at night merely because their prey—slugs and snails—do so. As the dew falls, these invertebrates, which would lose moisture in the daytime sun, come out to wreak their damage on the gardener's lovingly tended plants. Hedgehogs' other favourite snack, earthworms, leave their burrows in the damp night to feed on leaves. Earthworms are the principal food source for badgers, which also eat small mammals and, in autumn, fruit such as blackberries and elderberries. Shy and retiring, badgers sleep by day in underground setts and are rarely seen by humans, their only enemy.

Foxes are more easily spotted, in town as well as country, scavenging through bins or on the prowl for small mammals or birds. And during their winter mating season, the quiet of a frosty night can be shattered by the unearthly screams of a vixen attracting a dog fox. A similarly spooky night-time sound is that of the tawny owl's mournful too-whit-too-whoo. The barn owl glides over the fields as silent as a ghost, swooping to grasp a hapless dormouse or vole with its sharp claws and beak.

Most small mammals are vulnerable to these consummate hunters, and venture out only under cover of darkness, which provides at least some protection, to nibble on fungi and seeds on the woodland floor or forage among tree branches for nuts, berries and insects. The deciduous woodland, with its supply of tasty morsels, is a veritable larder for these small creatures—and those that feed on them.

BELOW *Badgers spend much of the day sleeping below ground in their labyrinthine homes, known as setts, and are rarely seen.*

impossible. The fact that a recent addition to the existing area of the graveyard is to be seen on the western side seems to substantiate this theory. The church was completed in the first half of the 14th century. It has a fine Perpendicular tower, windows from the 14th century and recently exposed ancient wall paintings.

It was after 8pm as we wound our way over the fields to West Handley. Lenticular clouds veiled the lowering sun and gave the impression of a close-approaching sunset. We still had to go several miles to our woodland haven above the Barlow vale.

We made quickly down through Unstone village and across the railway line by the old station footbridge. It was 9.15pm, and in failing light on that warm July evening we climbed the cornfields towards Bull Close. We could just make out the field poppies dotting the wheat as we ascended.

The western sky was bright pink, and wide banners of still cloud reflected the glory of that high-summer sundown. Under the trees we went, by Bull Close Farm, where the lights were already lit, and out above the edge of Monk Wood. Far below, the evening valley was still, and lights were winking from Barlow and Commonside and from as far away as Cutthorpe as we came to the dark trees at the edge of the golf course.

It was in the very last light that we located our cache of food, sleeping-bags and pressure stove. Dark clouds were blowing as we prepared our late meal at ten o'clock. There was a sudden crashing of undergrowth at the wood's edge not ten yards distant—a fox or badger which had sauntered towards us, unaware of our presence until the last moment. Darkness shrouded the tall trees that cut out the westward prospect, and we settled in our sleeping-bags for the short night.

THE DALE DIKE DISASTER

The first grey light of a cloudy dawn brought heavy spots of rain, and I curled lower in my bag. It was obvious that my high-altitude sleeping-bag cover, intended for bivouacking in the Himalayas, was suitable for only the slightest dew! At 6.50am the rain stopped. Wood pigeons and thrushes were calling as we breakfasted; by 7.30 a sunny sky was showing, and we set off smiling through School Wood and by Cowley Bottom. By now the clouds had cleared away towards the east, and we went along the ridge by Hills Farm in brilliant sunshine, out across the head of the Gosforth Valley and up Oxclose Lane to Dronfield Woodhouse.

For the rest of that lovely day we went northwards through South Yorkshire by Totley, Dore, Ringinglow and Rivelin. Over the high ground of Bradfield Moors and through Bradfield we reached the large, smooth hollow of Bradfield Dale.

Bradfield Dale, drained by the River Loxley, is the largest of the valleys west and northwest of Sheffield. It is more than eight miles from the source of the Strines Dike (one of the major headwaters of the Loxley) on Derwent Edge to the confluence of the Loxley with the Rivelin at Malinbridge, one of Sheffield's northwestern districts, and it is nine miles from the source of Hobson Moss Dike (under Featherbed Moss) down the Agden branch of Bradfield Dale to Malinbridge: both arms are considered part of this valley.

BELOW *In the idyllic twin villages of High and Low Bradfield peace and tranquillity reign—in sharp contrast to the hustle and bustle of industrial Sheffield, just six miles away.*

Bradfield Dale is a large hollow, and the complexity of its steep and sinuous lanes is well known to Sheffield folk. G. H. B. Ward—'the king of ramblers'—considered the views overlooking Bradfield Dale 'the choicest surprise view of dale and moor within six miles of any large industrial city'. It is a vista of the broad valley, wooded slopes towards the west beneath the high moors and the four large reservoirs in the Bradfield complex.

There are really two Bradfield settlements, near the place where the Agden valley branches northwestwards. Low Bradfield lies beside the flood plain of the Loxley. It is a collection of old houses and cottages, and a steep, high-walled lane climbs the valley side at a gradient of one in five to High Bradfield, which is the

true heart of the old village. A few hundred yards to the northwest of the church lies the mound of Bailey Hill. Some authorities have considered this mound and moat the remains of a Saxon moot hill used for assemblies, but the general opinion and probable origin is that this was a defensive site subsequently used by the Normans for a garrison soon after the Conquest. The ridge-mound of Bailey Hill measures 310 feet and reaches a maximum of forty-five feet above the base of the adjacent trench. The height from the trench mound to the top of the circular mound, on which a wooden structure was presumably placed, is eighty feet.

The adjacent parish church of St Nicholas stands in a fine position with wide views of Bradfield Dale. The tower is 14th century, with pinnacles, and the whole building is attractively embattled, which gives a defensive appearance completely in keeping with the situation so close to the windy hills. There was a church here at the beginning of the 13th century, but all evidence points to a complete rebuilding during the following century, the result of which we see today. Associated with the church was the Turie Library: about 225 books in Greek, Latin and English bequeathed by the Reverend R. Turie, vicar of Ecclesall, in 1720. The ravages of time and some carelessness seem to have caused a steady reduction in the collection, so that by 1966 there were only thirty-three volumes left, published between 1600 and 1707.

ABOVE *Dale Dike Reservoir is a picture of serenity on a hazy midsummer's day.*

From most places in High Bradfield there are good views down into the dale; views that include one or more of the four reservoirs that lie in the floor of this broad trench. Near the head of the valley is Strines Reservoir; below it is Dale Dike. The lowest, some distance below Low Bradfield, is Damflask, while Agden Reservoir fills the lower reaches of the tributary Agden valley. The most famous of the Bradfield reservoirs is Dale Dike.

Until early in the 15th century the small population of Sheffield was supplied with water by springs at the Ponds and at Westbar. In 1434 Barker's Pool was formed at the place called Balm Green, then a wooded suburb of the town, and this satisfied the area for 200 years. In about 1743 small dams were built in the lower reaches of Crookesmoor valley; thereafter other dams were formed in the same area. In 1830 an Act of Parliament created a water company, and dams were constructed at Crookes and Redmires.

Turning its attention to the Bradfield valley, the water company now began to build a reservoir above Low Bradfield, impounding the upper reaches of the Loxley (here called the Dale Dike), and this was finished in the winter of 1863–4. The rapidly expanding population of Sheffield needed more water immediately, so the directors of the water company resolved to fill the new Dale Dike Reservoir as soon as it was completed. The impounding wall was 1,200 feet long and almost 100 feet high in the centre; it held 700 million cubic feet of water, and the surface of the reservoir covered seventy-eight acres. The engineers responsible for this impressive dam believed, from tests carried out during construction, that the impounding wall could withstand ten times the pressure required of it when full of water.

It is recorded that on March 11, 1864 'a heavy rainfall filled the dam rapidly, and a high wind, blowing down the gorge, hurled the water against the embankment in heavy waves.' That afternoon the resident engineer carefully inspected the dam and then went back to Sheffield, satisfied that all was well. But an hour after the engineer's inspection a workman crossed the impounding wall and saw a horizontal crack in the outer slope. He reported this to the contractor. As no water was leaking, the contractor considered this to be simply a frost crack; however, he opened the outlet pipes and sent his son on horseback for the engineer. A short distance down the valley the saddle girth broke, and the young man stopped in Damflask to repair it; telling the people there of the crack in the reservoir wall, he set off again for Sheffield. Some of the population of Damflask (probably not a little anxious) set off in the gathering darkness to see for themselves.

It was ten o'clock by the time the resident engineer arrived, and the crack had now widened to such an extent that he immediately attempted to breach the overflow weir with gunpowder. His first effort did not work, and before another could be made the centre of the dam broke, sending a deluge of water down towards Low Bradfield. It was midnight. Contemporary records state that the flood water 'swept like an avalanche down the course of the River Loxley to Hillsborough, and down the Don through the town, deluging the valleys on both sides to the depth of many feet'.

In the region of Low Bradfield the water must have been from twenty to thirty feet deep as it swept all before it. The news of the cracking dam wall had spread quickly in the Bradfield neighbourhood and in Damflask, too, so that with the thunder of the breaking dam everyone thereabouts fled up the slopes to safety—all, that was, except an infant washed out of its mother's arms at Low Bradfield and a labourer at Damflask who had scoffed at ideas of danger, gone to bed as usual and drowned; he was found 'buried in debris far down the valley next day'.

Below Damflask hamlet, however, word of the dangerous state of the reservoir had not been spread, and it was in the lower reaches of the Loxley valley that most loss of life occurred. A record of the catastrophe written thirty-five years after the event tells of the sudden terror that struck men and boys on night shift in the works near Malinbridge: 'Upon them in the darkness the deluge came as a terrible surprise, sweeping away many of the works and overwhelming the workers in their bewildered attempts to escape.' A farmer by the name of Trickett, with his wife, several children, servants, father-in-law and a lodger, lived in a large stone house where the River Loxley joins the River Rivelin at Malinbridge. A neighbour living higher up the slope saw the foaming flood approaching 'like a mountain of snow'. The water struck the Trickett house and shook it 'like a cradle'. Lights were seen to flicker in the windows, and shrieks were heard from the terrified occupants. Then the whole house sank under the flood and was totally destroyed. Everyone was killed. Fifteen cottages nearby were swept away, too, and only three of their seventy inhabitants survived. That record of 1899 went on to explain that such destruction occurred all the way down the Loxley valley from Damflask hamlet to Malinbridge and Hillsborough, and 'scenes in the valley of the Don at Owlerton and Sheffield were scarcely less harrowing'. At Neepsend an Irish labourer got his wife and six children up onto the roof of

LEFT *Survivors of the 1864 Dale Dike disaster search for bodies in the ruined houses, in a sketch made for the* Illustrated London News.

his low, whitewashed cottage, but the flood rose quickly and lifted the roof off, carrying them all away to be drowned.

One of the reasons for the extensive damage as far down the Don valley as Sheffield was that the torrent came suddenly, without any warning. Loaded with much large wreckage, the water 'thundered against doors and walls like a battering ram'. Within half an hour the flood had passed, carrying many of the drowned miles downstream towards Doncaster. The scene it left behind was described as one of 'death and wreck and desolation almost unparalleled in the annals of English towns'.

Altogether 4,511 houses were flooded, thirty-nine of which were totally destroyed and 376 partly destroyed. There were 240 persons killed. After the Dale Dike disaster the Mayor of Sheffield launched an appeal, and quite quickly

£55,000 was subscribed, more than enough to meet all urgent claims. The water company was ultimately found to be fully responsible for the event and had to pay £373,000 for loss of life, personal injury and damage to property and trade. In addition it had to find an enormous sum to commence construction of a new dam. As a result, the company was authorised to add 25 per cent to its water rates for twenty-five years.

The cause of the collapse of the Dale Dike dam wall was never fully discovered, though a committee of 'five eminent engineers' decided that there must have been 'a landslip on the east side of the embankment, extending under a portion of the outer slope'. Before the dam collapsed, the water company was already engaged in building the Agden Reservoir immediately to the west of Bradfield, and this work now continued. In 1869 this, ultimately the second largest of the Bradfield reservoirs, was finished. Two years earlier the Damflask Reservoir was completed on the site of the destroyed hamlet of that name. This is the largest of these man-made lakes, with a surface area of 115 acres and containing 1,158 million gallons.

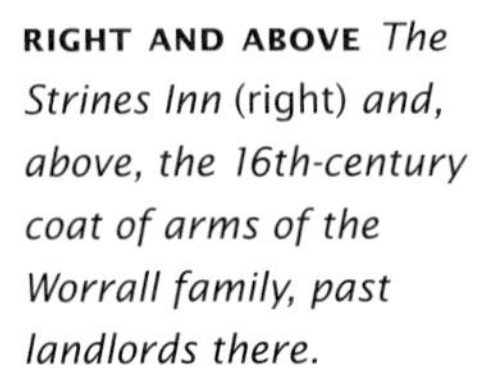

Work recommenced on the Dale Dike dam, and a new wall was built 400 yards upstream from the original site, reducing its capacity by a third. This was finished in 1875. The Strines Reservoir, near the very head of Bradfield Dale, was completed four years previously.

Overlooking the Strines Reservoir is the remotely situated Strines Inn. This building is known to have been the home of the Worrall

RIGHT AND ABOVE *The Strines Inn* (right) *and, above, the 16th-century coat of arms of the Worrall family, past landlords there.*

family early in the 16th century. The arms of this family are carved in stone over the doorway and show a lion rampant between three cups, an arm in armour holding a dagger and a crest on a helmet.

The inn dates from three building periods: the earliest now visible is probably 16th century; the next, the upper wing, is late 17th century; and the most recent is the smallest part erected in 1860.

A few yards north of the inn, at the top of the steep hill down to the Strines Brook, is an old roadside stone with 'TAKE OFF' inscribed on it. It was the place where the extra 'chain' horses were taken off after helping to haul a load up the gradient.

Strines has had its tragedies. Over 200 years ago a travelling tailor came up here on his rounds after doing work in Bradfield where he had been seen with some gold ornaments. On reaching Strines he decided to spend the night at the inn because darkness had overtaken him. He was never seen again; rumours surrounded his disappearance, and many believed the landlord to know more than he admitted, but the mystery was never solved. On another occasion, when the Worralls lived at Strines, a practical joke went wrong. Two young women dressed up as men and set out to impersonate the lover of one of the inn's maids. One of the girls was nervous and hung back in the shadows, but her more confident friend went round to the back of the inn and whistled to attract the maidservant. The Worralls heard the whistling, a window opened and a shotgun was fired at what was thought to be a burglar. An old book records that 'the figure was seen to reel and the shrieks of a young girl were heard.' Only then did the landlord realise the mistake. The dead girl's ghost is said to be seen periodically at the back of the Strines Inn.

THE LAST OF THE LODGES

At 6.15pm we reached the deep bracken above the Ewden Beck. Ancient oak woodlands which once covered most of the steep valleys to the west and north of Sheffield were removed during the Middle Ages as a source of charcoal for the local iron-smelting industry. Today only small areas of these natural deciduous woodlands remain, one such being in the middle reaches of the Ewden valley.

The Ewden Beck joins the Don where it meanders below Wharncliffe Wood between Stocksbridge and Oughtibridge. On the high ground overlooking the lowest part of the dale are two interesting settlements, one a village, the other a hamlet. The village is Bolsterstone, standing on a ridge on the northern side; an ancient site with the remains of a Norman castle and a squat-towered parish church looking out across the dale to the Pennine moors. The hamlet is Brightholmlee, which occupies a commanding position above the southern mouth of the Ewden valley; it is a collection of old cottages and farms, with an attractive set of gritstone troughs where horses and cattle are still watered beside the steep lane.

Two reservoirs were constructed in this lower part of the valley. The lower, More Hall, has a surface area of sixty-five acres. Yachting enthusiasts find it very useful,

RIGHT *Local sailing enthusiasts make the most of the huge expanse of water provided by More Hall Reservoir.*

and on a bright day the colourful sails make a grand sight below the frowning gritstone moors. The upper water is Broomhead Reservoir, which has a surface area of 123 acres. Its 1,100-million-gallon capacity makes it the third largest of Sheffield's water-supply reservoirs. Both Ewden reservoirs were completed in 1929.

The little village of Ewden occupies the sunny northern slope between the two reservoirs, and is largely a grouping of water-board dwellings. The coming of the reservoirs caused notable changes to some of the old buildings on the southern slopes of the valley. The ancient farm of Dwarriden ('the dwarf's dean', or hollow), just south of Broomhead Reservoir, was obviously important, for it stood where two old trackways cross. It was demolished by Sheffield Corporation. The ancient cruck barn has been retained as a storage shed and is unique owing to the great height of the stylobats (the stone bases for support of the cruck beams).

Nearer Brightholmlee are two farms with ancient cruck buildings still standing. By the beck in the valley below stood Broomhead Mill and New Mill (both recorded in the 13th century), and remains of lead and zinc sulphide workings, but all have disappeared since the coming of the reservoirs.

The ground steepens west of Broomhead Reservoir, rising 400 feet to the edge of the open moors. On this slope and almost surrounded by planted coniferous forest stands Wigtwizzle, formerly a hamlet of old farms but now reduced to one dwelling.

Wigtwizzle stands at the edge of Broomhead Park, a spacious sweep of greensward dotted with ancient trees, and an unexpected spot to find such a

dignified landscape; an oasis lying between the open moors to the west and the steeper dale country below it to the east. Broomhead Hall, built in 1311, was replaced in 1640 by a larger house erected by Christopher Wilson, a captain in the Parliamentary army. This must have been a most attractive building, but all that remains today is a pair of gateposts. In early summer, however, the gardens still exhibit a mass of colour as the azaleas and rhododendrons bloom in turn—an arresting contrast with the windy moors across the Langsett–Bradfield hill road.

This north–south road crosses the Ewden Beck by means of a steep hairpin bend and a narrow bridge. The road marks the boundary between the upper and lower parts of the dale. To the west the moors rise steadily to over 1,750 feet on the watershed of Derwent Dale. Immediately upstream of the bridge, however, the beck flows through a densely wooded cleft. Rhododendrons form a thicket difficult to negotiate as one walks up by the cascading waters.

Across the narrow defile of the dale, on the south side, is an impressive three-quarter-mile-long prehistoric earthwork and a cluster of Bronze Age tumuli. Here, too, is a stone circle which is difficult to find among the tall heather and summer bracken.

The uppermost reaches of the Ewden Beck wind through the peaty wastes of Upper Commons, a place that echoes to the call of the curlew, dunlin and stonechat in summertime, but a dark, bleak landscape in winter.

RIGHT *Verdant bilberry and purple bell heather flourish on the heights of the National Park's heaths and moorlands.*

BELOW *The Peak District is one of the most southerly habitats of the mountain hare, whose fur becomes white in the winter.*

The broad wilderness bounding the southern side of the upper Ewden is Broomhead Moor, formerly one of the richest grouse moors in Britain.

The monastic foundations of the Middle Ages were the first to manage these high, brown plateaus of the Peak District to any great extent. They established outlying farming settlements, or granges, in the valleys under the tops in order to use the moorland for the grazing of sheep.

Large private landowners followed the monasteries as the users of these heights, and with the growth of field sports it became increasingly fashionable to turn the wilderness into areas where game was introduced, maintained and encouraged to breed. The red grouse *(Lagopus lagopus)* and the mountain hare *(Lepus timidus)* were the favoured animals. They were well suited to the heather and bilberry and the severe winter conditions. Mountain hares were introduced from Scotland at the beginning of the 20th century and have adapted themselves well on the high plateaus. In winter they turn white, which renders them difficult to see against their world of snow and ice.

Wanderers were not only frowned upon, they were actively discouraged from setting foot upon these delectable heights for fear of disturbance to the birds and the hares, and for fear of any physical damage that might be caused to the moors, to boundaries, or to buildings erected at that time for the convenience of sportsmen and their employees. In 1886 the Duke of Norfolk became the owner of much of that vast and fascinating moorland to the east and north of the upper Derwent Valley which rises to the watershed extending from Derwent Edge, by Margery Hill to Howden Edge and Swains Head. The big house of the estate was the now-vanished Derwent Hall.

The considerable distances up the valleys and narrow cloughs, or ravines, were covered by the sportsmen, in due season, using ponies or on foot. Likewise, the dedicated countrymen employed as keepers, labourers and beaters reached the plateaus on foot throughout the year—whenever there was a job to do up on the moor. For the convenience of employers and employed, shelters were erected in convenient places on the heights. These came to be known as shooting cabins.

The pioneer ramblers enjoyed two things that today linger as little more than memories. The first was the thrill of avoiding the hawklike eyes of vigilant keepers, for no trespass was tolerated upon the plateaus far into this century, and any keen walker venturing there without permission did so at the risk of a chase over the heather. The keepers of the moors in the first third of this century were men dedicated to the task of preserving the plant and animal life in their charge.

The second feature of the high Peakland enjoyed by the early ramblers were the strategically placed shooting cabins. Many of these cabins or shelters fell into disrepair at an early date, and in the 1960s most of those remaining were ruined at the hands of an increasing number of vandals.

Fred Heardman of Edale remembers that there were once at least eight such buildings on the southern flanks of Kinder Scout. One was beneath Edale Head, high above The Cloughs, where there is one of the finest springs in the entire Peak

TRESPASSERS WILL BE CELEBRATED

After being turned off a walk on Bleaklow in 1932, a Lancashire group of the Communist-inspired British Workers' Sports Federation decided that the only way to press for access to the countryside was by a mass trespass. The event was well publicised in Manchester's newspapers, and on the bright, sunny morning of April 24 a crowd of around 400 turned up at Hayfield, on the western side of Kinder Scout.

They were addressed by Benny Rothman, a 20-year-old unemployed mechanic, at Bowden Bridge Quarry, before setting off for the 'forbidden mountain' of Kinder Scout. At a pre-arranged signal, they left the path and deliberately trespassed on the grouse moors, where they were met by a small band of gamekeepers. Scuffles ensued, and, as a result, six of the ringleaders, including Rothman, were arrested and charged with riotous assembly. Five received prison sentences. The severity of the punishment enraged and united the established rambling movement—which had been opposed to the trespass—and as public awareness increased, access restrictions were gradually lifted.

In 1949 the Labour government passed the National Parks and Access to the Countryside Act, and two years later the Peak District became Britain's first National Park. The Act also provided the mechanism for landowners to provide access to their land voluntarily, which soon affected 81 square miles of the Peak, including the former battleground of Kinder Scout. Fifty years later, in March 1999, another Labour government at last promised to bring in the long-awaited legislation for a statutory right to roam on open country.

ABOVE *A month after the mass trespass, local people gather in Derbyshire to demand countryside access.*

RIGHT *A plaque at Bowden Bridge Quarry marks the starting point of the 1932 trespass onto Kinder Scout.*

District. On a dark night long ago Fred and a friend arrived here intending to sleep within. The door was locked! Such a thing was unusual, but the visitors knew that access was possible through a trap door in the wooden floor. Through this trap door the keeper used to lower a stone jar of ale into the stream which flowed right under the cabin. During the night it rained hard, and by the next morning the stream was almost lapping at the trap door. How would they escape? Pushing their rucksacks ahead of them, they headed through the flood beneath the cabin's floor and bobbed out into the open in a decidedly bedraggled condition.

Another cabin that stood upon the southern flank of Kinder Scout was close beside the infant Grinds Brook which meanders in a gritty bed between the frowning crests of complex peat-grough scenery. The original cabin was built here by a man called Mike Tym, a notable Methodist who lived in the Vale of Edale and, now and then, had regrettable lapses into drunkenness. He was a stonemason and builder by trade and was instructed to repair the cabin. While there he delivered a lecture to his men on the horrors of alcoholism and the old cabin came to be known thereafter as Mike's Church. The new cabin replacing the original was constructed in two halves: one side for the shooters and the other for the beaters. This is a common theme throughout the Pennines, though most examples consist of two separate cabins. This new building came to be known as Four Jacks Cabin, as the Edale men who built it were called Jack Belfitt, Jack Tym, Jack Rowbotham and Jack Burdekin—the latter a member of a family who have lived in the district since the Domesday survey.

ABOVE *Edale resident Jack Belfitt stands in front of Four Jacks Cabin, Kinder Scout, which he built in the 1920s with three other men called Jack.*

It must be remembered that all these cabins were of value not only to the owners and their employees but also to any ramblers who cared to make use of the shelter they offered once much of the high plateaus became 'open country'. As an instance of this I recall the case of two girls who were crossing the Howden Moors some years ago. They became separated from the rest of their school party and wandered until, in failing light, they came upon the Abbey Brook cabin purely by chance. They took shelter here and passed a dark night of high winds and rain in comparative comfort—it is quite likely that the cabin saved their lives. No longer can the lost and exhausted make for the head of this deep-sided clough with any hope of a sheltering roof for the night. Indeed, such features marked on a map can be inconvenient and positively dangerous to the walker who spends energy in an attempt to reach cabins that no longer exist.

The coming of the Land Rover has meant that shooting parties and keepers no longer need the protection of cabins so much, but for serious walkers they can still be of considerable interest and service. It is the irresponsible vandal who has done far more than wind and weather could have done to reduce most of these buildings to either useless ruins or nostalgic memories. There are, however, two or three rarely visited and little-known ones that remain in good repair. I have no intention of divulging their whereabouts. If any reader does come across one of them I trust his good sense and judgment will guide him to treat them as if they were his own property. In such a way the handful of remote structures will continue for a long time yet as useful shelters for the true hill man, and as monuments to an age not long since passed when the Peakland bogtrotter was a pioneer who ventured into the plateau-land knowing that he would see fellow spirits—though the hawk-eyed keeper may not be far away in the next peat grough, or spying on the walker's progress from a distant tor silhouetted grotesquely upon the level skyline.

By 7.45pm we were off again in an attempt to gain as much ground as possible before nightfall, and in particular to leave the tenacious midges and the rhododendrons and bracken far behind. This jungle hindered progress, and as we went the clouds, now building up on the western horizon of Upper Commons, were getting denser and darker. In haste, we bivouacked behind a tumbled gritstone wall, the better to keep dry from the scudding showers that came and went throughout the night.

THE TOPS OF THE TORS

The next morning we experienced the most tedious and arduous walking of the journey amid the cotton grass of Sugdon Top, where the curlews called in the stiff breeze and pipits flitted from tuft to tuft. By 10.45, however, we had gained ancient Cut Gate which sweeps over the gritstone heights between Penistone and the coal measure country to Derwent Dale. On the watershed we met the first rambler of the journey, an old man with blowing white hair, and took breath as we admired the westward prospect between Win Hill and Holme Moss. It was a landscape of brightest green, of bilberry and bracken dotted with the pink of early heather. And so down to the Derwent we went, beneath the lonely Horse Stone, down to the river and across the county boundary into Derbyshire once more.

ABOVE *The meadow pipit inhabits open moorland. The male bird sings when in flight, changing tune on his descent.*

The afternoon hours of head wind and sunshine took us along the summit ridge of Bleaklow. We found two men floundering in the chocolate wastes between Bleaklow Hill and Bleaklow Head. They had set out from Edale that morning en route for the Scottish border but, near to exhaustion and caked in wet peat, had already lost the Pennine Way. We led them back to Bleaklow Head and set them on the undefined way towards Torside Clough and Longdendale.

The driest months in Longdendale are April, May and February in that order; the wettest are October and November. The fairly level plateau country and the high rainfall, allied to low rates of evaporation, mean that large parts of the gritstone areas of the South Pennines consist of bog, most commonly tussocks of cotton sedge but often mixed with heather, sphagnum moss and bilberry. The common incidence of the place name White Moss (as, for instance, a mile west of Wessenden Head) suggests that the cotton sedge has been established since ancient times—the common cotton grass (*Eriophorum angustifolium*) paints white many of the acid

BELOW *Huge millstones, abandoned in the face of technological progress, dot the landscape from which they were hewn.*

RIGHT *The millstone-grit escarpment of Stanage Edge has long been a favourite playground of rock climbers.*

moors of the southern Pennines in early summer when it blooms literally by the square mile. Such dazzling acres under a sunny sky are a pleasure to walk over, but so often the summer skies of the gritstone heights are darkened by palls of cloud and the widespread sheets of cotton grass blooms are soggy on close acquaintance.

We were now on the quagmire that interrupts the plateau between Bleaklow Head and the Higher Shelf Stones. The hundreds of tors on the face of Kinder Scout, on Bleaklow, on the heights to the north of wide Longdendale and on the extensive tracts of moorland forming Howden Moors, Upper Commons, and Bradfield, Broomhead and Derwent Moors command great interest. These outcrops of coarse, carboniferous rock are formed by the rotting of the rock along its lines of weakness (fault lines), the debris being slowly weathered away to reveal these features.

This tor formation was taking place before, during and after the Ice Age and is still taking place. In Peakland the tors stand in isolation upon the summits of the highest land. They are comparatively weak rock structures which must have remained just above the ice as it clawed powerfully at the sides of the plateaus and help to create the extensive gritstone 'edges', or low cliffs, which protect extensive lengths of the boundaries to these tablelands. On the northern side of the Kinder Scout plateau and on the wild and distant wastes of Bleaklow it is easy to discover the tops of new tors lying on the same level as the peat deposits. With the passage of time the peat will be removed at a faster rate than the gritstone and

BELOW *J. W. Puttrell of Sheffield, born in 1869, was one of the first men to practise gritstone climbing in the Peak District. The equipment available to Puttrell was very basic: today hard helmets are favoured over flat caps.*

slowly, over the centuries, new towers and turrets of coarse and blackened rock will rise above the general level of these heights.

Here and there are tors that toppled long ago, caught in midair and locked in precarious positions. As I have mentioned, a closely related feature of the tors are the edges—precipitous faces of millstone grit dropping from the top of the plateau to a usually steep heather- or bracken-covered slope that descends to a clough or greater dale. These rock edges reach heights approaching 100 feet, and where they have been exploited by quarrymen in the past some very impressive rock faces have evolved: edges have been used in recent times for the extraction of millstones both for corn-grinding and the sharpening of steel cutlery, weapons and implements in Sheffield, which is never far distant over the moors to the east.

On many of these former quarry sites—notably at Dove Stones, high above Saddleworth near the Lancashire–West Riding boundary, and at Millstone Edge above Hathersage in the Derwent Valley—and on the extensive broken faces of the natural edges, the early climbers of the district practised their art. Men such as J. W. Puttrell were wandering along Stanage Edge in 1890 in search of suitable rock for climbing. Edges that became attractive to those pioneers were Laddow Rocks, overlooking Crowden Great Brook in far northeastern Cheshire, and grimy Wharncliffe Crags, overlooking the confines of the Don valley between Oughtibridge and Stocksbridge.

ABOVE *The Salt Cellar tor, whose awkward shape has defeated many a scrambler.*

ABOVE *The Moatstone is one of several tors that stand in the peaty meres of the Peak's bogland.*

Wharncliffe Crags—virtually the birthplace of outcrop climbing—is undoubtedly the dirtiest climbing rock in the world, a distinction for which the steelworks of Stocksbridge must accept responsibility. Fire-breathing monsters inhabit the wooded steeps below the crags. The most notable feature here is the detached buttress known as the Bass Rock. It is really a tor. For more than three decades attempts were made to scale it by the steep front, but it was not until 1931 that Harry Scarlett climbed the centre crack and produced a first-class thirty-five-foot-high route of 'very severe' standard.

Stanage Edge also came into its own after the First World War, when Morley Wood and A. S. Pigott joined others who had previously found routes on this long escarpment. After the Second World War these same steep, coarse, rounded-hold cliffs were the nursery of such notable men of the mountains as Joe Brown and Don Whillans, who raised the standards attainable to an undreamt-of degree.

Perhaps the finest tors of all stand on the lonely crest of Derwent Edge and on the plateaus of Kinder Scout and Bleaklow. Derwent Edge overlooks the line of reservoirs in Derwent Dale. To the south of this are the several scattered tors seen so well from the road alongside those reservoirs: the rounded, dumpy trio called the Cakes of Bread, the shattered face of Dovestone Tor and the unusual Salt Cellar. This last rock is twenty feet in height, and the central part has been weathered to form a narrow stalk supporting the more resistant upper mushroom. Many have been the scramblers marooned on the top of the Salt Cellar after climbing onto it, unable then to make the more difficult descent.

Half a mile to the south of the Salt Cellar is one of the most interesting of all tors, called the Wheel Stones. A local name for this group of high rocks is the Coach and Horses. Looking from the western slopes of Derwent Dale near Ladybower Reservoir one sees, a mile in the distance and 900 feet above the surface of the water, a profile of a stagecoach drawn by galloping steeds.

Up on the smooth and peaty ridge of Bleaklow are numerous tors. Among the scattered Bleaklow Stones is the Anvil, a small tor similar to the Salt Cellar but so sharply etched by the elements that it could have been designed for use by Vulcan.

Along the northern edge of Kinder Scout are the various tors making up Seal Edge—rounded rocks resembling sea lions. Beyond Fairbrook Naze are the Boxing Glove Stones, upstanding rocks that look like a pair of boxing gloves. On the other side of the plateau there are the weird Madwoman's Stones, the castle-like turrets of Upper Tor above Grinds Brook, the Mushroom Stone and the most fantastic group of all—Whipsnade, or the Mushroom Garden. On a high, level shoulder between Edale Head and Crowden Tower (both tors), the exposed gritstone has been eroded into hundreds of small rock groups so as to resemble nothing less than animals in various attitudes. Come here in misty weather and it is quite easy to identify many of the beasts: the Dog, the Camel, the Hippos (in a peaty pool surrounding the rock group), the Sea Lion and so on. Wandering amid this moor-top maze gives a most peculiar feeling of otherworldliness.

High on the edge of Gibbet Moor and overlooking Chatsworth Park is the well-known Cannon Rock, a huge, rectangular block that sticks out high above the road and is a landmark for motorists. A couple of miles to the north, above Baslow Edge, the Eagle Stone stands twenty-five feet in isolation above the heather and is scored by countless scratches, many made by the young men of Baslow village long ago when it was customary to climb the Eagle Stone to prove one's manhood.

On the 1,200-foot top of Hathersage Moor stands a particularly impressive sight: the great bulk of the tor known as the Mother Cap. It is attractive because of its general tilt to the west, a leaning that suggests not imminent collapse but grace. Not far away, overhanging the main road to Sheffield, is that best-known of all Peakland tors: a large, flat, gritstone block, complete with 'eyes' and 'mouth', which has been called the Toad's Mouth for longer than anyone can remember.

All that windy afternoon we enjoyed spectacular views to the north and west beneath broken islands of whitest cumulus. From our viewpoint the blue, grey and white plumes of south Lancashire were pierced by sunbeams; it was a land of promise indeed.

A quick run down the steep 900-foot slopes at the head of the clough drained by the Shelf Brook, and soon we were overtaking a hedgehog on Doctor's Gate, the track that was the Roman road connecting Glossop and Brough. At 6pm we passed Mossy Lea Farm. Now it was evening, and, as we swung round to the south of Glossop on the lane by Moorfield and Gnat Hole, the profile of the church tower on Warhill and the dark outline of Cown Edge Rocks stood out in dramatic silhouette.

For three more miles we went south, along the Hayfield road. Then at 9pm we came to the gnat-filled wood on the eastern slope of Lantern Pike. We cooked our meal with the little summit far above our heads as the mackerel sky reflected the pink glow of the western sun. There was not a breath of wind, and we went to sleep as the last light bled from the sky behind our hill.

Once again a light drizzle fell at dawn the next morning, and we had a welcome mug of tea in our sleeping-bags. Soon the clouds were thinning, and long before we gained the top of Lantern Pike the sun was out.

My two friends and I had now travelled more than seventy-two miles, and this would be our final day. I wished that our journey would go on indefinitely in these wonderful conditions. From this 1,177-foot-high vantage point we could see the radio telescope at Jodrell Bank out on the Cheshire Plain; the massive bulk of Kinder Scout lay impressively behind us, topped by a gathering of dark cloud.

Down now to the sporadic conurbation that fills the floor of the Sett Valley—by Birch Vale, Pleasant View, Low Leighton and Newtown—then up a sunken lane onto the slopes of Black Hill.

By way of Kettleshulme and Windgather Youth Hostel and Cats Tor we reached Shining Tor at 2.30pm and saw our goal—Shutlingsloe—dominating the trough of Wildboarclough. To the south we were able to make out the blue profiles of the Clee Hills, the Wrekin and the long line of the Denbigh Moors.

So the three of us drew close to Shutlingsloe, lit now from the west, where the hill sheep graze. Our ninety miles were done, and overhead was as fine a sky of fair-weather cumulus as I think I have ever seen.

ABOVE *A climber boldly takes on Baslow's ancient test of manhood by scaling the Eagle Stone.*

ABOVE *The Toad's Mouth is one of many tors whose shapes resemble those of animals.*

CHAPTER TWO

PEAKLAND BOY

TWO MILES NORTH of Chesterfield's famous crooked spire in north Derbyshire lies the rather drab industrial-cum-residential sprawl called Whittington Moor. It is here, well out of sight, close beside a railway embankment, that the meandering River Rother is joined by a small stream which has wound down in a generally southeasterly direction for some seven miles through a valley whose historical importance and natural beauty are easy to underestimate. The stream is the River Drone, and its major settlement is the ancient market town of Dronfield, which lies near the head of the vale.

ABOVE *The spire of the Church of St John the Baptist is a prominent landmark in Dronfield, the author's home town.*

Here stand the Church of St John the Baptist (largely early 14th century), the ancient cruck barn thought to have been the dwelling of a 6th-century Anglian chieftain, and the early 18th-century manor house commanding the head of the High Street. This is the old heart of the town, but its original rustic character was largely changed by the coming of industrialisation and, in the third quarter of the 20th century, by large-scale residential expansion caused by overspill from nearby Sheffield.

There was much small-scale coal mining in the Drone valley, nowhere more intensive than in the Hill Top district to the south of Dronfield. Over the watershed to the north and northeast, tool-making developed into an important industry—little villages such as Ridgeway and Eckington becoming notable for the quality of their edge tools, particularly scythes and sickles.

In and about Dronfield are many fairly large stone houses, most of which date from the 18th century. Such dwellings include Chiverton House and Rose Hill. Some of these fine houses probably owe their existence to wealthy tradesmen. Many lead merchants lived in the little township in former times, perhaps because it was a more desirable locality than Chesterfield, a known centre of the Derbyshire lead trade.

Close beside the Drone, where it flows at the foot of Dronfield's parish churchyard, a foundry reputed to be the first to produce malleable iron castings was established in 1790. Samuel Lucas opened his works here and patented the process for the casting of malleable iron in 1804. On Christmas Eve 1971 the last castings were produced here, and subsequently the works was demolished. Only the archway that was the original entrance to the foundry remains.

The Drone flows southwards towards the Rother, hemmed in by high ground to both east and west. High upon the eastern heights stand the settlements of Summerley, Apperknowle and Hundall. Down near the valley floor, where the steep lanes from Apperknowle and Hundall meet, stands the village of Unstone.

MINING THE PAST

FROM THE DAYS of the Roman Empire until the mid 20th century, lead was mined in the Peak District. The industry was unregulated until 1288, when the entire area was divided into 'liberties', each one presided over by a bar-master. A miner could dig for lead ore anywhere—except churchyards, orchards, gardens or roads. Once a vein was found and registered with the bar-master, the miner had three weeks to get the mine operating, or else forfeit the claim. Stealing another miner's ore was punishable by heavy fines, and a repeat offender could soon find himself fixed by a knife through his hand to the windlass at the top of a mine shaft.

By the 17th century miners were reaching the water table. They fought valiantly to remove the excessive ground water, building drainage canals, or leats, like Mandale sough—a mile long and hacked out of the rock between 1797 and 1820. But even with the invention of steam-powered pumps to extract water, flooding remained an expensive problem. Take Mill Close Mine in Darley Dale, the last lead mine to remain active: in 1938 its 800 miners were producing 30,000 tons of lead a year. Each day, however, the pumps had to dispose of 7 million gallons of water. With the advent of cheap imports of lead, the industry became uneconomical and Mill Close shut down.

Today, it is the chemical industry that mines the Peak District, not for lead (which is still plentiful) but for fluorspar—a mineral used in the manufacture of such products as toothpaste and plastics. This valuable commodity was always extracted alongside the lead but was discarded as mere waste.

RIGHT *This carving of a lead miner can be seen on the exterior of St Mary's Church in the village of Wirksworth.*

LEFT *Lead ore—a valuable commodity since Roman times—is still present in the Peak District.*

ABOVE *Magpie Mine, near Bakewell, is a relic of an industry that is now consigned to the history books.*

An ancient bridle track goes up from Dronfield to Summerley, a tiny place with a couple of farms, a hall and several cottages. The name means 'summer pasture'. Summerley Hall was probably built in about 1300. The present house is the result of a major rebuilding after 1650 and is typical of several yeoman halls in the district built about the same time.

Half a mile along the lane to the southeast lies the larger village of Apperknowle—'apple tree hill'—which grew during the last century with the discovery of productive coal seams close to the surface here. Coal was sent down a cable-hauled railway to the main line at Unstone, and the course of this steep route can still be made out when a low sun etches the cuttings with telltale shadow. A further half-mile to the southeast lies Hundall, a hill-crest hamlet whose name means 'dogs' hill'.

In 1300 Unstone Hall was divided between the two daughters of the owner of the Summerley Estate. In the 15th century Unstone was held by the Bullocks. During the Civil War the Bullocks fell on hard times, but not so hard as to prevent the rebuilding of Unstone Hall in about 1653 as an L-shaped, gabled manor house.

Immediately downstream of Unstone the hillsides hem the river in, forming a wooded gorge. Here stood one of the village's two water mills, all but engulfed by tall trees beside the quiet Drone. Close by, the busy railway strides across the dale on its high, masonry viaduct, the most impressive feature on the journey between Chesterfield and Sheffield.

Downstream of the Unstone gorge the little Drone, often ochre-tinged from the disused colliery drains, meanders on to Sheepbridge. Here it is joined by

LEFT *Monk Wood lies between Dronfield and Chesterfield. In the past, monks used a trackway through the wood to travel between local monasteries.*

RIGHT *St Norbert (on the right of the picture), founder of the Premonstratensian monastic order, receives the Augustinian monastic rule of life from St Augustine himself. The Premonstratensian order gradually spread from its birthplace in Prémontré, France, to the rest of Europe, establishing an abbey near Sheffield.*

the Barlow Brook—its major tributary—and flows grey and rubbish-strewn past engineering works and railway sidings, to be swallowed unceremoniously by the Rother at Whittington Moor.

LOCAL HISTORY

You would never have thought that the rough lane winding south from Dronfield had once been the main route from Sheffield and the North. I never realised it, even though our house stood close by it; it was simply Highgate Lane, crossing the open, level land before descending as a track through the great wood to the mouth of Barlow vale and so to Chesterfield.

It is, in fact, a very ancient route, ten times older than the modern road that winds up by Unstone. Crossing the ancient way on the floor of the Drone valley is another of equal antiquity. This strikes westwards up Church Street and High Street and out into the open valley, leading to Holmesfield and Peakland proper. By coincidence, much of my life has been lived along two arms of these crossing routes—one to the south, one to the west, to the far blue hills which are the edge of the Pennines above Totley and Dore.

The southern and southeastern flanks of the high ground between Dronfield and Chesterfield were entirely (and still are largely) clothed with the trees of Monk Wood, one of the largest woods in Derbyshire. The ecclesiastical connection is simple. From Beauchief Abbey (now in a southern suburb of Sheffield) a trackway ran to its daughter penitentiary at Harewood Grange, above Holymoorside, some miles to the south. The Premonstratensian monks and others travelling between the two places would pass through Dronfield, up Hallowes Lane ('hallowed' lane?) and so through the woods, by way of Abbey Farm between Barlow and Cutthorpe, to ancient Linacre House. Here a rest would be taken before the last, long walk over the hills by Wadshelf and Upper Loads or by Chanderhill (maybe from the Middle English 'chauntour', a chanter or a chorister), Holymoorside and Cat Hole.

Where Hallowes Lane gives way to Highgate Lane stands what was formerly Hallowes Farm, now the Hallowes Golf Club. The present building, erected in 1657, is a very fine 17th-century yeoman farm. It is H-shaped, with gables on its wings and low mullioned windows tied to a long, uninterrupted stringcourse, the purpose of which was partly ornamental and partly to function as an 'eave' from which rain would drip clear of the lower wall and windows.

BELOW *Golfers enjoy a round at Hallowes Golf Club. The pond in the foreground was once the site of a tragic death; today it is nothing more sinister than a watery grave for stray golf balls.*

The Hallowes Golf Club took over the farmhouse in 1925. One major change was the removal of the high garden wall and the use of the stone to build an extension on the western end of the house. This has opened up the frontage so that passers-by can see the south front and the lovely stone dovecote, while the views from the house are now extensive, looking out over the links to a glimpse of faraway Peakland moors in the west. On the links, not far from the Hallowes, is a pond—a place of fascination and tragedy. On a frosty winter morning a long time ago, when the Hallowes was still a farmhouse, a youth went over to the pond to break the ice for the sheep to drink; as he did so the head of a woman broke the surface. She was a local woman who had been living at Hill Top in reduced circumstances.

The path associated with my earliest memories of this world of woodland is a continuation of Highgate Lane, the original route southwards towards Chesterfield. It must have been this track that King Egbert of Wessex followed in AD 829 on his way northwards from Tamworth, his capital, to meet King Eanred of Northumbria at Dore, three and a half miles to the northeast of Dronfield, just within the then-Northumbrian border. This extension of Highgate Lane into the wood has the indescribable aura of a living past, a charged atmosphere which is apparent even to the stranger.

Just beyond the edge of the golf course are the ruins of Highgate House. It is a long time since this place was inhabited, but there are people still living who remember when it was. The last occupants were a local family called Booker, and 'Teddy' Cooper recalls that there was a drift mine in the upper part of Loundes Wood and coal was brought up the slope by a narrow-gauge tramway. Ponies drew three full tubs at a time to the vicinity of Highgate House, and there the coal was loaded into carts and taken down to Dronfield and district. He used to climb between the laden tubs and enjoy the ride to the top of the slope, and slowly down again with the tub wheels sledging on runners.

LEFT *Being small and strong, pit ponies were invaluable for hauling coal to the pit head.*

Beyond the inconspicuous ruins of Highgate House the lane turns down through a deep cutting, hedged on either side above steep banks near to which the tramway ran. The isolated smallholding by the lane is called Ouzelbank Cottage; it looks out to the south over a broad meadow which was surrounded, until the 1950s, by the upper reaches of Loundes Wood. Over on the far side is a spring of clear water emptying into a trough, which Dronfield people have visited for a very long time to fill bottles that were carried home to be used as a tonic for the delicate and aged. I used to go regularly with my mother to collect the spring water in lemonade bottles for my grandmother. The spring still flows, but most of Loundes Wood has gone.

From Ouzelbank Cottage a path leads steeply down to the east, to cross the railway at Unstone station. I remember that when I was four and five years old we used to go down that way quite often to meet my father on the main road below the station. He would stop the car and we would have a ride home. Alternatively one could continue down through Brierley Wood, keeping to the ancient route, and so reach the mouth of broad Barlow vale near Sheepbridge Works. Even though it is a dirty place, this old-established engineering works has the advantage of being close to the wood and the open fields, and it was the proximity of small coal pits in Monk Wood and by the Sud Brook that caused the construction of two railway tracks. These tracks wound up their respective valleys between the trees, bringing fuel to the Sheepbridge blast furnaces.

Lees Common, a farm of considerable antiquity which was modernised in 1960, is the home of Sir Eric Mensforth, a former Master Cutler. I can remember seeing the new perimeter wall for the farm's orchard being built many years ago by an old craftsman from Barlow. The wall is unique in this district, for it consists of alternate layers of stone and turf. The roots in the turf have continued to anchor the soil and this in turn supports the stones.

ABOVE *A Redfern family tree. These initials were carved by the author's father in 1925, and were later joined by those of his mother and himself. The tree has since been cut down, but the author was first able to preserve the carving on film.*

Not very far along the track towards Barlow stands Monkwood Farm. Teas used to be served in its orchard, and in those days the place was virtually surrounded by the wood. It is a typical Barlow vale farmhouse, with walls of local sandstone and a roof of large stone slabs in the traditional manner. To our delight a swing hung from an old pear tree in the orchard, and if it was wet we sheltered in the open cart shed facing the southwest. The place was probably rebuilt in the 17th century, but it is of older foundation as it was known at an earlier date as 'the Mounks house'. Perhaps the monks stayed here and farmed the open fields towards Barlow while their herds of swine were fattened on nuts and roots gleaned in the encircling woods.

A short distance towards the west along the track known as Middle Riding is Robin Hood's Well. Whether the celebrated outlaw ever drank from this watering hole must remain a subject for conjecture, but it is almost certain that he travelled in this region, en route between his Sherwood country and the higher parts of Peakland with which he is so closely linked by tradition. The water issues from a hollow, long surrounded by several trees, notably a venerable pair of hollies, a little way above the track. Upon these shading holly trees were some very old initials, with rather indistinct dates: in 1925 my father carved his initials clearly; two years later my mother carved hers. In 1948 I did the same and so the trunks could be said to have comprised a complete family tree.

Along the Middle Riding there are no open views, but towards the northwest a little valley develops to the left and across it is the 530-foot-high eminence of Broom Bank. From its top the views are suddenly revealed over Barlow Lees and central Barlow vale, backed by the blue haze of the hill slopes rising towards Grange and the moors. On the southern flank of Broom Bank are the ruins of the colliery of the same name, one of many that were developed in the lower reaches of the valley during the last century and which gave employment to many of the inhabitants of Barlow, Unstone and Dronfield.

On the northern flank of Broom Bank the bluebells are particularly dense: they have colonised a great part of the hollow falling from the Middle Riding and often bloom at the same time as the wild crab apple blossoms nearby, making a lovely contrast of deepest blue with palest pink. Indeed, bluebells and bracken, cuckoo calls and the soft and drowsy cooing of wood pigeons, a glimpse down some enigmatic ride between silver birches at the end of a warm evening and the many scents of fungi on a September walk, these and a whole miscellany of other sounds and smells and sights are, for me, Monk Wood past and present.

WHITTINGTON'S GLORIOUS REVOLUTION

Of all the lesser heights of Peakland and its wonderful fringe my favourite is Glasshouse Hill, the dominating eminence of the Drone valley. Its maximum

FABULOUS FUNGI

THERE ARE AN ASTONISHING 10,000 species of fungi growing in the British Isles, from microscopic moulds to huge bracket fungi. Non-flowering plants with no chlorophyll, fungi are unable to produce their own food. Instead, they obtain nourishment from dead organic matter such as leaf mould or wood, or grow parasitically on living organisms. Fungi have a useful role to play in aiding the formation of humus but can be destructive: the honey fungus, for example, is anything but sweet: it is a serious pest that kills many trees every year.

ABOVE *A colourful collection of fungi gathered from the British woods and fields. But beware—the pretty red and white fly agaric toadstool is poisonous.*

Children's books often have whimsical illustrations showing elves living in toadstools, or fairies dancing inside mushroom rings, but fungi have sinister connotations too. Psilocybin mushrooms have hallucinogenic properties, and, if eaten, trigger a range of side effects including raised blood pressure, nausea and numbness. There is also an old country belief that toadstools are composed of all the evil elements of the earth.

This fear is well-grounded in some instances. The aptly named death cap and the destroying angel are lethal if eaten. Also poisonous, but rarely fatal, is the distinctive scarlet and white fly agaric which is unlikely to be mistaken for an edible mushroom. There are many species that can be cooked and enjoyed, but anyone considering eating wild mushrooms should ensure that they identify them properly first. Although some species mature in the spring, the best time to gather fungi is in late summer and early autumn, after rain. Gastronomic treats include the common field mushroom, the cep, the chanterelle and—the king of fungi—the truffle.

RIGHT *Honey fungi growing round the roots of a tree is an ominous sign—this pest destroys its host.*

ABOVE *Glasshouse Hill dominates the horizon seen from a Derbyshire country lane banked with hawthorn.*

height is 664 feet above sea level, so that on the grounds of altitude alone it cannot claim any distinction. But, owing to the haphazard forces of weathering, it has been left at a position where, in relation to the surrounding ridges and valleys, it assumes a central point of focus in views from almost all angles.

For eight years Glasshouse Hill was the focal point of my view as I walked homewards down Stubley Lane from Gosforth, and in that time I came to know intimately the wonderful pattern of fields through every season. During autumn each yellow stubble field on that northwestern flank above and below Windmill Lane turned to brown as each in turn was ploughed. Every spring the exotic pattern of green was renewed as young corn grew to rival the permanent pastures and meadows; and as summer came and went the colours assumed the variety of a patchwork quilt, rearranged each year. The meadows were mowed and cleared of hay to leave a yellow-brown rectangle; the pastures remained green; the cornfields slowly lost their vivid verdant hue and by late summer shone burnished in the afternoon sunlight—golden pockets set about by dark green fringes of hedgerow and woodland.

From the upper reaches of the Barlow vale, Glasshouse Hill peeps over the intervening ridge above Monk Wood, its topmost fields normally set with corn and offering gold to the late-summer sky. From Unthank Fields close by Rose Wood, the important role played by Grasscroft Wood in the configuration of Glasshouse Hill is clearly seen. The wood grows right across the southern flank from 500 feet to within a few feet of the summit. The uppermost trees overtop the summit so that their profile accentuates the dome-shaped crest, making it seem quite conical. It is a crook-shaped hill in the true tradition of Peakland profiles, subtle rather than dramatic, suggestive rather than accentuated.

Richard Dixon came to the district soon after 1710 to found a glassworks, and Whittington became an important industrial centre. Whittington glass was a lovely product, possessing a pale-blue cast, and was used to make tumblers, vases and other pieces, particularly cruets, in collaboration with the Sheffield plate trade. Several factors caused the decline of glass manufacture here, and it ceased finally about 1815.

ABOVE *The Whittington glass industry produced elegant cut glass, such as this cruet, for over 100 years during the 18th and early 19th centuries.*

As for Whittington itself, the name stems from the Old English—'Hwita-ing-tun', literally 'Hwita's farm'. The village has a number of associations with events and, more particularly, people of note.

At a house called Elm Wood, by the road towards Handley, lived the caricaturist Phil May. He was born in 1864 and worked as an artist for *Punch* before his early death on August 5, 1903. Subsequently Elm Wood became the home of Henry Brearley when he worked for the large steel manufacturers Brown Bayley Ltd of Sheffield. Previously Brearley had worked for Thomas Firth and Sons Ltd, and while so employed had invented stainless steel. It was because of this discovery that the patent for Firth Stainless Steel was procured.

In May 1783 Joseph Brotherton was born at Old Whittington. He became connected with a powerful political party in Manchester, and in 1827 was elected first MP for Salford. Perhaps his fight against the notorious Corn Laws stands out as the greatest contribution he made in a very active life. To the memory of this life of public service a statue of Brotherton stands in Peel Park, Salford, bearing the following words from one of his speeches to Parliament: 'My riches consist, not in the extent of my possessions, but in the fewness of my wants.'

By coincidence, in the same year that Phil May was born in Yorkshire (1864), there was born at Old Whittington a child destined to become a great English artist. Joseph Syddall was born into a Whittington family of joiners. His talents were well-known locally and he created copiously, though his work is not now widely known. Much of it, however, was tragically destroyed during the Second World War. He designed the Great War memorials at Old Whittington and Dronfield, and both stand as memorials to his genius. The one at Old Whittington, with its crosses on all four faces, was executed by Tom Moxon who lived in the village.

Whittington was involved in the Revolution of 1688. The Catholic James II had succeeded his brother, Charles II, in 1685, and his efforts to emancipate the Catholics were one factor in the rebellion. Among the powerful noblemen who wished to see James off the throne so that all threats of Catholicism could be removed was the Earl of Devonshire. A tradition exists concerning the first meeting of many that led to the revolt against the unpopular King. It states that the

BELOW *Revolution House in Whittington, depicted on a banner celebrating the centenary of the 1688 Revolution. It was here that a group of treacherous peers of the realm plotted to overthrow King James II.*

Earl of Devonshire's harriers were taken to Whittington Moor—then an infertile area of common and river confluence—so that everyone in the district would be busy following the chase. According to an old account, 'when the pack were in full cry, and the field in hot pursuit, his lordship and friends drew away from the hunt, and rode to the Cock and Pynot, to deliberate upon the means by which to procure King James's overthrow.'

The little party was ushered into a private parlour—ever afterwards known as the Plotting Parlour. It is known that besides the Earl of Devonshire, those at this meeting to plan the overthrow of the King included the Earl of Danby and John D'Arcy (son and heir of Conyers, Earl of Holderness). It is not certain that other supporters of the proposed revolution, Sir Scroop Howe and Lord Delamere, were actually present on that day. Seated in high-backed chairs around a small table, the group examined a map of the country and agreed upon the wording of the invitation to William, Prince of Orange, to take the throne once James had been expelled. William was a grandson of Charles I and had married James II's daughter Mary.

It was agreed that the Earl of Danby was to give the signal for the rising in the North of England, and Devonshire was to raise an armed force in the Midlands. In 1694 he was created the first Duke of Devonshire by William.

William landed at Torbay on November 5, 1688, and before he entered Exeter the Earl of Devonshire had reached Derby with a small group of followers and declared before the mayor his support for William. It was soon clear that William was taking all before him, gathering ever more support as he passed from Bristol to Salisbury and on to London. James fled for France.

ABOVE *William of Orange and his wife Mary were crowned King and Queen in 1689. As the daughter of the deposed King James II, Mary was appointed to the unprecedented position of joint sovereign with her husband.*

At the time of the revolution the Cock and Pynot Inn, where the secret meeting took place, was a long, low building with six rooms on the ground floor. Due to decay and dereliction the northern section was finally demolished, leaving the present squat building, commonly known as the Revolution House, with its thatched roof and pretty dormer window. Long ago the licence of the public house was transferred to the newer building behind the Revolution House. This is now the Cock and Magpie Inn (pynot is the old name for magpie) while the Revolution House has become a public museum run by Chesterfield Borough Council.

And so with the passing of time the village has changed its character. Whittington Hall—once a notable house of the gentry—has now been converted into flats; a new road bypasses the hillside part of the village near to the church. Perhaps that is a good thing, for it leaves the upper portion of Whittington as a backwater. There were several small collieries hereabouts, and a great number of village men worked at Sheepbridge Works, a mile and a half below in the Drone valley. From the top of Glasshouse Hill it was a dramatic sight to watch at night as the great blast furnaces at Sheepbridge were tapped. The blackness of winter midnights was suddenly shot through with orange, red and rose. If there were low clouds about they were caught in the glare and reflected the shimmering light, an illumination with satanic overtones backed up by the distant noise of clashing metal and great activity. That nightly spectacle of the many manually controlled furnaces vanished years ago, to be replaced by the vastly less romantic automatic blast furnaces. Now those, too, have gone, and no more is the night sky resplendent with heat, light and colour.

The compensation, of course, is the greater western vista, up the valleys to the north and west, to the setting sun and its incomparable and never-repeated finale of light on cloud and sky. Go up behind the village on a crisp autumn evening, up the fields towards the crouching wood of Grasscroft which crowns the crest of this most conspicuous Derbyshire hill. As the sunset banners unfurl in the west the grey-blue bulk of Grange Hill, Eastmoor beyond and those familiar steeps of home about Monk Wood change to an ever-darker solidity, washed with a brush and colours so soft that at times they melt into the haze of the Drone valley below and into the sky above. It is possible to imagine the inhabitants who lived all their quiet lives just below in the village, most of whom now lie in the shadow of the trees and St Bartholomew's Church.

BELOW *A breathtaking sunset over the Drone valley brings the day to a glorious close.*

GEORGE STEPHENSON, RAILWAY PIONEER

LEFT *Labourers take a break from the construction of the Dove Holes Tunnel on the Rowsley–Buxton railway line,* c. *1862.*

ENGINEER, INVENTOR and 'father of the locomotive', George Stephenson was born in 1781 near Newcastle-upon-Tyne. Never formally educated in his youth, Stephenson began work in the local colliery at the age of eight. During his teenage years he worked as an engine stoker—at this time there were only stationary steam engines to pump out mines and haul trucks—and found he had a talent for mechanics. In 1803 he married and had his first and only child, Robert, who would grow up to be his assistant and a great civil engineer in his own right.

Stephenson rose to become the chief engineer at the local colliery of Killingworth, and in 1814 he was commissioned to build his first steam locomotive, the *Blücher*, which could draw a 30-ton load of coal at 4 miles per hour. He went on to build improved versions of it for various different collieries. Then in 1825 his career accelerated when, for the new Stockton to Darlington railway, he built a locomotive that could transport 450 passengers at 15 mph. The following year he began work on the Liverpool and Manchester Railway and in 1829 his *Rocket* won the prestigious Rainhill trials to choose a locomotive to run on the line. Meanwhile, he continued to run the locomotive-manufacturing company that he had established in Newcastle in 1823. Until his retirement in 1845, he presided over a number of large projects as both engineer and consultant, bringing railways to cities such as Birmingham, Derby and Leeds.

Stephenson and his locomotives were at the forefront of the railway boom. By 1838, 500 miles of railway track had been laid in Britain, and by 1850, two years after Stephenson's death, this figure had increased to 5,000 miles. The era of cheap public travel had arrived. In the Peak District the first railway was the Cromford and High Peak line, which opened in 1830–31. By the mid-19th century the area was linked with the rest of England via lines running along the Derwent and Wye valleys and Longdendale. Stephenson's legacy had changed the face of Peakland—and of civilisation—for ever.

BELOW *A railway ticket from 1832, valid for a trip to Warrington on the Liverpool and Manchester Railway.*

ABOVE *A model of Stephenson's* Rocket, *which won the 1829 Rainhill trials to find the most efficient railway locomotive.*

LEFT *John Seymour Lucas's portrait of George Stephenson shows him standing proudly in front of one of the railways that his engineering genius helped pioneer.*

RIGHT *The opening of the Liverpool and Manchester Railway in September 1830 was a grand occasion. George Stephenson designed the first locomotive to run on the line.*

MY RAILWAY AGE

On a dark winter night of hard frost and flashing stars the slow beating of a class 4F 0-6-0 locomotive sounded louder and clearer than usual as it climbed the long bank. It must have been hauling a particularly heavy train of coal or iron ore, for I remember that the bedroom walls shook as it climbed northwards to the watershed. The throaty barking continued, it seemed, for hours, echoing from beneath Wreakes Lane Bridge and on into the cutting, leading ever nearer to the dread blackness of the tunnel mouth. Up there, a mile away from home, was the sinister vault where evil and torment held the day. Wraiths came and went through the briars and willowherb on sunny afternoons; on black nights it was an area beyond description—a place of loud labours, foul air and black-faced, angry gangers. I drew down closer between the sheets, and only then, after the familiar whistle followed by the sudden death of noise, did I know that the train had reached the portals of that palace of the demon king and vanished within—never to be heard again.

ABOVE *As a young boy the author was entranced by steam engines and the work involved in running them. Here, a fireman stokes a locomotive's boiler with coal.*

I wouldn't have changed places with the driver of that night goods train for any prize on earth. Yet, by day, down to the colliery sidings we would fly if there was any chance of a goods train resting there. The experience never failed to give an indescribable thrill as we were asked aboard and climbed the greasy steps to the wonderful alcove between fiery furnace and heaped coals; there the all-pervading aroma of steam and oil transported me on a magic carpet of delight to dreamlands of faraway and unknown main lines, where exotic machinery belched fire and columns of grey-black cloud into the blue sky. I remember, even at this distance in time, that one particularly benign driver allowed me to pull the regulator and set his great locomotive on its way, out of the siding and onto the gradient towards the tunnel. Before reaching the stone road bridge over the line we were set down and we waved farewell with proud and thumping hearts.

It was the lack of a convenient railway link that had delayed the industrial development of my native Dronfield. George Stephenson chose the neighbouring Rother Valley to take his main line between Derby and Leeds because it offered fewer physical problems. The North Midland Railway Company opened that line on May 11, 1840. At Masbrough, close to Rotherham, there was a junction with the Sheffield and Rotherham railway line which ran the four miles up the Don valley to the Wicker station on the northern side of Sheffield. During the next quarter of a century mounting pressure was brought to bear from influential sources in and around Sheffield for a better railway link for this expanding industrial centre. A meeting of interested parties was held in Sheffield on December 5, 1863. The outcome was a proposal that a new line should be driven from Chesterfield to Sheffield, to be the main line and so cause the town at last to stand astride a convenient and efficient railway route.

The new route was planned to leave the existing line a mile north of Chesterfield station, at a place that has come to be known as Tapton Junction. On the top of the steep rise to the east stands Tapton House, where George Stephenson came to live in the prosperous years before his death in 1848. The

new route followed the valley drained by the River Drone for several miles, ascending towards the high ridge that forms the major obstacle. It was this high land that had turned Stephenson up the Rother Valley in the first place.

Great embankments carried the line above the flood plain of the meandering Drone by Sheepbridge station and Sheepbridge Works. A mile and a half north of Tapton Junction, on the steadily ascending incline, the contractors were forced to construct a tunnel eighty-eight yards long as a condition of permission to cross the land. The landowner insisted that a right of way across the line must be given by the Midland Railway Company by means of a wide belt of land for the passage of farm animals and local inhabitants. This tunnel was called Broom House Tunnel, taking its name from the landowner's house nearby. In August 1969 it was removed by British Rail, as maintenance costs were proving prohibitive. The line now runs through a wide cutting, where a century ago the railway contractors found and marketed coal during tunnelling operations.

Less than a mile to the north the valley of the River Drone narrows. Here the railway had to cross the valley and gain the far bank in order to maintain a direct course. The answer to the problem was the erection of Unstone viaduct, an impressive structure of seven graceful arches in mellow stone. Immediately to the south of the viaduct the Midland Railway constructed in about 1878 a branch line which wound about to the east of the main line to serve the several collieries that were then being worked. The tall brick winding house of one of these still rears up through the woods near Dronfield—a forgotten turret where, in childhood fantasies, brave knights came to rescue imprisoned maidens.

ABOVE AND TOP
The Midland Railway Company issued posters (top) *promoting the delights of Derbyshire to encourage tourists to travel by rail. The company, which ran trains from London to Carlisle, adorned its carriages with a decorative coat of arms* (above).

From the platforms at Dronfield it was always a thrill to watch steam-hauled trains approaching the long, straight one-in-ninety gradient from Unstone. A great column of creamy smoke and steam would rise into the clear sky on a frosty morning as a heavy freight train came northwards. The lower line of exhaust and the rocking front of a fast-climbing express was even more exciting. We always tried to reach the down platform in time to watch the high-speed passing of the Glasgow-bound Thames–Clyde Express at 12.30pm. Sometimes we were late out of school and heard its close-approaching rhythmic roar, but usually managed a mad scramble onto the platform to watch the majestic passing of the fastest down train of the day. Of course, the sudden and explosive appearance of a London-bound express on the up line, coming into sight round the curve beneath the stone bridge at the northern end of the station, was very impressive, but the greater speed and shorter time it was in view made the impression less memorable.

One mile north of Dronfield the line entered an ever-deepening cutting into the high ridge that forms the watershed between the upper reaches of the Drone and the Sheaf. This ridge had deterred Stephenson thirty years before, but now work was started on the tunnel. It is Bradway Tunnel, and measures 1 mile 267 yards in length, largely through millstone grit. Eight shafts were sunk to facilitate tunnelling operations on eighteen headings. The great problem was water: 16,000 gallons per hour flowed from the workings. All this had to be pumped from the headings by engines erected at each of the eight shafts, and was 'of such purity' that it was taken by pipes to Sheffield to form 'an unfailing supply for all station purposes'. The eight shafts were retained to form smoke shafts for exhaust purposes, and the familiar plumes of black coal smoke would drift over Middle Birchitt and Bradway golf course.

The northern portal of Bradway Tunnel is set in a very deep cutting, made through sandstone and shale. Shortly the line swings into the Sheaf Valley, and in four miles reaches the Midland Railway Centre which was built at the same time as the railway to be Sheffield's major railway station. In 1894, incidentally, the Midland Railway Company completed its route from Sheffield to Manchester via the Hope Valley. To gain access to this Peakland valley the line reaches the head of the Sheaf Valley—near to the northern portal of Bradway Tunnel—and goes beneath Totley Moss by way of Totley Tunnel, the second-longest main line railway tunnel in Britain. It leaves the Hope Valley by way of the Vale of Edale and continues through Cowburn Tunnel to Chinley and so towards Manchester.

One of the most memorable characters I have ever known was Rowland Hill. Even in great age he looked like a Viking warrior—tall and broad-shouldered, with a great hook nose, flowing white mane and matching walrus moustache. Old Hill, for that is what everyone called him, found work with the Midland Railway in the hills of north Derbyshire, and that naturally led to work in the numerous tunnels there: Cowburn, Totley, Bradway, Clay Cross. He had worked in the smoky darkness of all north Derbyshire's longest railway tunnels. Besides a strong constitution, Old Hill retained a sharp mind and numerous memories.

'In wintertime I used to have to walk down t' middle, between t' tracks, with a long 'ickling pole held up t' roof and fastened in a belt round mi waist to support some o' weight—that were to knock off ice, and some o' them icicles used to rattle down and clout y'u on t' head!' He grinned as he reminisced, and recalled that a mate held a paraffin lamp up towards the roof so that he could see the icicles which had to be dislodged before the trains could be allowed to pass through. 'Do y'u remember owd Haslam, 'im as got buried in t' ballast near Bradway tunnel-mouth?' he continued. 'I was 'im as found 'im! Ay, a light engine came up and bowled him o'er before any on us saw it. And he were t' horn blower for our gang!'

The Midland Railway Act of July 12, 1869 had allowed for the construction of the Sheepbridge branch. A line came from the old main route near Tapton

Junction, through Sheepbridge Works, and forked near the confluence of the Sud Brook with the Barlow Brook. One line wound upwards for over a mile and a half to Engine Hollow, near Barlow village; the other line ran for almost a mile into the lower reaches of Monk Wood. Both lines served the several small collieries developed at that time in these quiet hollows. The rusting lines and white-painted crossing gates remained, until quite recently, a silent track winding mysteriously out of sight between hazel and willows. It seemed to be waiting breathlessly for some 0-6-0 tank engine of old to come churning along the line, but none came; a level trackway, like a forgotten Roman road, is now all that remains to remind one of the activity that once enlivened those woods.

TRAINS ACROSS THE PEAK

In 1846 a scheme was drawn up to join Ambergate, on the Derby–Chesterfield line built earlier by Stephenson, to Cheadle, on the edge of Manchester, with a railway that would pass through the heart of the limestone valleys of Peakland. It had the grand name of the Manchester, Buxton, Matlock and Midland Junction. The

GLORIOUS CHATSWORTH

CHATSWORTH HOUSE, seat of the Dukes of Devonshire, is the grandest of the Peak District's many impressive stately homes. The house is set in a superbly landscaped bowl of wooded parkland and spectacular gardens on the banks of the River Derwent, and from certain vantage points the palatial house appears to float, perfectly reflected in flattering mirrors of water.

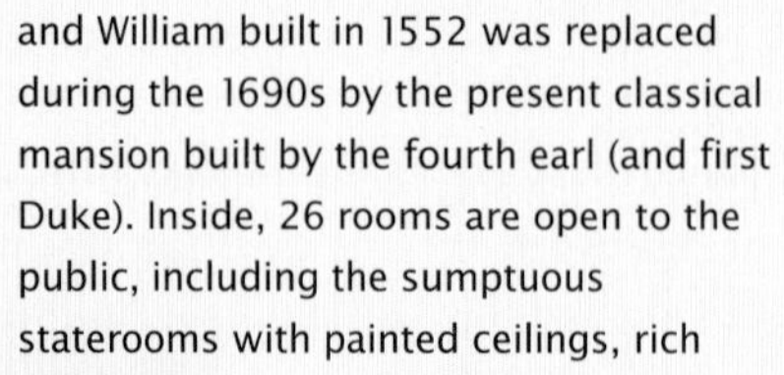

Chatsworth's history began in 1549, when Bess of Hardwick persuaded her second husband, Sir William Cavendish, to buy the surrounding land. Their son became Earl of Devonshire in 1618. The large Tudor house Bess and William built in 1552 was replaced during the 1690s by the present classical mansion built by the fourth earl (and first Duke). Inside, 26 rooms are open to the public, including the sumptuous staterooms with painted ceilings, rich tapestries, sculptures, silver and porcelain. Among the hordes of valuable and fascinating items on display, visitors remember especially the astonishingly realistic trompe l'oeil violin by Jan Vandervaart, apparently hanging on the back of a door, and two magnificent vases made from local Blue John stone. Like many of their predecessors, the present duke and duchess are avid art collectors. Modern art by Lucian Freud and Elizabeth Frink rubs shoulders with old masters by Rembrandt and Van Dyck. Family portraits include works by Pietro Annigoni and John Singer Sargent, but none is more enchanting than Gainsborough's painting of Georgiana Spencer, who married the fifth duke.

ABOVE *Thomas Gainsborough's portrait of Georgiana, Duchess of Devonshire, wife of the fifth duke, graces the Great Dining Room at Chatsworth House.*

During the 18th century Chatsworth's formal gardens and parkland were remodelled in the fashionable 'natural' style by Capability Brown. Ambitious water features form a distinctive part of the gardens. These include the Cascade (a long, stone waterfall staircase) and several eye-catching fountains. The Emperor Fountain is the world's tallest gravity-fed water-jet; the jokey Willow Tree gives visitors an unexpected wetting; and a kinetic water sculpture features a nine-foot-high bronze lily which opens and closes. During the 19th century Sir Joseph Paxton, the sixth duke's gardener, designed a series of elegant glasshouses, the forerunners of his Crystal Palace masterpiece. Unfortunately, not all of these have survived, but a splendid modern greenhouse displays plant specimens from around the world.

southernmost section was soon completed, linking Ambergate to Rowsley; here there was a very fine station where passengers alighted to continue their journey by coach and horses to Chatsworth, by far the finest house in Peakland.

To Sir Joseph Paxton and his patron, the sixth Duke of Devonshire, must go much of the credit for Chatsworth's beautiful gardens. The architectural garden of flowers beneath the west front of the house was laid out by Wyatville before Paxton came to Chatsworth, while it was the Duchess Evelyn who planted the narrow gorge or ravine below the grotto pond after the First World War. But between them, Paxton and the sixth duke were responsible for some of the finest features—especially the great Emperor Fountain, fed by water from the lakes up on Eastmoor's edge.

Formerly, the way to Chatsworth was a steep descent off Eastmoor close to the Hunting Stand, and travellers regularly remarked on their relief on that descent. In 1697 Celia Fiennes rode from Old Brampton and hated every mile of the wilderness way, until, quite suddenly, she saw 'the duke's house' and noted its position as being 'just at the foote of this steepe hill which is like a precipice just at the last'.

LEFT *Almost every visitor is taken in by the astoundingly lifelike trompe l'oeil violin and bow that 'hang' on the back of a door in the music room.*

BELOW *The painted hall, decorated in 1692 with scenes from the life of Julius Caesar, is the setting for a local children's party every Christmas.*

LEFT *Chatsworth House, seen from beyond the bridge built by James Paine in 1762. A sumptuous mansion of yellow stone, the house glows in the late afternoon sun and is reflected in the waters of the River Derwent.*

For a long time the rugged profile could be seen rearing up behind the house and gardens, but during the 19th and 20th centuries the planting of thousands of trees has driven the wild moorland out of sight. Up there, by the Emperor Lake, one is at the edge of the moor, and quite suddenly it is possible to look down over the waterfall to that loveliest of contrived landscapes: the water descends like a curtain between the massed rhododendrons and along the top of the aqueduct to cascade suddenly to the rocks below, from where it leads beneath the garden wall to emerge in the Cascade House. From there the wild torrent is a curtailed and cultured watercourse, gently progressing towards the south front.

As far back as 1845 permission had been granted by the Duke of Devonshire to take the railway northwards from Rowsley through Chatsworth Park to Baslow, providing that the entire length of the line through Chatsworth Park was covered. By 1860, however, when the line was ready to be extended beyond Rowsley, this Duke of Devonshire was dead and the new duke refused to entertain such a proposal. An alternative route had to be found, and the only feasible one was to go up the Wye valley to Bakewell. This meant going through the grounds of Haddon Hall, a mile above Rowsley. Negotiations with the Duke of Rutland of Haddon Hall commenced, and finally it was arranged that the line would pass through Haddon Hall Park, behind the hall, provided that no trees were felled or lopped and that the line was hidden in a tunnel for its entire passage through the park.

Keepers were set to watch the grounds, to prevent and report on any damage done by the contractors and their navvies. One of the principal objects of this exercise was, of course, to prevent the taking of game. The line was excavated from the hillside, partly by a cutting and partly by tunnelling. The cutting was then arched over with masonry and filled in with rock and soil to form a continuous tunnel—the present Haddon Tunnel—of 1,058 yards.

To the north of Haddon Hall the railway line contours high above the flood plain of the Wye and passes to the east of Bakewell. To satisfy the insistent demands of influential local inhabitants stations were built at both Bakewell and Hassop—though the latter was some distance from the village of that name. It was one of the first stations to be closed in this part of England some years ago. The line then climbs steadily through the limestone countryside round Longstone.

Where the branch line winds up to the west, along Ashwood Dale to Buxton, was situated Blackwell Halt, which had the distinction of being the smallest British railway station. The main line was driven on up the limestone valley called Great Rocks Dale at a gradient of one in ninety. The summit is reached two miles up this incline, 1,000 feet above sea level, at the southern portal of Dove Holes Tunnel (2,860 yards long). Today this valley is heavily industrialised—the longest quarry face in Europe stands above the railway on the western side—and kilns belch smoke and fumes by day and night.

The line then descends by way of Chapel-en-le-Frith to Buxworth. Here, late in 1866, sixteen acres of clay and shale slipped down the slope, damaged the railway construction works and severely damaged the new five-arch viaduct.

LEFT *Bakewell station closed in 1967, and local businesses now use the building as offices.*

Even so, the line was finally completed and opened to passenger traffic in February 1867.

Since this line was closed to traffic in 1967 I have walked the central, most dramatic, section of the route on several occasions, examining details of construction and scenery en route. A deep cutting through dark-grey limestone leads one to the southern portal of Headstones Tunnel. Towards the north the line curves round to the right, cutting out any sight of the other end until one is well advanced along the tunnel's 533-yard length. Ahead is one of the most dramatic points on any British railway: the lines emerge from Headstones' northern portal and almost immediately cross the arches of Monsal Dale viaduct. Had this line been projected today I am quite certain that permission would not have been given for such an intrusion upon the green slopes of Monsal Dale. Ruskin was outraged, but his was a voice crying in the wilderness of Victorian 'railway mania'. The line crosses the dale and thereafter is virtually hidden by another long, deep cutting in the limestone.

Beyond this the line passes through limestone spurs above the River Wye by means of Cressbrook Tunnel and Litton Tunnel, again good fun on foot. On the approach to Miller's Dale station the railway was carried over the river again by means of Miller's Dale viaduct. This is a structure with three arches, each of ninety-foot span and carrying the lines almost 100 feet above the river and the road. Then comes the difficult passage of beautiful and intricate Chee Dale, involving the negotiation of three tunnels and sudden downward glimpses to the dale of woods and white limestone outcrops. The construction work involved at this point was excessive, but the railway traveller had a most interesting ride, with ever-changing glimpses of a typical limestone dale close at hand on either side of the carriage alternately. After the opening of this line it was described as carrying the traveller 'through perhaps the most interesting series of railway works to be found in England'.

CHAPTER THREE

FARMER'S LAD

UNCLE BEN WAS sixty-six when I first met him. It was a mellow September day, and the gnats were still biting. I remember that because he had a knotted handkerchief on his head in a valiant effort to keep those tiresome insects at bay. Having come to my new job on the farm that very morning I found things rather strange, but the farmer was friendly, and after drawing a trailer up between two manure heaps with the tractor, he had suggested that I didn't take too much notice of Uncle Ben who was to load up on the other side.

The old man had lived and worked on his brother's farm all his life. He was thin and angular, his face aquiline, and he walked with a bad limp caused by a hip injury sustained when he was young. He was very, very deaf into the bargain, and this affliction, too, had been with him since youth. The result was that Uncle Ben was a sour old thing. Until one got to know him well—or perhaps until he got to know you well—any communication was difficult, to say the least. He was not given to showing interest in anyone, but was quick to point out faults and grievances in sudden outbursts of undulating sound, largely because his deafness denied him tone and volume control.

'Naw! Naw! Chuck it on t' trailer,' he screamed over the load of manure on that first morning long ago, when I threw a forkful too energetically, causing it to clear the trailer and land at his feet. The gnats and this raw youth were certainly testing his patience. Mugs of steaming coffee came out at eleven o'clock, but Uncle Ben ignored such time-wasting hindrances so I stole quick gulps from my mug while he wasn't looking. He was always like that: a cup of tea brought up the fields to where he was creosoting a henhouse would be left until stone cold unless he thought no one was watching, and then he would consume it quickly. I never discovered whether it was obtuseness or virtuous example-setting.

In earlier days, long before I knew him, he was the horseman on the farm, and managed, despite lameness, to cart manure up the lane to some outlying land two miles away high above the valley, while in summer he carted the hay and corn down to the farm. These climbs and descents were normally accomplished at full speed, Uncle Ben attempting to control the horses from a seated position at the back of the shafts. His roars and screams were well known to the people living along his route to the top of the lane. Once, a pair of particularly lively mares threw him from his precarious perch below a load of manure and he lay in the hedge bottom until the careering horses were seen by a farmer's wife farther up the hill; he was subsequently rescued, screaming oaths at his vanished team. Autumn ploughing must have presented the ageing cripple with severe problems, though he was able to walk with his short leg on the 'land' and his good leg in the furrow, and the work was completed in a surprisingly short time.

By the time I got to know him, his bad hip regularly caused severe pain and he had a day or two in bed every week. His bedroom overlooked the farmyard, and I could hear his agonised groans through the open window as he attempted to turn over. To a stranger these sounds would have been most disturbing, but we knew that the noises were far more dramatic than the pain that caused them. At dinner time Uncle Ben's place at the table was vacant and a bowl of cold rice pudding or 'pobs' (bread and milk) was taken upstairs to him. His bedroom was directly over the kitchen where we ate, and I tried not to choke as he was helped to sit up in bed amid a cacophony of groans and roars. No one else around the table took the slightest notice of the vocal exhibition overhead.

Things were just as embarrassing when he took his midday meal with us. The meat course would be taken away and his niece would ask in a raised voice if he wanted some rhubarb pie or rice pudding, or whatever the sweet consisted of, her spoon poised for immediate action. Uncle Ben would contemplate the dish for some time while his niece's patience dissolved; finally he condescended with great benevolence—always with those same words: 'Go on, then, I'll try a bit.' Needless to say, he rarely refused a second helping. On the few occasions when he did refuse he replied with contempt, 'No! I don't want no more.'

Of all the jobs on the farm his chief preoccupation in later years was cleaning out the large free-range poultry-breeding houses that dotted several fields round the holding. Some of these were almost a century old and needed

BELOW *Before the days of tractors and baling machines, farmers relied on the horse and cart to transport mown hay from field to farmyard.*

regular attention, so every summer saw Uncle Ben groaning on sticks across the fields, carrying brushes and buckets and stirrup pump, armed with creosote to do battle with rot and red spider. Despite a knotted handkerchief held down with an old cap, he finished each such day with a well-stained face that gave the impression of a rich suntan which must have been very sore. With long-handled brush and bucket, an apron of sacking and that handkerchief round his head, he looked for all the world like a desert-weary sheik whose camel had trotted off.

On such days a return to the farmhouse for dinner was out of the question so a tray would be sent across the fields to the battleground. I never discovered where Uncle Ben took dinner when out in the fields, until one memorable day when I happened to go into a large henhouse that stood in an elevated position and was called the Knob. Upwards of 200 Rhode Island red fowls made their home here, and at least half that number were gathered in the house on that day. There seemed to be no trace of the warrior as I entered, but after a few seconds he came into sight between an interested group of hens. He was seated on a pellet box in the far corner, surrounded by the quietly clucking flock. One hen stood on the dropping-board by his shoulder, seeming to whisper in his ear; another perched on his head and looked down into the bowl of rice pudding.

Every week he did a complete round of the henhouses to clean them out, using a cut-down hoe to scrape the dropping boards and a dustpan to fill up sacks. These he left outside and it was my duty to go round the fields later and collect these sackloads up in the cart or muck spreader. After heavy rain, when the sacks were soaked and sticky, or after frost, when the muck was frozen solid inside, it was miserable work. Only the carting of water in icy weather and the hand-cutting of kale and lifting of mangolds in similar conditions were comparably unpleasant.

ABOVE *The Rhode Island red was introduced to Britain from America in 1909, and is now the most popular breed of domestic chicken in the country.*

The flocks had wheat night and morning, strewn from a bucket when the eggs were collected. What a picture those massed birds made at feeding time, and what patterns one could make across the field by scattering the grain in curving lines. When the sun shone on the backs of the masses of pecking Rhode Island reds, with the arrogant, agile black leghorn cockerels standing by, the scene was truly beautiful.

As the grain bucket emptied, so the egg bucket filled. Trap nesting was carried out in a couple of cotes nearest the farmyard (the 'dairy' and 'second' cotes): this necessitated collecting the eggs five or six times daily, lifting the birds from the trap nests, reading the number on the leg ring and resetting the traps. In this way the best-laying birds could be selected from records made over a lengthy period of time.

All this round-the-field tramping was far more onerous in the mud and rain of winter. Nevertheless, carrying full buckets of eggs in the teeth of a westerly gale or pulling one's feet from the squelchy ooze on a January afternoon as the light failed at least had the bonus of a respite as each cote was reached, offering welcome shelter within as the eggs were collected and grain thrown down on the straw. At such times of bad weather the hens were not let out, and once each door had been shut behind one the poultry work was finished for that day.

At all other times the pop-holes used by the birds had to be fastened at nightfall, when all had retired to their perches. This was particularly tiresome when dusk descended later in the evening, though I had usually gone home and was not involved. On many occasions my employer had an anxious return from an evening outing, hoping to reach the pop-holes before Reynard came on his nightly prowl.

Now and again a hen would for some reason stay out, perching optimistically in a holly tree or hawthorn hedge. Such birds were rarely seen again; often, though, we would discover a handful of bloody feathers or a leg cast aside in the long grass. What was feared most of all was the nightmare of a fox entering a cote by a broken window or by pulling netting away from a gap in the boards. The result was brutal murder. Scores of birds had their heads snipped from their bodies and strewn about the hut, where utter confusion reigned. Foxes will kill as many birds as possible in such an attack, apparently for the sheer joy of the exercise, and rarely carry off more than a couple of carcasses for consumption in a safer place.

With the passage of the years the free-range system of keeping breeding hens lost ground to more labour-efficient methods. New deep-litter houses appeared at

THE RISE AND FALL OF BATTERY FARMS

CHICKENS WERE FIRST farmed intensively in America in the 1930s. The idea quickly spread across the Atlantic to Britain, where farmers were being encouraged to feed a growing population while keeping costs low. Chickens were housed in rows or 'batteries' of cages to facilitate feeding and egg collection. It wasn't long before turkeys and pigs were also being subjected to battery farming.

After the Second World War battery farming became more and more automated until machines not only fed and watered the animals, but also controlled light, insulation and ventilation to encourage maximum growth or egg production. For the past 30 years, however, campaigners for animal rights and concerned consumers have pushed for free-range farming, where livestock has space outside to roam and forage.

Finally, in June 1999, the European Union signed agreements banning battery cages for chickens by 2013, after which free-range conditions or 'luxury' cages must be provided.

Concerned consumers are increasingly demanding not merely free-range but also organic produce, despite it costing slightly more. Organic farmers allow animals the freedom to roam, and, although they may use antibiotics to treat an individual sick animal, they never use them routinely to prevent illness, and do not use growth hormones. Artificial fertilisers, herbicides and pesticides are also banned. Recent furores over genetically modified food and the cattle disease BSE have greatly helped the organic cause—indeed, there has never been a single recorded case of BSE from an organically raised dairy or beef herd.

RIGHT *In 1998 top chefs Anton Edelman and Aldo Zilli joined forces with the animal welfare group Compassion in World Farming to campaign against battery farming.*

LEFT *Free-range farms like this one will become increasingly common as battery farming is phased out across Europe in the 21st century.*

the edge of the Home Field, but the empty hen cotes can still be picked out from the surrounding high ground; their dark profiles bring back memories of busy days as they decay gently in the shelter of the tall trees that break the west wind.

RARE BREEDS OF DERBYSHIRE

The regional specialisation of farm-animal breeds in the past—of the large white pig in the West Riding of Yorkshire and the shorthorn cow in County Durham, for instance—is well known, and many carry the name of their county of origin. Sadly, the passage of time has tended to reduce the number of breeds and a rather dull uniformity prevails. Efficient performance is certainly an important criterion, but the ubiquitous Friesian which is seen in ever-increasing numbers means that the day may dawn not too far distantly when the red and white and blue-roan dairy shorthorn and the pretty Ayrshire will be as rare a sight as is the Shire horse today. Regionality is giving way to overall uniformity and, what is after all the point of agriculture, efficiency.

But before all memory of well-loved things perishes with those who knew them it is worth hesitating and looking at the contribution made by Derbyshire over the centuries to the kaleidoscope of farm animals. Today it is easy to overlook this contribution, for the county never produced a breed of cow or sheep or pig that became of really widespread importance; nevertheless, the county has had a share in shaping as wide a range of breeds as any in Britain—sheep, fowl, horse and cow. Only two of these breeds remain at all important in a world of agriculture notable for its increasing lack of colour: they are a hill sheep and a horse.

Within the confines of Peakland several breeds of sheep were developed long ago. Among these was the Penistone, a breed of hardy hill animals whose origins are lost in the mists of time that shroud much of the wide uplands of northernmost Peakland. No pure Penistone sheep exist today, but the breed will long be remembered for the remarkable feat that two animals performed at the beginning of the 19th century. A few sheep were taken to a farm in Kent, three soon disappeared and two eventually reappeared at home on the moors! Their horns hung for a long time in Hope parish church.

A very old breed of sheep that does remain, though in very small numbers, is the whitefaced woodland. This lovely old hill breed can be traced back to the Middle Ages in the highest Peak District. A century and a half ago there were eighty or more breeders with some very large flocks. I have seen old photographs of flocks of these big, heavy animals with grey faces and large, spiral horns. But crossing with other hill breeds, notably the Swaledale, and a general decline in popularity have resulted in this colourful breed nearing extinction.

A breed that is still represented by an active breed society and which appears regularly in sheep classes at local shows is the Derbyshire gritstone, formerly known as the Dale o' Goyt after the western hollow of its origin. Purebred flocks have been kept in this region for more than a century, and the breed became popular in the hills of northeastern Cheshire, southeastern Lancashire and south Yorkshire. The Duke of Devonshire became the first president of the Derbyshire

RIGHT *A gritstone wall pens in the Dark Peak's native sheep, the Derbyshire gritstone. This hardy breed is the largest of Britain's hill sheep.*

BELOW *Although rare, whitefaced woodland sheep, with their distinctive pink nostrils and curling horns, are still farmed in Derbyshire and Yorkshire.*

Gritstone Sheepbreeders' Society when it was founded on October 15, 1906. There were about thirty members at that point, but the number has now more than trebled. This sheep has a pretty, speckled face, but one of the reasons that it lost favour over the years was that it did not maintain the age-old rule 'polled for grass, horned for heather'. The breed is polled (hornless), and this was often thought of as being a bad point—a bias based on tradition, for the Derbyshire gritstone has a rugged constitution and is a stubborn resister of disease.

One other breed of sheep associated with the county is the Portland. It probably originated in southwestern England, but for a long time there has been a purebred flock kept in the lovely wooded grounds of Calke Abbey on the boundary with northern Leicestershire.

It was about 100 years ago that A. F. Wragg, the schoolteacher at Edensor (the 'model' village in Chatsworth Park) developed the first specimens of the redcap breed of poultry, a breed that has been linked with Derbyshire ever since. Mr Wragg crossed a golden spangled cockerel—a breed then named moonies and originally imported from Hamburg—with a hen of the well-known fighting breed of old English game.

The redcap breed was initially kept in the neighbouring Peak District villages of Birchover and Elton, but its popularity spread throughout the county and later to most parts of Britain. In appearance the redcap is a light breed, not unlike a leghorn. Its plumage is brown and black, and its outstanding characteristic is its picturesque red comb. In the days when the breed was more popular, it was used for both egg production and table purposes, since it possessed a surprising amount of meat on the breast. A good free-range pullet will average 200 eggs per annum, and under such management the eggs are particularly rich in albuminoids.

Redcap cockerels are still in some demand for crossing with other breeds to improve the quality of breast meat and eggs. The pugnacious character of these cocks has led to their popularity in certain parts of the world for fighting purposes: they are capable of making a good showing against fighting gamecocks.

Mr Harry Fox of Matlock handled and bred redcaps for seventy years, and was acknowledged as the leading authority on this now rare breed. Mr Fox had considerable knowledge of exotic birds, too: he advised on the stocking of a private bird collection at Calver which includes flamingos, and obtained a pair of Australian black swans for Riber Castle, Matlock, on the hilltop above the farm where he was born.

So to the cow. The only breed of importance that has come out of the county is the blue Albion. This blue and white animal is now virtually extinct, because

ANIMAL PASSIONS

CRUEL SPORTS involving animals have been practised in Britain—popularly perceived as a nation of animal lovers—since at least medieval times, and were outlawed only in the 19th century. Probably the two most popular sports were bear-baiting and cockfighting. In bear-baiting, mastiffs or other dogs were set loose against a bear tied to a post by a rope or chain. To make the fight more even, the bear might be blinded or have his claws drawn. The contest ended when the bear had fought off his assailants or, more usually, had been savaged to submission or death. These bloodthirsty shows were held at fairs or as regular spectacles at 'bear gardens'.

Especially popular with gamblers, cockfighting involved a combat between two cocks, whose legs were fitted with razor-sharp metal spurs. The fight took place in a small arena, or cockpit, where people of all backgrounds—some the worse for drink, others just drunk on bloodlust—would lay their bets and roar on the combatants. A champion bird could be a money-spinner, so training was taken seriously: one owner in 18th-century Chester is said to have built up the strength of his best fighters with a diet that included eggs, barley, milk, butter and rhubarb.

Cockfighting, bear-baiting and the kindred sport of bull-baiting were banned in 1835. Even so, some illegal sports, such as fights between dogs, or dogs set against badgers or even cats, still sometimes happen today in Britain, and there have been successful prosecutions in recent years for such inhumane activities.

LEFT *William Hogarth's engraving shows people from all walks of life at a cockfight. Cast over them is the shadow of a debtor who has been hung in a basket above the arena.*

of its inability to breed completely true to colour: Mendelian laws dictate that the expectation from a cross between two blue animals will be one black and one white to every two blue offspring. There are, of course, blue and white and blue-roan animals still to be seen, particularly on the limestone uplands of the west; these are not pure blue Albions but are the type of animal from which the breed developed. This colouring has also long been common in the breeding of the dairy shorthorn. So that though it is broadly true to say that the blue Albion is extinct, there will continue to be animals of the same type and marking, while the versatile dairy shorthorn remains as a viable breed.

ABOVE *Blue Albion cattle were bred in Derbyshire from 1920 to 1940 by crossing Welsh black cattle with shorthorns. Cattle of similar colouring still exist today, but it is unlikely that any purebred blue Albions remain.*

The Suffolk Punch, Clydesdale, Percheron and Shire are the heavy horses of this country, and it is the last breed—the most notable and oldest—with which Derbyshire claims the closest affinity. The Shire is the national heavy horse. It originated in times beyond the scope of detailed history: Queen Boudicca won battles against the Romans because of her superior British horses, the ancestors of the quiet Shire of recent times.

The Shire was developed largely in the north Midlands—in the Shires—and it is possible to claim south Derbyshire as the headquarters of Shire-horse country. Here, in the Ashbourne district, where the sound limestone land seems to give the fullest expression to the inborn qualities that go to the making of a good Shire, the biggest success of everyday farmers in the breeding of good strains of the horse was seen. As evidence of this fact let it be remembered that here the greatest Shire stallion, the famous Harold, was bred.

There is still an important annual show and sale of Shires here at Derby, and the heavy-horse classes are still well-supported—albeit by breeders and farmers who use their animals for utilitarian purposes far less than previously. The sight of a pair of Shires drawing a single-furrow plough across old pasture, lea or stubble is now rare; the last local farmer to use horses regularly for this task was Jim Smith of Lower Birchitt Farm in the upper Drone valley. Now his horses have gone and the old plough lies rusting.

The long and arduous life of the horseman on a large farm is generally unknown by the majority in these easy days. Old Jim Shepherd was the last horseman at Broomfield, near Derby, and one of the last of the traditional breed of horsemen in this part of the country. I well remember his short, wiry silhouette in the muddy yard of Lime Farm on wet December mornings at 6am. His paraffin lamp swung across the yard to the brick-arched stable doorway and sent long, frightening shadows slipping round that big and draughty yard. We lads unloaded the frosted kale from a cart with bare hands for the cowman to fork to the dairy herd, and if we got in old Jim's way at that short-tempered time he would snarl and bark and disappear inside the stable. The yellow light reflected warmly off the straw and made the smooth contours of the three proud animals in his charge flow like liquid gold. No matter how angry he had been with the ignoramuses in the mucky yard beyond the warm glow of his lantern, he rarely had a hard word for his charges within. With soft sounds and a special language understood by both parties, he quickly had them groomed, fed and harnessed up for the morning's work.

Old Jim had the typical temperament of a professional farm horseman: working quietly and steadily, uttering firm orders to his animals, chewing tobacco and punctuating his words with pauses while he spat on the ground to one side. The horses finally went from Broomfield, and their going nearly broke Old Jim's heart; very soon he had joined the long line of colleagues who had gone before him.

GENTLE GIANTS OF THE LAND

THE HEAVY HORSES of Britain are a nostalgic reminder of work on the land in a slower, quieter age. For much of their history, though, these peaceful creatures were closer to the sword than to the ploughshare. Throughout the Middle Ages they carried knights in full armour into battle. But, as the nature of warfare changed, strains of heavy horse were bred for agriculture, and by the early 18th century horses had ousted oxen as the main draught animal.

There are four main types of heavy horse in Britain. The Suffolk Punch, renowned for its stamina and longevity, is descended from the warhorses brought to England by the Normans in 1066. The massive Shire, the heaviest of the breeds, was developed from Flemish strains crossed with these Norman animals. Mighty in size and strength but exceptionally docile in temperament, it was used across the 'Shire' counties of the English Midlands. Scottish farms depended on the Clydesdale, also a Flemish breed, but less bulky and more agile than its southern cousins. The Percheron is

LEFT *A pair of Percherons ploughs the land in the 1930s, before the triumph of tractors made horsepower all but obsolete.*

ABOVE *In the Middle Ages horses carried knights clad in heavy armour into battle. This manuscript shows the Battle of Barnet.*

THRESHING DAYS

The rick yard of the farm where I worked lay at a steep angle, and the stacks of corn were built with care and not a little skill on great baulks of timber; their roofs and eaves were horizontal so that one end of each stack stood higher than the other.

It took considerable time and effort for the threshing men, with their steam traction engine, to manoeuvre the threshing drum and stationary baler into position, for these had to be perfectly level so that the drum could thresh out the grain properly. The fact that they arrived towards dusk on a winter's evening, having just completed a thresh on some farm not far distant, didn't help. At last the drum would be chocked up with wooden blocks and wedged into a level position below the corn stack, with the baler pushed into position behind it, and the contractors would get on their tall, blue tractor and go homewards in the darkness.

We were at work early the next morning. I had the milking finished a good half-hour earlier than usual and did the yard jobs more quickly than was normal; in the

another Norman horse, which saw active service on the battlefields of the First World War.

These gentle giants provided the major source of power on British farms from the mid-19th century until the 1940s, when the tractor was in its swift ascendancy. Work on the land was intensive: fields had to be ploughed and weeded with a cultivator. By the 1840s the seed drill, drawn by two or three horses, was replacing seeding by hand. Mechanisation of harvesting in the second half of the 19th century meant the introduction of a further array of horse-drawn implements, including reapers, mowers and haymakers.

The breeding of heavy horses slowed down in the early years of the 20th century as demand for horses declined with the rise of the motor vehicle. But dedicated societies have kept these noble breeds alive and today they draw huge crowds at county shows. Some breweries use Shire teams for deliveries, and the great beasts can still occasionally be seen pursuing their stately course across the land.

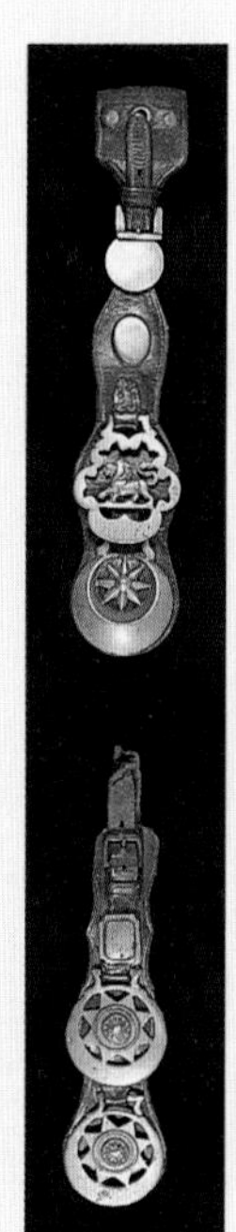

ABOVE *Horse-brasses were originally worn on a horse's harness to fend off evil spirits, but today are purely decorative.*

LEFT *At a heavy-horse parade in Burton-upon-Trent in Staffordshire, immaculately groomed horses pull brewers' drays.*

meantime the contractors arrived and unsheeted the drum and baler, attached the driving belts and went round with grease gun and oilcan.

The threshing contractor maintained his traction engine in perfect condition. At regular intervals during the day's thresh he would polish up any brass or paintwork that had gone dull. Care was exercised in refuelling so that no coal dust spoiled the look of the pressure and water gauges. The shining boiler and brightly painted wheels were a joy to behold as the fearsome locomotive moved the threshing implements—drum, trusser and, later, stationary baler—from farm to farm throughout the winter months. It was ironic that such a pristine machine had such a dirty task as threshing to perform. In due course steam gave way to the diesel engine, and the tall, blue tractor did all that the belching locomotive had done previously, though with less need for care and attention—and less romance.

During the contractors' preparations Uncle Ben would as likely as not be dragging sackfuls of empty corn bags to the grain-delivery spouts at the back of the drum. He always made sure that there were several large, loosely woven sacks by the chaff outlet, for his job was to bag as much chaff as possible for use later in the poultry houses. A thick layer of chaff on the floor of a free-range poultry house made a good base for a shallower layer of straw.

With a whine the belts would begin to turn and soon the drum was humming. Work began. The contractor climbed the ladder to the top of the drum, knelt on the platform and began to feed the first sheaves from the roof of the stack. Up on the stack were a couple of men who had previously removed the neat thatch of wheat straw—it always seemed a shame that the time and energy used in thatching the stack were undone in a matter of moments when the threshing set arrived.

ABOVE *Grains of wheat* (left) *are protected while they grow by a sheath or husk. Threshing removes the husk, which then becomes known as chaff, seen here* (right) *mixed with unthreshed grain.*

These two stack men now maintained a steady flow of sheaves, thrown carefully to the contractor on his platform. At the rear of the drum the farmer and his younger brother saw to the bagging of the grain and had the heavy job of carrying the two-hundredweight bags up the stone steps to the corn chamber which was perched above the little cow shed at the top of the yard. The contractor's son saw to the wiring of the straw bales, and my job as often as not was the carrying and stacking of these bales. Uncle Ben took up his position at the chaff spout between the drum side and the end of the stack.

The speed with which the sheaves of corn were fed into the drum by the contractor dictated the speed at which the rest of the team had to work. If the grain and straw were dry and the stack men fed the sheaves to the drum smartly, the corn carriers and the men on the straw baler had to work quickly to keep up. This applied equally well to Uncle Ben in the dark and dusty confines at the side of the machine. When he had filled most of the bags with chaff and these stood about him, their necks tied with twine, he used the few remaining bags in rotation to fill the empty space at the rear of a large wooden shed called the Food Room where all the poultry foods were stored. His problem was that by the time he had dragged a voluminous bag behind him up the rick yard, emptied it in the

Food Room and returned to the scene of activities the next bag would be full. It needed only a slight delay on one of these slow and apparently painful journeys for the chaff to build up in the feeding chute and jam the chaff fan and riddle.

Many were the times that Uncle Ben could be seen ripping the overfilled bag off the attachment hooks and attempting to free the blockage by pushing his arm up the chute. A sleeve full of dust and chaff was inevitably the result. Once I saw him poke his indispensable walking stick up the chute; there was a sharp crack and the handle of the stick was withdrawn without the shaft! Over the passage of the hours the pile of loose chaff that had evaded Uncle Ben's efforts to capture it grew about his feet and threatened to bury him. His temper deteriorated in proportion to the increase of loose chaff.

The welcome midmorning break saw us sitting below the stack, glad to have five minutes' quiet and rest. The valiant chaff bagger sat on a full bag, his face and clothing grey with dust and filth. As often as not his cap lay awry at this stage and he instructed me to 'fetch a few bags from cart shed afor' we start again!' His aim was to avoid a repetition of the near rout just suffered, only prevented by the appearance of his niece with a tray of mugs and that familiar steaming earthenware jug.

ABOVE *Many farmers in Peakland employed Ned Morgan's threshing machine in the mid-20th century. Contracting machinery was a huge expense for farmers, and all the family would help out on threshing days to ensure the job was done quickly.*

Some of the farms the threshing outfits went to were the homes of generous people; other farmers were miserly or their wives parsimonious. One place which my friend Ned Morgan visited for many years had a farmer's wife who counted minutes of work lost as money well and truly thrown away. 'There were no intervals on that farm, not with her watching from behind the curtains!' he said. One of her tricks (witnessed by a keen-eyed youth looking through the kitchen window one day when the corn was being threshed) was to pour the tea for the midmorning break into the assembled mugs from a great height, thus cooling it down so that there would be no delay while the men drank it. Not content with that, she was seen to bend down and blow on each steaming mug in turn before her daughter was despatched with it into the rick yard. The daughter, as keen as her mother where time and money were involved, always raced up the ladder with the tea for the band cutter and his mate so that they would not waste seconds in climbing down to ground level and then, maybe, sit down on sheaves or bales out of the biting wind.

After our break the drum was soon humming again and the baler clacking rhythmically as the straw was rammed tight. Having filled all available storage space with chaff, Uncle Ben now began the longer pilgrimage down the rick yard, across the road and into the brookside pasture field where the excess chaff was burned, along with the riddlings raked at intervals from under the drum. Someone helped him now by changing the great loosely woven bags on the chaff spout when they were full. As the day wore on and the chaff expert grew weary, the assistant carried the bags into the field where Uncle Ben was firmly established, stick in hand, controlling the conflagration. 'Naw, naw! Chuck it right on top o' fire!' he screeched in a voice hoarse with the dust of the day.

And when the day's thresh was completed and the contractor had cleaned down his tackle and moved away into the dusk, and when I had done the belated afternoon milking, Uncle Ben could still be seen tending the great yellow heap in the field, while a tall, white plume of smoke curled into the frosty sky, tinged pink with the dying sun as it set beyond Burrs Wood.

FIELD PATTERNS

Fields form a major part of our landscape. Where the soil allows, the ingenuity of man has, down the centuries, imposed cultivation on heath and moor and marsh and woodland in fields of unlikely shape and form, of every size imaginable and with a tremendous variety of names.

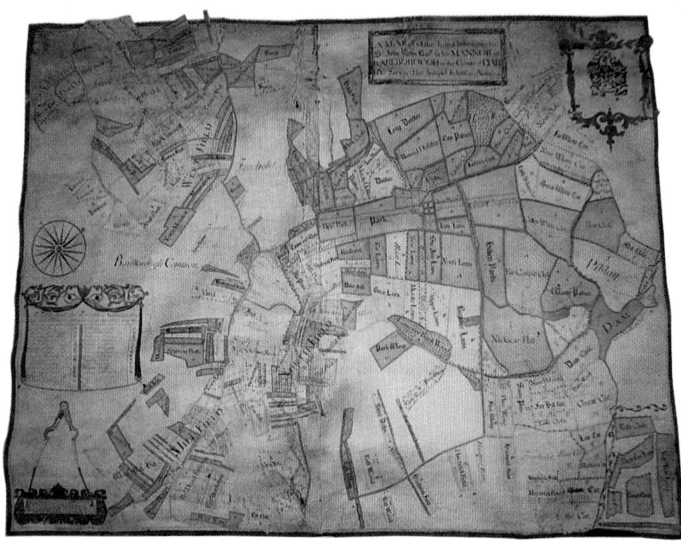

ABOVE *Marked on this 1723 map of Barlborough Hall Estate in Derbyshire is the disused medieval three-field system and the individual acreages into which the three fields were divided over time.*

The first fields were open fields, created in the Middle Ages and usually numbering three to each village. If their form has passed into oblivion, their identity often lingers on in local place names, as at Turlow Fields, near Hognaston, and Hatton Fields, near Hatton, both in south Derbyshire. Two of the three great fields attached to a manor grew cereal crops, while a third of the acreage would lie fallow each year, to rest the soil and to control weeds and pests.

This was, of course, before the wide-spread use of the so-called 'fallow crops', such as turnips and swedes. The coming of these useful plants meant that the farmer could make the idle third of his land productive, for he could 'clean' the soil between the wider rows as the root crop matured. It also meant that he could at last supply freshly grown vegetable matter to his overwintering livestock and so avoid the formerly inevitable slaughter of the majority of his animals as winter set in.

Such farming systems were all well and good when the lord ruled his manor, but farms became independent and at an early date some land was broken up into individual acreages. Fences, hedges and walls began to spread across the land, chequerboard-fashion or snakelike.

The breakup of the great fields accelerated considerably towards the close of the 18th century. Enclosure was first carried out by means of private Acts of Parliament, then later by private agreement between individuals and finally in a fully organised way by enclosure awards.

The result of general enclosure of the land was a revolution in way of life and in landscape. In the past villages were largely groups of farmhouses, from which the men went out to the great fields on most days of the year. After enclosure this pattern sometimes remained, and it is still possible to find villages or hamlets made up largely of farmhouses. But in some areas enclosure resulted in the farmers moving lock, stock and barrel to new houses, and buildings being erected on their portion of the original open fields, now enclosed by wall and hedge.

When enclosure came it took two main forms: apparently haphazard, patchwork enclosure by walls and hedges and fences in an endless variety of shapes and areas, and regular, usually rectangular, enclosure of land. Why these two contrasting patterns, often in close proximity within one parish? The answer is not too difficult to find.

WALL TO WALL

ONE OF THE FIRST things to strike visitors on entering the Peak District is the amazing network of dry-stone walls which spreads up hill and down dale.

Most of these walls were constructed between 1750 and 1850 as part of the nationwide enclosure movement. At that time, common land on the edges of villages was enclosed by large landowners empowered to do so by various Acts of Parliament. Groups of parliamentary surveyors and commissioners gradually parcelled up the ground, erected walls and, over the 100-year period, planted around 200,000 miles of new hedgerows. It has been estimated that there are 26,000 miles of dry-stone walls in the White Peak alone.

Interestingly, there was just as much of an outcry when these walls and hedges were installed as there is today when they are demolished. John Clare, the Northamptonshire nature poet, famously fumed:

Inclosure, thou'rt curse upon the land
And tasteless was the wretch who thy
existence planned.

Enclosure fields tend to be large, and can usually be identified by their regular, rectangular shape and the long, straight roads with wide verges—along which cattle were driven to market—that run across them. Older fields are usually much smaller and asymmetrical. Recent research by Sheffield University has established that some walls at Roystone Grange near Ballidon in the White Peak are older still, and can be dated back nearly 2,000 years to Roman times. Certainly built to last, some of these walls are still in use today.

RIGHT *Many people had to leave their villages to seek work in towns when the common land on which they had always grazed their animals was taken over by private owners during the enclosures.*

RIGHT *Reversed-S-shaped fields, dating back to medieval times, are still in evidence on the Holmesfield parish boundary.*

BELOW *This illustration from a medieval manuscript depicts farmers ploughing with a team of oxen. For over 3,000 years draught animals did the heavy work that is now so easily done with a tractor.*

The haphazard form was the result of enclosure that came piecemeal, over an extended period of time, and which adhered to the original boundaries of the great open fields and woodlands. The common shape of the plough strips of the medieval open fields was a reversed S, owing to the fact that a team of eight animals required considerable space in which to turn at the headland. By curving the furrows at the end of the field, the ploughman could get his team round in the shortest distance and with the least confusion. It is known that almost all medieval ploughs had a fixed share and mouldboard on the right-hand side of the implement—as in modern times—so that the soil was turned over to the right. With a leftward turn at the end of a run, the ploughman could keep the mouldboard firmly against the furrow slice, helping to prevent it from dropping back into the furrow that had just been opened up. Having turned his team to the left, at right angles to the line of ploughing, the ploughman and his assistant could then manoeuvre the animals and plough sharply round to the right (clockwise) so that it was comparatively easy to enter the fresh ground to be ploughed. And so the reversed-S form was ideal for ploughing the field strips.

The hedges or stone walls often followed this curve and can still be seen in many parts of Derbyshire. The finest example known to me is on the Holmesfield–Barlow parish boundary, 950 feet above sea level, in the vicinity of the so-called Meek Fields, near Moorhall in the north of the county.

It is likely that the reversed-S shape of cultivation had become a thing of the past by the end of the 16th century, partly as a result of improved ox breeding, which resulted in larger and stronger animals so that a smaller team was required to haul the plough. Also, the development of conservation of winter 'keep' (largely hay) meant that towards the end of the Middle Ages the animals began spring ploughing in better condition than formerly.

Curving plough strips became obsolete. The fields on either side of this particular field near Moorhall are not of the reversed-S shape so it is quite likely that at the breakup of the open-field system this particular strip was retained as a headland or as a means of access to land on the far side. At a later date it would have been closed off from the adjoining land by the stone walls seen today.

BELOW *In the 19th century enclosure laws resulted in open moorland being carved up into large square or rectangular fields, such as these on Cracken Edge in the Peak District.*

Then we come to the other form of enclosure, the regular, usually rectangular, form. Such enclosed land is best seen near Loades (above Holymoorside village, to the west of Chesterfield) and adjoining the extensive and ill-drained moorland known as Leash Fen. These fields are relics either of the parliamentary enclosure awards of the early 19th century (which resulted in the breakup of the great open fields of the ancient three-field system of arable farming) or of the systematic enclosure of former rough moorland known as intake land.

Some of the intake fields are very large, and the walls (being hill country) form rectangular patterns. Again in Derbyshire, in the parish of Hayfield, there is land called The Intakes; at Hazlebadge there is Intake Farm; at both Bakewell and Cromford there is an Intake Lane; and just over the county boundary in northeast Cheshire there is that bleak hilltop area near Chisworth called Ludworth Intakes.

All these and many more originated as moorland and were taken in with the help of the 'graver's spade'. A team of cultivators usually consisted of two men, the graver using the large 'graver's spade' and his mate (the putter-over) turning over the sods he cut. It was a slow and laborious job, but it won land that would otherwise have long remained unproductive; it also gave men work when work was in short supply.

A great intake field at Mossy Lea, near Glossop, is known as the Duke of Norfolk's Garden because it was cultivated by local mill workers when there was no other employment. The Duke of Norfolk's agent gave them the task of breaking up the moorland and enclosing it with high gritstone walls against the future encroachment of heather and bracken. There was little hope of the ground being much improved thereby, but the men did not starve and they retained their dignity; at least they had not been reduced to paupers or had to rely on the parish.

Similarly, on the Pennine Way the winding road that comes up the slope from Mankinholes, often referred to as the 'Long Drag', was a route planned by John Fielden of Dobroyd Castle on the western slope of the valley adjacent to Todmorden. This philanthropic mill owner had the hill route made ostensibly

RIGHT *Mill workers reduced to penury by the Cotton Famine of the 1860s exchange vouchers for goods. Embargoes on American imports during the American Civil War caused a shortage of cotton in England.*

so that a carriage could be got to the summit of Stoodley Pike, but the real purpose was to give work to mill workers who would otherwise have starved in the notorious Cotton Famine, caused by the blockade of cotton exports from America during the Civil War.

One of the finest examples of intake land in the North of England is that occupying the site of the former Holy Moor three miles west of Chesterfield. According to a document dated 1584 in the Portland Collection, the district was called Howley More, a name perhaps coming from the earlier Norse *haugr* (a hill or height) and the Old English *leah* (a wood or woodland clearing). Such a 'hill clearing' would have been taken in for cultivation quite early, but the regular pattern of rectangular fields came at about the same time as the general enclosure of the open fields, between one and a half and two centuries ago.

Not far to the north of Holy Moor are similar fields in close proximity to the upland hamlet of Wadshelf, a cold place facing the eastern lowlands at the very edge of Eastmoor in north Derbyshire. From the environs of adjoining Wigley there is a very clear view of these rectilinear enclosures. And 'enclosures' is a word used advisedly, for according to the Domesday Book this land was formerly the cultivated land of Wada, and divided into three great fields: North Field, Nether Field and Wheatcroft Field. At the very beginning of the 19th century several of the original strips had already been enclosed: nine strips round the northern and western fringe of the Nether Field, among others. Then in around 1830 the total area of these three open fields was enclosed, largely by stone walls surrounding rectangular portions.

Several large volumes could be written about the names, location and derivation of fields of even a limited region. Field names are an essential part—and a fascinating one at that—of the rich heritage of the countryside of these islands.

Most of the names of fields date from relatively early times and tell us something of the land use and state of agricultural husbandry of the era. Some field names describe characteristics of the land enclosed, of which here are a few examples.

In the parish of Parwich are Bad Flatts, Baldstones and Froghole. The latter suggests that the land is wet and poorly drained, whereas not so far away, in the parish of Brassington, there is a field known from at least 1620 onwards as Shining Cliff, describing the unbroken slope of dry land lying on limestone rocks. In the parish of Bradley, near Ashbourne, there are some interesting names that suggest former friction and strife: take, for instance, Encroachment and Slang. As examples of self-explanatory names there are (in the same parish) Three-cornered Piece, Top Croft, Six Acres and Ox Close. In every parish there are many field names that take more understanding. In Bradley parish, again, there is a field called Poison Piece—probably land containing water much polluted by an element such as lead, where livestock did not thrive or even died.

Field shapes often give rise to particular names. Some Derbyshire examples are Cleaver-shaped Half Acres, Boot Foot and Rump of Beef. Wry Neck and Teakettle Handlepiece seem especially apt and attractive. Then it was fashionable to name enclosures after distant places—for patriotic reasons or to impress the neighbours? In the parish of Ashover, south of Chesterfield, are North Brittain and Carolina. Elsewhere may be found New York, Land's End and Jericho.

Fields forming parts of old charities abound throughout the county, and we find them in connection with names such as Sacred Fields and Charity Field. Lastly, there is the mysterious side of the story of field nomenclature: fields and enclosures with picturesque but puzzling names such as Blue Button, Gingerbread Piece, Save All, Hundred Year and Three Week. We may never know the real explanation for the many truly fanciful field names, but perhaps it is just as well for our rural heritage to retain some secret charms.

CHAPTER FOUR

LIFE AT THE EDGE

THE DANE VALLEY is one of those places impossible to appreciate except on foot, a beautiful upland valley in the gritstone of western Peakland with a very particular character. I tend to think of it as a miniature of the upper reaches of Swaledale, for its narrow confines are not really like any other valley of the region.

The source of the Dane lies at 1,650 feet on the gently shelving heather moor at Whetstone Ridge, less than one mile south of the Cat and Fiddle Inn, the second-highest public house in England, which stands beside the Buxton–Macclesfield road. Almost immediately the peaty stream forms the boundary between Cheshire and Derbyshire; after a couple of miles, at Panniers Pool Bridge, the river becomes the frontier between Cheshire and Staffordshire and continues as such until it leaves the hills. For all those ten miles, from moor-top source to plain level, the Dane courses through a beautiful area of steep slopes and hidden bowers and maintains an atmosphere all its own. This characteristic charm is a product of the unique topographical shapes and the gritstone forming them; also responsible are the pattern of hill farming, the unchanging countenance of ancient habitations and, not least, the old place names which blend so well with this locality.

ABOVE *The River Dane thunders over rocks at Panniers Pool, which takes its name from the packhorses that used to water at the riverside.*

There are shooting butts still in use in late summer and autumn on the high ground where the Dane rises. In the uppermost reaches of the valley proper are the remains of Dane Bower and Reeve Edge Quarries, where gritstone was once extracted for building material.

There was much sporadic coal mining hereabouts in the 19th century, and on the slope directly to the south of the Buxton–Congleton road Dane Bower Colliery still has its blunt chimney intact, an attractive memorial to this isolated pocket of Victorian industry. Sheep pens stand below the chimney, close beside the infant Dane. The river curves on down near Holt and Sparbent Farms, and then passes under Panniers Pool Bridge where the three counties meet. This spot is traditionally associated with the medieval courts summoned to hear evidence against trespassers in Macclesfield Forest. This preserve, like the Royal Forest of the Peak, was held strictly in the grip of the forest laws and stretched as far south as Bosley, where the Dane winds out of the hills and enters the plain, and northwards to Marple.

Below Three Shire Heads, at Panniers Pool, the little Dane trickles on for a couple of miles down gritstone steps to Gradbach. Here is the amazing gorge cut by the Dane through the enclosing gritstone edges rimming The Roaches basin—an important geological syncline (or downfold). It seems that at one time the river flowed at a much higher level, and rapid down-cutting through the sandstones and soft shales has created this gorge, now well wooded in parts.

THE ROYAL FORESTS

TODAY, WE THINK OF a forest as a large area of trees, but during the Middle Ages the word was not synonymous with woodland. The forests of England were uncultivated areas, often heaths or treeless grazing land, that had been set aside for the personal use of the King. The practice of establishing vast estates on which the royal family could indulge its love of the chase was introduced to England by the Norman King William the Conqueror.

All the venison in the forests—red, roe and fallow deer, and boar—was the King's property, and any unfortunate poachers caught by wardens were tried at a special forest court. At first, punishments were vicious and included mutilation and even death; but attitudes softened as time passed, and by the 13th century these harsh penalties had been replaced with fines. These were an important source of income for the King, as were the sale of timber and the granting of licences for such diverse privileges as grazing animals, felling trees, mining and hunting other beasts such as wild cats, rabbits and wolves.

This revenue became less important after Edward I (1272–1307) established a national taxation system, and over the centuries the royal chases were cultivated by the common people as the need for land rose with an increasing population. The Crown also granted tracts of its land to individuals and monasteries, and by the 17th century the royal forests, which had once covered a third of the country, had all but disappeared.

RIGHT *Peveril Castle served as the administrative centre and gaol for the Royal Forest of the Peak.*

BELOW *King John and his hounds enjoy the royal privilege of hunting a stag in a Royal Forest.*

Gradbach is an area of scattered farms, cottages and the remains of early industry: the fast water of the Dane attracted mill builders to this part of the valley. Gradbach Mill was built in 1640, but it is uncertain what was produced here for the first 140 years. However, in 1780 the Dakeyne family purchased the mill, and for a century they manufactured sewing-silk and did some weaving. About 1885 the mill was sold to Sir John Harpur Crewe of Calke Abbey, south of Derby, and was thereafter used for sawing timber.

For many years Gradbach Mill lay empty and derelict, but once its thirty-eight-foot water wheel was the largest pocket water wheel in England. Each of its ninety-six water pockets had a capacity of thirty-five gallons, and—through its gearing—one revolution of the giant wheel caused the driving shaft inside the building to revolve 2,500 times. The gearing, shafting and wheel have gone, but the overgrown water channel remains where the Dane water ran down towards the mill and did its pollution-free work before rejoining the main stream.

Several crystal streams on the hillside near the mill have provided the mineral-rich water for a thriving watercress business. In *Dane Valley Story* (1953), Clifford Rathbone claimed that Joseph Sigley of the Mill House was the only person in the country who had a market stall exclusively for the sale of watercress (at Macclesfield).

When silk thread was being produced at Gradbach, and the Dane Valley was experiencing its industrial heyday, it is recorded that there were fifty or so cottages in the neighbourhood, which have since completely vanished from the landscape. The power of the river was superseded by the power of steam, and this remote location made transport expensive so the workers drifted to the towns on the edge of the plain, to Leek and Congleton and Macclesfield. With a dwindling agricultural population, the Methodist chapel at Gradbach (now Love Lane) Bridge—which held its first service at Easter 1849—is now closed, along with the village school.

Where the Back Brook swerves down from the east and joins the Dane below Gradbach there is a particularly beautiful hanging wood, part of Back Forest, on the southern slopes. Up here is the site of a remarkable landslip called Lud's Church. In the 17th century the Staffordshire historian Dr Plot described its narrow confines as capable of holding snow all summer through—one enterprising Quarnford man emptied a sackful of old snow taken from Lud's Church onto the market square at Leek on July 17 three centuries ago.

During the 14th and 15th centuries, the Lollards, followers of John Wycliffe, a 14th-century religious reformer, sought refuge from the ecclesiastical authorities in this remote district. Their leader and pastor was the illustrious Walter de Lud-auk. On one occasion, in about 1405, fourteen Lollards were worshipping here at Lud's Church—an ideal hide-out for their services—when they were surprised by soldiers out searching for them. The lovely Alice, Walter's grand-daughter, was mortally wounded in the struggle, and the rest of the congregation surrendered and were taken away. Walter de Lud-auk died, a prisoner in chains, in London, far from the quiet hills where he had been relatively free to follow the uninhibited, reformed ideals of Wycliffe.

BELOW *John Wycliffe, a 14th-century religious reformer, spoke out against corruption in the Church and issued the first English translation of the Bible.*

Lud's Church is still a secret sort of cleft, much of it draped with mosses and lichens which give a peculiar, almost unique, lighting effect. Visitors came from far and wide in Victorian times to see this chasm and its magic light; then the visitors seemed to die away, and for many years Lud's Church was left almost to its own devices. In recent years, however, the number of people seeking it out has greatly increased, and the padding of countless feet on the floor of the ravine and up its walls is having a damaging effect on the vegetation. The church is ever so subtly having its curtains of green—and, therefore, its singular light—destroyed by unintentional wear and tear. As so often happens in a marvellous and natural place, the source of interest is causing its own destruction by attracting too much attention in a massively over-populated island such as ours.

ABOVE *The Lollards, followers of John Wycliffe, were deemed heretics by the Church and were hanged and burned for their beliefs, as illustrated in this 16th-century woodcut.*

TOP *Lud's Church is an impressive 50-foot chasm, part of a landslip that occurred many centuries ago. The gorge, being difficult to reach, was used as a meeting place by the Lollards.*

The Dane flows on westwards below Lud's Church and is soon joined by the Clough Brook draining Wildboarclough. Below the confluence with the Clough Brook, the Dane Valley winds on to the southwest, bordered now by thick and attractive woodland. Up on the slope to the west of the valley is the village of Wincle. The ancient route between Cleulow Cross and Heaton goes steeply down from Wincle to cross the Dane at, appropriately, Danebridge. On the steep hill below Wincle church stands the 16th-century Ship Inn, with its hand-painted sign depicting Sir Ernest Shackleton's vessel *Nimrod*. Across the valley from Wincle stands Swythamley Hall, former home of the late Sir Philip Brocklehurst, who was a member of Shackleton's British Antarctic expedition of 1907. The painting of the *Nimrod* at the Ship Inn was commissioned by Sir Philip Brocklehurst's mother to commemorate her son's Antarctic adventures.

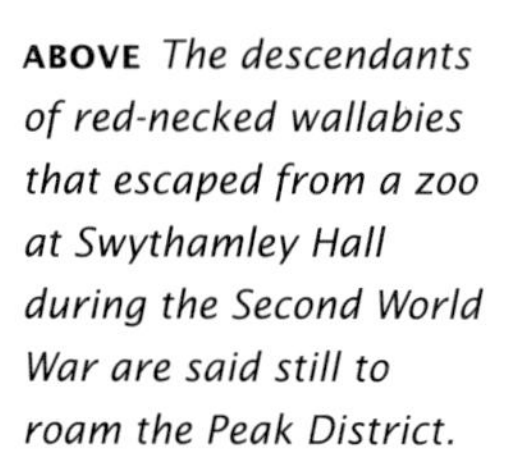

At one time there was a considerable collection of exotic animals in Swythamley Park, and tales have been told of climbers on The Roaches nearby reaching the top of that escarpment and coming face to face with a yak or a brown bear. The wallabies that escaped from the park years ago have found life in this quarter of Peakland singularly amenable, and they may still inhabit remote corners of the moors, though they are rarely seen.

Wincle Grange, on its unseen hillside above the Dane, was erected in the 15th century, and, despite additions, is certainly one of the oldest and least-altered dwellings in the South Pennines. It owes much of this

ABOVE *The descendants of red-necked wallabies that escaped from a zoo at Swythamley Hall during the Second World War are said still to roam the Peak District.*

RIGHT *Towering Ramshaw Rocks form part of the wide expanse of gritstone outcrops known as The Roaches, a name derived from the French word for 'rocks'.*

lack of disturbance to its remote position, unseen by most folk on this, the 'wrong' side of the hill on which it stands. There is a track leading across from Wincle village and paths down into the roadless tributary valley of the Shell Brook, but no main road is nearer than the Leek–Macclesfield route (A523) two miles distant and 400 feet lower to the southwest. From Wincle Grange there is a clear view to Bosley Cloud, three miles away across the broadening Dane Valley to the southwest. This is the westernmost ridge of the South Pennines and presents a dramatic scarp face or 'nose' to the north, overlooking the plain near North Rode and Bosley villages. Up on the Cloud is the only true Neolithic chambered tomb not situated on carboniferous limestone; it is called 'the Bridestones'.

Downstream of the confluence with the Shell Brook, the Dane Valley suddenly widens and the river flows under the Leek–Macclesfield road at Hugbridge, the old crossing between Staffordshire and Cheshire, for the Dane has acted as the boundary all the way down from Three Shire Heads. It is thought that the original bridge here took its name from the Norman Hugo de Mara, who held Bosley in 1080.

So the Dane winds on across the Cheshire Plain, leaving the brown uplands behind. The highest gritstone hills are visible from far out into the plain, dominated by Peakland's most shapely hill, Shutlingsloe (1,659 feet), which is capped by a bed of hard gritstone tilting at about thirty degrees towards the west and from which there are some of the best views in this part of England—as far as the estuary of the Mersey in clear conditions.

TAMESIDE

The confluence of the River Goyt with the River Tame marks the point where the Mersey comes into being. Some think the Goyt is the true headwater of the Mersey, while others argue that the Tame is the major parent river. I favour the Goyt, thus placing the actual source of the Mersey on the open moor close to the Cat and Fiddle Inn, but I do not claim any particularly strong reason for this.

The Tame reaches the Goyt at Stockport, where a Roman ford carried the Buxton (Aquae Arnemetiae) road northwards. In Norman times there was a castle here, overlooking the beginnings of the Mersey.

It is, though, the upper reaches of the Tame Valley that are Pennine in character. The steep-sided valleys are dotted with settlements and the scars of quite early industrial development. The Huddersfield Narrow Canal and the main railway route between Manchester and West Yorkshire pass this way.

Up on the open tops above the Tame Valley one can see a long way in clear conditions: out over the plain of south Lancashire in one direction and across into the gritstone heights of the South Pennines proper in the other. These open little hills contain several interesting antiquities which make useful objectives when planning a walking route. At 900 feet above sea level, a mile northwest of Diggle and overlooking the little moorland valley which goes down towards Delph from the Pennine Way on Standedge, lie the remains of Castle Shaw Roman fort. It is a modest earthwork, all that exists to mark the presence of Roman forces in this head valley, and was probably associated with the protection of a Roman route from Manchester (Mamucium) to York. The fort is of two building periods: an outer turf and clay rampart enclosing two and a half acres and dating from about AD 80, when the Roman general Agricola was governor of Britain; and the smaller, inner fortress which measures only sixty yards by fifty yards and is slightly younger. It is thought to have been abandoned in the reign of Hadrian, around AD 125, for by this time the native warriors had been subdued hereabouts and Roman forces were required in the areas nearer Scotland which were still giving trouble.

Five miles to the south and overlooking the eastern slopes of the Tame Valley are the remains of Buckton Castle. The site is 1,123 feet above sea level and immediately to the southeast of Mossley. This is not a castle ruin in the generally accepted sense, but a weathered earthwork of uncertain age. An old tradition had it that there was buried treasure within this castle, and in 1730 over 100 people are reported to have gathered here and carried out 'vigorous digging' over several days. No treasure was found, but twenty or so years after the great dig various ornaments and a chain of gold beads were found quite accidentally beside the old road (now the B6175) down the slope to the west of Buckton Castle. In about 1800, more gold beads were found quite close to the earthwork.

ABOVE *The conical peak of Shutlingsloe overlooks Clough Brook valley.*

On a bleak autumn day I walked over from Tintwistle, by way of Swineshaw Reservoirs, to the place where Buckton Castle comes into full view high above the Carr Brook; and there, far below, the winding dale of the Tame lay suddenly revealed. Mossley is the central settlement in this vista, backed by the stone-walled hills towards Oldham. From all the high points in this area a dark tower is conspicuous on the heights just west of Mossley. This is Hartshead Pike. It seems likely that this site served as a beacon in ancient times and that there has been a stone structure here for centuries—certainly long before 1758 when the structure is reported to have been rebuilt. Lightning was probably responsible for the serious damage reported in 1794, when 'the tower became rent from top to bottom'. The tower fell into ruin over subsequent years, but on September 17, 1863 the foundation stone of a new structure was laid sixty-seven yards from the ruins of

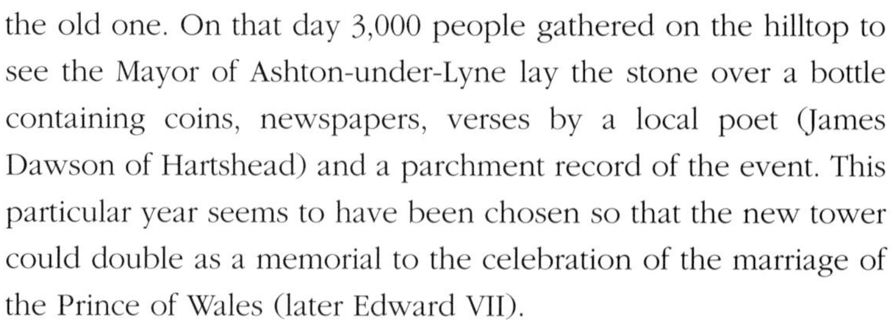

the old one. On that day 3,000 people gathered on the hilltop to see the Mayor of Ashton-under-Lyne lay the stone over a bottle containing coins, newspapers, verses by a local poet (James Dawson of Hartshead) and a parchment record of the event. This particular year seems to have been chosen so that the new tower could double as a memorial to the celebration of the marriage of the Prince of Wales (later Edward VII).

ABOVE *Parishioners of Mottram in Longdendale have a steep walk up to the church of St Michael and All Angels, whose imposing crenellated tower stands high above the village.*

In the last few miles before its confluence with the Goyt at Stockport, the Tame must once have flowed through attractive, rural lowland. First industrial development and then sprawling suburbia have engulfed much of this flood plain, so that the stranger wandering near Bredbury or Hyde nowadays would get little impression of its former beauty. There are, though, one or two remnants that give the game away, but they must be searched out.

Take, for instance, Hyde Hall, a few hundred yards north of the tightly meandering river between Haughton Green and Denton. It exhibits two distinct building styles: the earlier part probably dates from the 13th century and is half-timbered; the later addition, maybe early 17th century, is in dressed stone and includes the porch over the main entrance on the west side.

Close beside the River Goyt near Bredbury stands Goyt Hall, another half-timbered house which was erected about 1570. Another old building lies back off Huddersfield Road, Stalybridge. This is Stayly Old Hall, an Elizabethan yeoman farmer's dwelling in dark stone.

Not geographically part of Tameside, but sufficiently close to include here, is that part of lower Longdendale centred on Hollingworth and Mottram in Longdendale. The outstanding architectural feature of the district is, without question, the parish church of St Michael and All Angels, Mottram, popularly known as the cathedral of east Cheshire (though now in Greater Manchester). Few churches stand more conspicuously and dramatically above the settlement they serve than St Michael's does on its conical hilltop above Mottram. The little stone town lies mainly to the west and northwest of this eminence, and the view from the churchyard is of a multitude of rooftops and dark hills, and the stern grandeur of Longdendale away beyond Hollingworth. On this hilltop, where the church now stands, a battle took place in the 12th century between King Stephen and Matilda, daughter of King Henry I, who contested the former's claim to the throne. Civil war raged for several years, and this engagement at Mottram was just one of many; the war finally ceased with the Treaty of Winchester whereby Stephen was allowed to keep the throne on condition that Matilda's son should succeed him, which he did (as Henry II) in 1154 to become the first of the Plantagenets.

Most of St Michael's dates from the 15th century. Apart from the tall, dark tower, the best features are the two chapels within the building. On the north side is the Hollingworth chapel, formerly the property of the old family of Hollingworth (or Hollyngworth) which took its name from the next settlement up Longdendale. On the south side is the Staley chapel. It contains two important sepulchral effigies in sandstone representing Sir Ralph Staveley ('Staley' and 'Staly' are more recent spellings of the name, hence Stalybridge) and his wife, who lived at the beginning of the 15th century.

ROYAL STRIFE

DESCRIBED BY a contemporary chronicler as 'nineteen winters during which Christ and his saints slept', the reign of Stephen (1135–54) was scarred by civil war against his cousin Matilda, daughter of King Henry I.

The seeds of strife had been sown in 1120, when Henry's only male heir drowned at sea. Anxious to settle his succession, he made his English and Norman barons, including Stephen, swear allegiance to Matilda. Yet when the King died in 1135, support for her evaporated: the barons resented the idea of serving under a woman, and the Normans were wary of her second marriage to Geoffrey Plantagenet of Anjou, a region hostile to Normandy.

So when Stephen secured the English throne after his uncle's death, there was little opposition. But he soon proved to be an indecisive king. His barons became unruly, and when Matilda pressed her claim to the throne in 1138, some threw in their lot with her. The result was a civil war marked by small-scale sieges and raids, and fluctuating loyalties among the barons. In 1141 Stephen was captured in battle, but later released in exchange for Matilda's half-brother. In 1144 the Angevin cause was strengthened when Geoffrey conquered Normandy. Finally a resolution came about when Stephen's son died in 1153; Stephen came to terms with Geoffrey and Matilda, and agreed to accept their son Henry as his heir in return for keeping the crown during his lifetime. The following year, however, Stephen was dead—and Henry was the first Plantagenet King of England.

ABOVE *The Great Seal of Matilda shows Henry I's heir on the throne, even though she was never actually crowned Queen.*

BELOW *King Stephen is captured by the forces of his cousin Matilda at the Battle of Lincoln in 1141.*

The exposed churchyard (it catches every wind that blows) contains many interesting, often amusing, epitaphs. Take, for example, the one near the northeast corner of the church which refers to body snatching:

To wretches who pursue this barbarous trade
Your carcases in turn may be convey'd
Like his, to some unfeeling surgeon's room
Nor can they justly meet a better doom.

One fruitful parishioner is recorded as being 'father, grandfather, and great-grandfather to 147 persons'.

From the northern edge of this graveyard there is a very good view of upper Longdendale, where the gritstone moors crowd in at Tintwistle and on towards Woodhead. This is perhaps the most mountainous-looking defile in all the South Pennines, having the scale and proportions of real mountain country. A mile to the north of Mottram, slightly set apart, Hollingworthhall Moor rises to 1,309 feet and separates Longdendale from the Tame Valley. Looking out from the wilder moors above Glossop, particularly Chunal Moor and Cown Edge, I have always been attracted by Hollingworthhall Moor. On cold days its friendly profile has been a welcome sight after hours of travail over the ground of highest Peakland, and it provides some wonderful vistas out to the western horizon across Greater Manchester, from a sufficient distance to make the city seem colourful, even romantic.

Hollingworthhall Moor takes its name from Hollingworth Hall. The Normans realised the potential of the site, for a hunting lodge was built here from which boar and deer could be conveniently hunted in the wilderness of upper Longdendale. The setting is typically Pennine and protected by sycamores and beeches, but the heart has gone out of the place: all that remains are a fine gateway, old trees, a farm and what were the stables erected in the 19th century. Where the hall stood there is a sweep of rough grass, and the wind is usually moaning in the old trees which have outlived it.

Another old house, much closer to Mottram, is Mottram Old Hall. It seems to have been associated with Hollingworth Hall and was, in fact, bought by Captain Robert de Hollyngworth early in the 19th century. It has been much altered over the years, and what we see today is an early 19th-century exterior, though the stables nearby are 300 years old.

One more old building near Mottram is worthy of a mention, this one located on the western slopes of Harrop Edge looking out of the lower Tame Valley towards Hyde. Matley Hall Farm has an unusual courtyard, enclosed by the farm-house (1733 over doorway) and by buildings that were once labourers' cottages. It is stated that the old house has nineteen windows, no two alike (more a case of haphazard modification than contrived uniqueness).

To Mottram in Longdendale in August 1948 came one of Britain's foremost 20th-century artists, persuaded by a friend who already lived there to 'give it a try'. Laurence Stephen Lowry did not like Mottram and loathed this, his 'dreadful' last home; for many years he meant to leave, but he said he did not know where to go—or where he would like to go! He explained with resignation to a friend, 'I have no scenic sense,' so it did not really matter where he laid his head at night.

However, Lowry's move to Mottram in Longdendale was followed by the production of several 'unindustrial' landscapes, so it is perhaps correct to say that his new surroundings—the horizon of dark moorland profiles—did have some effect on his work. These landscapes include *Agricultural Fair, Mottram in Longdendale* (1949), *The House on the Moor* (1950) and *Heathcliff's House* (1950).

Though I corresponded with this outstanding northern artist, there was no opportunity to meet him before his quite sudden death in 1976. A year later I returned to Mottram and walked down the hill from the church and along Stalybridge Road. Lowry's house, The Elms, stood drab, dark and very empty on the west side of the road. It backed onto open fields where ponies were grazing. Beyond, the tops of the giant tower blocks of Hattersley New Town rose.

LOWRY: AN ORDINARY MAN

CANVASES DEPICTING matchstick-thin figures scurrying along the streets of a bleak industrial landscape are instantly recognisable as the work of L. S. (Laurence Stephen) Lowry. Today, such scenes sell for hundreds of thousands of pounds in the top auction houses of the art world. But Lowry himself never courted fame and fortune.

Born in 1887, Lowry led a simple life: he never smoked, drank, married, drove a car or travelled abroad. He worked all his life as a rent collector and clerk—even after he had won huge success—and walked the streets of Salford observing the comings and goings of everyday people. It was only in the evenings that he got the chance to record his observations on canvas. Nevertheless, Lowry was prolific from a young age, and attended evening art classes religiously for some 20 years. In addition to his famous urban scenes, he painted seascapes, rural landscapes and the occasional portrait.

ABOVE *Lowry was still painting well into his 80s; during his lifetime he is believed to have produced over 3,500 works of art.*

It was quite by chance that Lowry found public recognition. In the late 1930s some of his works were noticed by an art dealer while at a framer's. Before long the Tate Gallery in London was buying his work; he was made a Royal Academician in 1962; and in 1967 the Post Office celebrated his talent with a stamp. Lowry continued painting until only a few months before his death in 1976. Salford honours his memory with The Lowry, a new multi-million-pound arts venue which houses a permanent exhibition of the artist's work.

ABOVE The Canal Bridge, *painted in 1949, displays Lowry's trademark smoking chimneys and peopled streets.*

The garden was overgrown after years of semi-neglect; thistledown was blowing in the autumn breeze.

I was informed by a short, fat man further along Stalybridge Road that souvenir hunters were now taking pieces of Lowry's garden wall. Yes, he knew the artist well. He had once asked him why he always painted tall, thin people and received the reply, 'Well, you'd always draw short, fat ones, wouldn't you?'

Resting on the eastern side of Harrop Edge in the golden autumn sunlight, I could see upwards of thirty pylons striding across the hills round about, cutting up the scenery. The landscape is so steep and varied, though, that it still looks good framed between the swinging, curving wires. A mile to the north I strode over heather the colour of old wine on Hollingworthhall Moor. Mist was clinging to the far, high moors of Peakland proper; this haze also helped to conceal part of the urban sprawl westwards to Manchester and Oldham, Lowry's own, earlier industrial scenery.

THE DROWNED FARMS OF DERWENT DALE

During the latter part of the 19th century several large towns which were responsible for providing reliable sources of pure water cast interested glances into the longest and most sinuous of Peakland's gritstone dales, the beautiful upper Derwent Dale. This valley was cut out of relatively impervious gritstone and had steep slopes and a small human population. Dams built across its width would collect large reserves of water which would then flow south, aided by gravity, towards Derby, Nottingham and Leicester.

The Derwent Valley Water Act of 1899 enabled the first instalment of work to begin, involving the construction of two large masonry dams—Howden and Derwent—between 1901 and 1916. The Act of 1920 authorised the building of the much larger Ladybower Reservoir lower down the dale. Construction of Ladybower Reservoir, which contains 6,310 million gallons, began in 1935 and continued through the Second World War.

One of the major problems facing the Derwent Valley Water Board before a start could be made on the first two dams was finding the most suitable source of gritstone for the dams and other masonry works. Eventually Bole Hill, up on the high ground north of Nether Padley, some ten miles from the construction site, was chosen. Here was an outcrop of coarse gritstone known as Rivelin Grit, characterised by a rosy-pink coloration.

The top workings of the quarries reached to 1,000 feet above sea level and 600 feet above the Midland Railway line between Sheffield and Manchester, just west of Totley Tunnel and close to Grindleford station. It was estimated, when work began at the very beginning of the century, that there were 2,400,000 tons of sound Rivelin gritstone suitable for building at the site. The quarry expanded to cover an area of fifty-two acres and employed about 600 men.

A great asset of the site was that, by constructing linking railways and an inclined cableway down to the Midland Railway line, it was possible to transport the stone for three and a half miles on that route, up the Derwent Valley to

Bamford. From Bamford the Derwent Valley Water Board built its own railway up the dale, past Ashopton village to the site of the Howden Reservoir impounding wall near Marebottom Farm. The massive piers carrying this line across the mouth of Ouzelden Clough, on the western bank of Derwent Reservoir, are revealed in drought conditions and give a small indication of the huge cost of construction at Howden and Derwent, estimated in 1905 as being some £6–7 million when completed.

The flooding of the upper dale by Howden and Derwent Reservoirs resulted in the inundation of thirteen of the lovely old farms that nestled in sheltered corners where tributary streams joined the Derwent. These included Westend Farm, which stood near the confluence of the River Westend with the Derwent and served as a rest house for travellers using the Glossop–Penistone packhorse track. Then the village of Ashopton vanished under the rising water when Ladybower Reservoir began to fill in March 1943. One arm of this new lake flooded the lower Ashop valley, and the other filled Derwent Dale almost as far as the great impounding wall of Derwent Reservoir.

BOMBS AWAY!

RESERVOIRS DOT the woods and valleys of the Peak District and provide the surrounding industrial towns of Sheffield, Manchester, Nottingham and Derby with abundant water. But one spring the reservoirs in the picturesque Derwent Valley briefly gained a whole new purpose.

The Second World War had hardly touched this quiet corner of Britain, but in April 1943 the roar of low-flying aircraft broke the usual peaceful air. The locals were at a loss as to the purpose of these operations until the following month when they heard that the valley had been used as a training ground for a top-secret military operation: on May 16 and 17 the Allied forces had breached the Möhne and Eder dams of the Ruhr Valley, Germany's industrial heartland, with an amazing invention—the bouncing bomb.

LEFT *In 1993 Britain's only airworthy Lancaster bomber flew over Derwent dam on the 50th anniversary of the dam raids.*

RIGHT *The crest of 617 Squadron bears the appropriate motto of:* Après Moi le Déluge—*After Me the Flood.*

Aviation designer and inventor Barnes Wallis had devoted many months to perfecting the device. To be effective, it had to be dropped with great precision, so the crème de la crème of the RAF and Allied air forces were brought together to form 617 Squadron. An outstanding young pilot, Guy Gibson, led the operation, which was hailed as a great success, notwithstanding the loss of 53 men from the 133-strong squadron.

The story of the bouncing bomb was made legendary by the 1954 screen spectacular *The Dam Busters*, the filming of which brought low-flying Lancaster bombers to the reservoirs of the Derwent Valley once more. In 1986 the real Dambusters revisited their training site, when a memorial to the brave members of 617 Squadron was unveiled.

RIGHT AND BELOW *The 20th century saw the Upper Derwent Valley transformed into a miniature Lakeland. The Howden and Derwent Reservoirs* (pictured right) *and their southerly neighbour, the Ladybower Reservoir, were huge construction projects—the Derwent dam* (below) *took 14 years to build; they are now popular beauty spots.*

In Derwent Dale was the picturesque village of Derwent, where a medieval packhorse bridge crossed the river close to the parish church and Derwent Hall. The earliest records relating to Derwent refer to the founding of an abbey grange by the canons of Welbeck Abbey, Nottinghamshire, towards the end of the 12th century. This grange was established on what is now the eastern bank of Howden Reservoir and remained an important outlying farm in the possession of the Premonstratensian order for three and a half centuries. After the Dissolution of the Monasteries in the 16th century Derwent came into the hands of the Cavendish family, and later still it was owned by the local family of Balguy, who erected the fine Hall close to the point where the monks had built the packhorse bridge. The Balguys were followed by the Newdigates, who sold the estate to the Howards, Dukes of Norfolk, in 1886. The Howards used Derwent Hall as a shooting lodge, and people still living in the vicinity remember the large shooting parties that came there each autumn before the Second World War.

The hall was dismantled as Ladybower Reservoir was being built. The attractive stone gateposts, topped with Tudor-style balls, were removed to the entrance to

ABOVE AND RIGHT *The inhabitants of Derwent* (above) *had to leave their homes for good in the late 1930s to make way for the Ladybower Reservoir. The shops and houses were demolished before being submerged, and in the dry summer of 1989 the mud-caked ruins of the village briefly saw the light of day again* (right).

Woodthorpe Hall near Holmesfield, a dozen miles away, near the eastern edge of the National Park. The packhorse bridge was also taken down, and carefully re-erected at Slippery Stones, four miles upstream of its original site. It carries the Glossop–Penistone track over the river and is still much used by ramblers.

The Premonstratensians had established a chapel near the packhorse bridge in the village. It was replaced in about 1757 by what J. Charles Cox described as an 'ugly little building'. Just 110 years later, 'this mean edifice, which had neither antiquity nor beauty to recommend it' was demolished and replaced with a parish church.

As the waters rose ever closer towards the village, the interior of the church was stripped. The doors at the main entrance were taken to replace those at the parish church of Old Brampton, near Chesterfield. The war memorial was removed to a site beside the new high-level road across the dale.

During dry summers the water in each reservoir is reduced, and sometimes a few of the remains of Derwent village and of some of the ancient, isolated farms are revealed. A heap of stones marks the site of the church, and the drive to the hall still winds down by the Mill Brook, where a water mill formerly stood, a reminder of the Premonstratensian monks who farmed here in the Middle Ages.

LOVEFEASTS AND LANDSLIPS

Another dale, smaller and fortunately less well known to the general population than Derwent, is that drained by the River Alport.

Travellers using the A57 between Sheffield and Manchester—the famous Snake Road—are likely to miss seeing the mouth of Alport Dale as they cross it by Alport bridge. Such oversight is due to the large trees that overhang the road, the river and the bridge.

To get a really good view of the lower dale, one should take the old track up the hillside opposite. This leaves the Snake Pass at Alport bridge, crosses the River Ashop by a ford and swings up the slope of Blackley Hey at the northeastern corner of the Kinder Scout plateau. The track is actually a Roman road, connecting the fort of Navio in the Hope Valley with the fort of Ardotalia near Glossop. If one looks back to the north a quarter of a mile from Alport bridge, the broad mouth of Alport Dale is revealed. Steep and grassy slopes rear up 800 feet as high, smooth sentinels of this fine valley. Deciduous trees crowd beside the twisting course of the River Alport, and the dale swings away to the ever-wilder heights of heather and peaty wastes. In the middle distance, looking from the Roman road, plantations of conifers can be seen as punctuation marks on the far slopes, before the dale turns to the left and out of sight two miles above Alport bridge. High on the right slope a rugged area of exposed rock can be made out. This feature is Alport Castles and is best seen at close quarters.

To explore this little-known Derbyshire dale of the gritstone plateau country one must, of course, walk. A public footpath twists up to Alport hamlet from the Snake Pass at Hayridge Farm.

The stone barns that dot the lower pastures here are typical of the North Country, with great doorways for the quick entry of loads of hay in this high-rainfall district. Adjoining them are shippons and calf pens for overwintering cattle. Such a barn is passed to the left of the track a quarter of a mile above the Snake Pass, and in a further three-quarters of a mile the remote hamlet of Alport is reached.

The name Alport is derived from the Old English for 'old town' or 'old fortification'. The tiny settlement now consists of two farms: Alport Farm and Alport Castles Farm. The track curves round to the right to avoid a large barn, the place where the historic Lovefeast takes place on the first Sunday of every July.

With the passing of the infamous Act of Uniformity of 1662, many clergymen were ousted from their livings on Bartholomew Day, August 24, in the same year. Some of them made for the safety of this remote dale. Here they assembled 'to worship God according to the dictates of their own consciences'. In the 18th century John Wesley is said to have preached in this very barn while travelling between Lancashire and Yorkshire.

ABOVE *Alport Castles Farm still hosts the annual Lovefeast on the first Sunday in July. This religious festival dates back to the 18th century when nonconformists such as Wesleyan Methodists had to meet in remote locations to avoid persecution.*

It was natural, then, that the early Wesleyans should establish their annual Lovefeast at this romantic spot. The ceremony includes the singing of hymns and the partaking of plum loaf and water. No longer is the Lovefeast attended by a great crowd, many of whom had walked miles across the hills; those still participating arrive at the Snake Pass by car.

A path drops to the River Alport behind the barn. By following the river downstream a short distance, a footbridge can be used to cross to the eastern slope of the dale.

The path climbs eastwards up the steep, grassy slope for half a mile to the crest of Birchinlee Pasture at 1,600 feet above sea level, and then down to the mouth of the River Westend, where it enters Howden Reservoir in popular Derwent Dale. High up on this flank, 600 feet above the river and dominating this section of the dale, is the rugged scar of Alport Castles, Britain's largest landslip.

The millstone grit that forms the surface layers of the plateau here comprises a bed of hard sandstone overlying a thick shale series which is comparatively soft. Constant weathering of the underlying shales has resulted in undermining and the collapse of the harder sandstone above, an effect best seen on the east face of Mam Tor at the head of the Hope Valley five miles distant. Here at Alport Castles a great wedge of the plateau has broken away from the face behind and very slowly fallen out towards Alport Dale. As it has moved out and downwards over the centuries, a huge 'bow wave' of earth has formed in front of it. One can scramble up the tower, as the top of the breakaway block is known, and look at the extensive face of millstone grit acting as a backdrop for the sweep of Alport Dale as it winds northwards towards the heart of Bleaklow.

ABOVE *The ring ouzel can be identified by the light crescent on its chest. Each year it journeys from the Mediterranean to spend summer on the rocky outcrops and desolate moors of the Peak District.*

From the foot of Alport Castles a path can be followed to the north, a route that contours at about 1,400 feet above the narrowing dale. Eventually, where the last conifer plantation ends on this side, a good path develops. In a side valley nearby called Glethering Clough dippers and ring ouzels may be seen in summer. And in May and June the call of the cuckoo is commonplace in the dale.

Out of sight from the path, just below Glethering Clough, is a small waterfall, where the Alport plunges into a secret pool beneath a rowan. Waterfalls are not common in the Peak District, and this is the lowermost of three that enhance this dale. The path winds for half a mile above Glethering Clough, then the other two falls appear in quick succession. The uppermost is the finest, and after heavy rainfall on Bleaklow is a dramatic sight.

The situation is a lonely one, just below the level of the exposed gritstone plateau. In the shelter below these falls were found the bodies of Scouts who had succumbed to exhaustion after the spring weather suddenly deteriorated during a walk some years ago. The remoteness of this dale head is emphasised when it is recalled that the bodies were not located for a considerable time, despite a well-organised search over a wide area.

A mile above the waterfalls the sides of the dale open out to form a broad basin. Here is the confluence of the Alport and its main tributary, the Hern Brook. This place is called Grains in the Water, an ancient name evolved from the Old Norse *grein* (literally 'a fork of a river'). The broad basin is called The Swamp. In summer the moor grasses and bilberry bring colour, and it can be a sun trap on a still, bright day; then the only sounds are the calls of curlews, dunlins and rock pipits, and the trickle of the Alport.

Less than a mile to the north of Grains in the Water is Alport Head, where the little river is born under the peaty crest of Bleaklow Hill. This wide wilderness of Bleaklow is a dark waste of chocolate peat. A mile to the west is Bleaklow Head (2,060 feet), where the Pennine Way comes over from the head of the Snake Pass en route for Longdendale.

OPPOSITE *The rocky outcrop of Alport Castles is all that remains after a landslip many centuries ago in Alport Dale.*

WALKING THE WATERWAYS

BELOW *Canal banks teem with wild flowers during the spring and summer months.*

Canals, whether in good repair or derelict, make excellent walking routes. In summer the flora in and beside them is a great source of interest, likewise the animals. In winter a walk beside a South Pennine canal makes an easy route below the heights when it is raining or foggy. Not least, there is the fascination of looking at the architecture and engineering, the industrial archaeology, still visible along every mile of canal.

In the canal age of two centuries ago, there were few parts of England that presented such formidable problems to waterway engineers as the complex contours of the southern Pennines. The geological accidents that produced the South Lancashire, Yorkshire, Nottinghamshire, Derbyshire and north Staffordshire coalfields had given rise to important industrial conurbations separated by high ground which was difficult to traverse. Consequently, brilliant engineers made their names—and some their fortunes—during the construction of waterways across or near these hills. James Brindley (1716–72), William Jessop (1745–1814) and Benjamin Outram (1764–1805) are the best known.

Only three canals actually crossed the main watershed and so connected in a direct way the lowlands on either side of the Pennines. The first was the Rochdale Canal (1804), then came the Huddersfield Narrow Canal (1811) and finally the Leeds and Liverpool Canal (1816). The other waterways built adjacent to these uplands had termini in valleys or traversed a flank. A glance at a canal map of this part of England shows their reasonably even distribution on the perimeter of the high ground.

THE CHESTERFIELD CANAL

Few British industrial towns are as far from the sea as Chesterfield, yet neither this nor the fact that high ground surrounds the district on three sides prevented the construction of a major waterway in the late 18th century, at the commencement of the canal age. The story really begins in 1769 when James Brindley was asked to make a survey by lead-, coal- and iron-mining interests in northeast Derbyshire. By August of the same year Brindley had prepared a plan for a canal

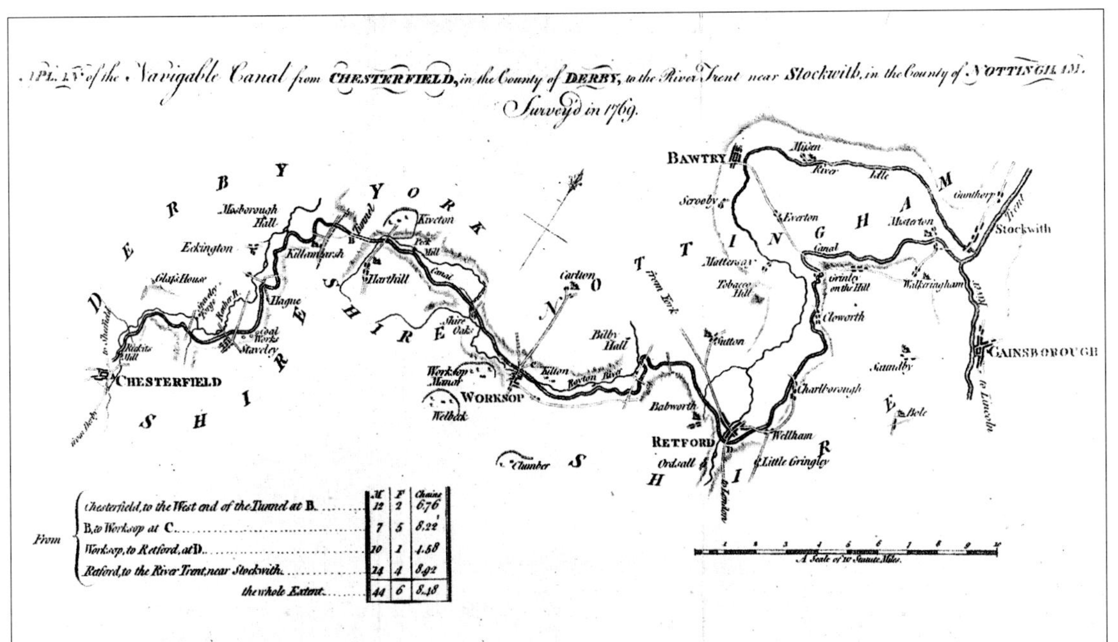

From	M	F	Chains
Chesterfield, to the West end of the Tunnel at B.	12	2	6.76
B, to Worksop at C.	7	5	8.22
Worksop, to Retford, at D.	10	1	4.58
Retford, to the River Trent, near Stockwith.	24	4	8.92
the whole Extent	44	6	8.48

ABOVE AND ABOVE LEFT *James Brindley* (above) *was one of the greatest engineers of the canal age. He oversaw the construction of 365 miles of canals in all, including the 45-mile-long Chesterfield Canal, which he surveyed in 1769* (above left).

of just over forty-five miles from West Stockwith on the Trent, near Gainsborough, by way of East Retford, Worksop and Staveley, with a steady climb (using thirty locks) from Worksop to the broad magnesian limestone ridge at Norwood (where a tunnel saved further ascent), and so into Derbyshire and up the valley of the River Rother to Chesterfield (another nineteen locks).

In the spring of 1774 the central section came into service, and the downstream portion as far as East Retford by late summer. This new communication link had an immediate effect on the townspeople of East Retford, reducing the price of coal from fifteen shillings and sixpence to ten shillings and sixpence per ton.

In May 1775, when it was opened to traffic, the Norwood Tunnel was the longest canal tunnel in the world, measuring 3,182 yards. The opening was something of an event: a contemporary account records that 'three vessels sailed through…with no less than 300 people on board, attended with a band of music.' That journey took a minute over one hour and marked a great opening up of adjacent parts of the Derbyshire coalfield.

The Norwood Tunnel was constructed in a straight line, 'being so truly directed that a person standing at one end may see out of the other'. It is no longer possible to check the accuracy of this statement, because in 1908 mining subsidence caused the collapse of the tunnel, and both entrances have long since been blocked with bricks and mortar.

As with most British canals, the coming of the railways in the first half of the 19th century dealt this waterway a shattering blow. Revenue was £12,636 in 1848—about the time that 250,000 tons of magnesian limestone was carried by barges from quarries at Anston, near the canal between Worksop and Killamarsh, for the rebuilding of the Houses of Parliament. By 1888, however, revenue had slumped to a mere £4,734, and in 1905 the forty remaining boats were carrying

ABOVE *Decorative canal memorabilia, such as this jug commemorating the opening of the Chesterfield Canal, are now collectors' items.*

only 15,000 tons of coal and 11,000 tons of bricks, the major commodities at that time. During the previous thirty-four years almost continuous repairs had been necessary to maintain Norwood Tunnel in a safe condition, such were the ravages of mining subsidence. Then in 1908 came the collapse of the tunnel. Since then the fourteen miles of waterway between Norwood Tunnel and Chesterfield have been defunct, save for the occasional horse-drawn coal barge which continued to use the narrowing channel into the 1930s.

When, in 1955, the brickworks at Walkingham (three miles up from the Trent) closed, all commercial traffic ceased, and in 1962 the canal was officially abandoned. Since that time vessels have been exclusively pleasure craft. Half a mile above Worksop Lock is Morse Lock (the fifty-ninth below Chesterfield), which marks the present official head of navigation and where a new turn-round point has been constructed. This has made the ten-mile section between East Retford and Worksop more popular with boaters.

Nevertheless, a walk along the old towpath, which winds down the Rother Valley from Norwood Tunnel to Chesterfield, is most interesting, because it covers

ARTERIES OF TRADE AND PLEASURE

TWO HUNDRED YEARS AGO, as early industry began to boom, canal mania gripped Britain. Canals were ideal for the cheap transportation of raw materials for industry and manufactured goods. Entrepreneurs competed to develop the new commercial transport routes, and the first 'packet boats' were launched to carry passengers.

James Brindley's construction in 1759–61 of the Bridgewater Canal sparked off a widespread building programme undertaken by gangs of labourers called navigators, or 'navvies', and within 80 years Britain was crisscrossed by a web of more than 4,000 miles of navigable waterways, with Staffordshire at its hub. Coal was the main cargo, but canals also carried corn and all kinds of agricultural and industrial products. The goods were loaded onto narrow boats measuring some 70 feet long and less than seven feet wide, towed by horses which plodded along the towpath wearing crocheted bonnets to keep flies out of their eyes.

By the 1840s economic competition from the railways had forced many canal workers to make their homes

ABOVE *Canal-boat exteriors and equipment, such as water cans and buckets, were often decorated with rose and castle motifs.*

LEFT *Almost half the floating population at the turn of the 20th century was made up of bargees' children.*

largely 'unknown' territory with some surprisingly sylvan sections, and provides a new viewpoint of this part of north Derbyshire.

Norwood Bottom Lock, with its broad pool and footbridge and attractive whitewashed dwelling, which was until 1909 a public house, marks the bottom of the flight of thirteen locks that carried vessels up the slope to the western portal of Norwood Tunnel, one mile distant. It is certainly one of the steepest flights of locks in Britain. Then, at the bricked-up tunnel mouth, one may pass beneath the motorway and walk along the line of the tunnel to the eastern portal and so on through delightful, wooded country by way of Turnerwood to Shireoaks and Worksop.

THE CROMFORD CANAL

With the opening of the Erewash Canal in 1779, Langley Mill and adjacent districts of the Nottinghamshire and Derbyshire coalfield became linked with the Trent, and a tide of industrial expansion rose up the Erewash valley. Nine years later interested parties met to discuss the possibility of extending this canal beyond

aboard the narrow boats, both to avoid paying rent on land and so that they could employ their wives and children as unpaid helpers. A whole family might live in a verminous cabin only nine feet long. Boat children had scant education and were expected to do heavy work from a young age. To brighten up their surroundings, families decorated the vessels with bold colours and distinctive lettering, creating the symmetrical designs, roses and castles that have become the hallmarks of canal boats.

As faster, more efficient forms of transport developed, many canals fell into disuse and decay. Few are now used for carrying cargo, but since the 1970s many miles of waterways have been restored for cruising and other forms of recreation. Linking towns and cities with tranquil stretches of countryside, today's canal network is used by thousands of pleasure boats, many of them built in traditional narrow-boat style. Walkers and cyclists can explore towpaths, and some families are once again choosing to live on boats, giving a new lease of life to the historic waterways and their colourful craft.

LEFT *A barge loaded with raw materials for Josiah Wedgwood's pottery factory floats past his home, Etruria Hall, on the Trent and Mersey Canal.*

RIGHT *Holidaymakers float along the sun-dappled waters of the Macclesfield Canal in Cheshire aboard brightly coloured barges.*

Langley Mill, in order to provide cheap transport for coal, iron and carboniferous limestone. There was even a suggestion of making some sort of trading link with Manchester across the watershed of the southern Pennines.

The necessary Act of Parliament was passed in 1789 and William Jessop and Benjamin Outram were made responsible for the engineering. The resulting Cromford Canal was completed by 1794; it wound up the Erewash valley from Langley Mill, turning westwards to Ripley, along the lower reaches of the Amber valley to Ambergate and thence northwards for five miles to Cromford. Here were Sir Richard Arkwright's cotton mills, just beside the head of navigation, which benefited greatly from the presence of such convenient transportation.

The Cromford was a successful business venture, and by 1841–2 goods traffic had risen to 320,000 tons. There was even a privately operated passenger service between Cromford and Nottingham for many years, whose vessels used the now-derelict Nottingham Canal beyond Langley Mill. In the early years of the 19th century there had been a plan to extend the canal beyond Cromford, via Bakewell and the upper Wye valley, to join the Peak Forest Canal at Buxworth, near Chinley, and so give a through route from the Trent to the Mersey. The engineering problems involved caused this proposal to be dropped and instead the Cromford and High Peak Railway was constructed and opened in 1831. The engineer was William Jessop's son, Josiah. The railway left the canal one mile south of Cromford, at the place that came to be known as High Peak Wharf; here goods were transferred between waterway and railway. The thirty-three-mile-long line crossed the limestone plateau and reached 1,264 feet above sea level southeast of Buxton. It then descended into the Goyt Valley to link up with the Peak Forest Canal at Whaley Bridge.

ABOVE *'Legging' a craft through Cromford Canal's Butterley Tunnel was a challenging and exhausting task for boatmen.*

Competition from the railways affected the Cromford Canal after 1850, and when the Midland Railway purchased it in 1870 only a little local traffic was using it. As with the Chesterfield Canal, the Cromford had a long tunnel on its middle section: the 3,000-yard-long Butterley Tunnel, passing underneath Ripley. After several roof collapses towards the end of the century, it was finally closed by a serious collapse in 1900. Thereafter the upper half of the canal, between Butterley Tunnel and Cromford, was used a little, but the entire waterway was finally abandoned in 1944. Since that time the lower section between Butterley and Langley Mill has become utterly ruinous, and most of the canal's length in the Erewash valley has been filled in altogether.

LEFT *The tall, slender chimney of Leawood Pumphouse once spouted clouds of steam as it worked flat out to feed water into Cromford Canal.*

It is the five miles at the head of this canal that remain in the best condition. Much restoration work has already taken place at Cromford Wharf and a mile to the south at High Peak Wharf. Immediately south of this are two of the most interesting features of the Cromford Canal: the imposing Leawood Pump of 1849, which could raise twenty-four tons of water from the adjacent River Derwent to the canal every minute using steam power; and William Jessop's single-span Wigwell Aqueduct over the Derwent, which collapsed soon after construction and had to be rebuilt more solidly. The towpath is maintained, and the section from Whatstandwell to Ambergate is now a nature reserve.

THE MACCLESFIELD CANAL

This waterway traverses the western fringe of the Peak District for twenty-six miles, from the Trent and Mersey Canal at Kidsgrove to the Peak Forest Canal at Marple, Cheshire. It was the last of the waterways mentioned here to be

constructed, opening to traffic in 1831, and was designed by Thomas Telford. The canal was once a vital link between Macclesfield and Stockport, bringing raw materials to the mills and taking away the finished textiles. Now it is a quiet backwater, used mainly by holiday craft. It passes through attractive countryside for almost its entire length.

The walk along its towpath makes a good day's expedition and offers broad views out to the west across the Cheshire Plain. The hills are apparent to the east for the entire journey: Mow Cop, the Cloud, Gawsworth Common, Kerridge Hill, Nab Head and the moorlands about Lyme Park. The canal is very popular with pleasure-craft users as it forms one arm of the noted Cheshire Ring Canal.

Another feature of the Macclesfield Canal is the number of beautiful accommodation bridges of local stone, some with curved ramps to enable the boat horse to cross to the other bank without being disconnected. Here and there are white-painted swing bridges (as at Oakgrove, south of Macclesfield) which must be opened and closed by the boat crew.

Between Macclesfield and Congleton the canal descends 110 feet in one mile as it goes southwards. This is achieved by the twelve Bosley locks. South of these again, where the canal turns westwards for a couple of miles, there is an airy aqueduct high over the River Dane where that river flows out of the hills and on towards the plain.

Only a mile or so west of the canal, above Bollington, is Adlington on the River Dean, a most interesting spot. Here, on the site of a pre-Norman hunting lodge,

ABOVE *Accommodation bridges, as they were called, allowed horses towing boats to cross the canal without being unhitched.*

BELOW *Adlington Hall's unusual architecture combines a neo-classical portico with Georgian brickwork and 15th-century half-timbering.*

ABOVE *The village of Pott Shrigley—a cluster of stone cottages and a church—nestles in a secluded wooded hollow.*

stands beautiful Adlington Hall. The Legh family have lived here for nearly seven centuries. The approach from the lane skirting the northern side of the park brings one past the impressive stable block (now serving as luxury flats) and out under mature trees to the black and white east front of the house.

Adlington Hall was once moated—the remains of this are still visible—and the oldest part of the house is one of Cheshire's best half-timbered buildings. At the centre of the house is a courtyard, from which one gets a good impression of the Elizabethan half-timbering and the red brickwork dating from the alterations of 1757. One of its most interesting features is the 300-year-old Smith organ on which Handel played while staying at Adlington.

On the opposite side of the canal from Adlington, under Nab Head, lies Pott Shrigley, one of the most attractive villages in all this South Pennine country. It stands amid high trees and steep, patchwork slopes, and the unusual name is derived from the word 'shriggel', 'a wood frequented by shrikes', and 'pott', 'a pool', though Pott is also a local family name, so the actual origin is something of an enigma: 'Pott's wood where shrikes are common' perhaps?

The outstanding architectural feature of the village is the tower of St Christopher's Church. The building is unusual because it is mainly constructed of millstone grit, which is rare for a Cheshire church; more particularly, its tower is very large for such a modest building. With its beautiful pinnacles and battlements framed by mature deciduous trees, it would do credit to a much bigger town church. There was a chantry chapel here from 1491, but an older building definitely once stood on the site, and the very tall cross in the graveyard was probably the original preaching cross, once so common, from which the early priests conducted their services.

Two miles due south of Adlington is the village of Prestbury, on the banks of the River Bollin. It is affluent and attractive, but in a rather twee sort of way. Almost a suburb of Macclesfield and Manchester, it is a dormitory village of the type we associate more with the wealthier parts of Surrey or Kent than with the lowland fringe of the southern Pennines.

Prestbury means 'priests' fort', and the remains of a Saxon cross and an Anglo-Danish chapel in the churchyard of St Peter's suggest that there has been a centre of worship here since perhaps the 5th century. In fact, in the Middle Ages this relatively small village commanded an extensive parish which included Macclesfield and Bollington. The passage of time reversed these roles: the development of industry and the Macclesfield Canal enlarged canalside Bollington, for instance, so that in 1834 it achieved the status of an independent parish. Prestbury is many people's dream of an ideal place to live, and it has retained its railway station on the main line between Macclesfield and Manchester, while latterly busy Bollington has now lost its railway link.

ABOVE *The main street of the pretty village of Prestbury is lined with picture-postcard whitewashed cottages.*

A well-known feature overlooking the canal from Kerridge Hill above Bollington is White Nancy at the northern end of the ridge. This takes the form of a tall, whitewashed structure shaped like an old straw beehive. An ordnance beacon of brick apparently stood here before 1810, and in a local history of the Macclesfield district (published in 1825) it is stated that a Mr Gaskell of nearby Rainow built 'a round building, clothed in white, called Northern Nancy'. The name Nancy probably came from the several females of the Gaskell family who had that Christian name; also the horse that was used to drag the slab of stone that formed the seat within the building was called Nancy, possibly after those same ladies. Although the building is now sealed, from it, in clear weather, shipping is visible on the Mersey.

Almost eight miles north of Macclesfield the canal flows under an arched towpath bridge and meets the Peak Forest Canal at Marple.

ABOVE *Canal users slowly and carefully navigate their craft along the narrow Marple aqueduct, almost 100 feet above the River Goyt.*

THE PEAK FOREST CANAL

Opened at the commencement of the 19th century, this fourteen-and-a-half-mile waterway was built between Dukinfield Junction on the Ashton Canal—at the heart of an industrial area bordering eastern Manchester—and the Buxworth Basin, near Whaley Bridge. The Cromford and High Peak Railway came down to Whaley Bridge, where a half-mile branch of the canal from near Buxworth had its terminus at an interesting warehouse which now houses a small museum. In this terminal building, goods and passengers were transferred between canal and railway.

A walk along the entire length of the canal from Whaley Bridge to Dukinfield Junction makes a rewarding day's outing, and there are trains back to Whaley Bridge from Guide Bridge, a mile from Dukinfield Junction. But the most interesting section of the canal is that from the junction with the Macclesfield Canal at Marple, running northwards for three miles to Romiley. A series of sixteen locks in quick succession carry the waterway 210 feet down to the famous Marple aqueduct. The three arches of the aqueduct, designed by Benjamin Outram and a local engineer, Thomas Brown, carry the canal slightly less than 100 feet above the River Goyt. Opened in 1800, it is one of the best-looking aqueducts in the country.

CHAPTER FIVE

ARTISTS, ROYALISTS AND ROGUES

WHEN THE EIGHTEEN-YEAR-OLD J. M. W. TURNER was sent by Walker, the publisher, to Derbyshire and neighbouring counties to make topographical drawings, he travelled northwards to Sheffield by coach from London. The year was 1793. His first sight of the town would have been from the top of the steep ground immediately to the north of Norton village, where the old main road (Derbyshire Lane) skirted Meersbrook Park. It has been suggested that Turner knew instinctively that he was not likely to find a better view of Sheffield than this: that sudden, broad vista over the Sheaf valley to the major buildings of the town centre, with Shirecliffe and Wincobank Hill in the background. Whether he searched the high ground round the town for a better viewpoint is not recorded, but, in the end, it was from the edge of Meersbrook Park that he produced his drawing which ultimately appeared in the *Copper Plate Magazine* of 1798.

ABOVE *Turner was just 18 years old, but already a well-known artist, when he painted this panorama of Sheffield from the heights of Meersbrook Park.*

Sheffield is more closely surrounded by hills and steep ground than any other industrial city in Britain. Although there are many good viewpoints, this one on the southern side at Meersbrook is generally accepted as being the finest because it is lit from behind for most of the day and is sufficiently close to the city centre to reveal details of industry and architecture, including easily recognisable features such as St George's Church, Portobello Street of 1821, the town hall of 1890–97, some of the university buildings and the more recent, tree-girt Hallam Tower Hotel. None of these featured, of course, in Turner's drawing. The characteristic crocketed spire of the early 15th-century parish church (raised to the rank of cathedral when Sheffield became a city in 1914) would then have been the most conspicuous feature of the town's skyline as seen from the edge of Meersbrook Park.

Meersbrook House is a red-brick mansion built in about 1780 by Benjamin Roebuck, son of the Sheffield cutler and industrialist John Roebuck. In 1890, it was opened by the Earl of Carlisle as the Ruskin Museum of the Guild of St George. Its fine collection of rare minerals, natural-history items and works of art was originally given to help 'educate and enlighten the working classes' of this once dark and dirty industrial town.

In a guidebook of 1899 the ornithological collection, primarily the celebrated Eyton Collection, was held to be the most complete set of coloured bird illustrations and drawings in existence. Most of the drawings and paintings were produced for this museum by artists trained by Ruskin, and, appropriately, the original sketch by J. M. W. Turner of that best view of Sheffield from near the top of the park was included. However, by 1953 the decline in numbers of visitors to the museum caused it to be closed, and the Ruskin Collection was transferred to Sheffield City Museum, Library and Art Gallery. Meersbrook House is now the headquarters of Sheffield Corporation Recreation Department.

BELOW *Sheffield has spread closer and closer to Meersbrook over the years, but the park still provides an impressive view of the city.*

ABOVE *The Bishops' House in Meersbrook Park, now a museum of Tudor and Stuart life, is itself a piece of history.*

Up at the top of Meersbrook Park, close to the place where the view of Sheffield is at its best, stands the Bishops' House. This is a 16th-century half-timbered building erected on a stone base. Such black and white structures are now rare in this part of England, and this is the best example remaining on the eastern flanks of the South Pennines. Centuries ago, when oak, straw and reeds were readily available on the lower ground, there were many half-timbered and thatched-roofed dwellings. They were largely replaced by stone and, as manufacturing spread, by easily made bricks. If one looks down towards Heeley in the Sheaf valley, the closely packed houses of Victorian and Edwardian development are evidence of the wealth accumulated by brick-makers at that time.

Why is this lovely old building alongside Norton Lees Lane called the Bishops' House? It is likely that the house we see today was the home of William Blythe and his family. The Blythes are enduringly commemorated as Norton residents by William Blythe's monument in the Blythe chapel in Norton parish church. It is known that he had a coat of arms in 1485, and that two of his five sons became bishops. The elder of these two brothers, John, became warden of King's Hall, Cambridge in 1488, was later appointed Master of the Rolls and in 1494 was consecrated Bishop of Salisbury. Other posts he occupied were the chancellorships of Cambridge University and of Ireland. He died in 1499 and was buried behind the high altar of Salisbury Cathedral. The younger brother, Geoffrey, was educated at Eton and Cambridge, where he followed John as warden of King's Hall in 1498. In 1502 Henry VII sent him on diplomatic work to Hungary, and on his return in 1503 he became Bishop of Lichfield and Coventry. It was Geoffrey Blythe who founded his family's chantry chapel in Norton church.

The name Meersbrook seems to have been derived from Anglo-Saxon for 'a boundary', and until 1934 the stream formed the boundary between Derbyshire and Yorkshire and before that Mercia and Northumbria. All the land to the south and west of the stream lay in Derbyshire, in the parish of Norton. In 1934 this large parish was transferred to the city of Sheffield.

A last look back at Sheffield from the top of Meersbrook Park brings to my mind the recent description by R. C. Scriven of his native town:

> When I was born in Sheffield it had a dramatic infernal beauty by night. On all its hills the cones of blast furnaces were tilted at random intervals and the lurid crimson glow of their fires glared like the eyes of demons.
>
> The smoking, reeking witch's cauldron of Edwardian Sheffield, Bessemer's mistress, the honest tart with her sleeves rolled up, was my Sheffield. Today it has some of the purest air in polluted England.

You can certainly appreciate that on a nice day in Meersbrook Park, from somewhere near the Bishops' House, seeing Sheffield backed by the broad hills of the South Pennines, the lovely gritstone country.

CHANTREY LAND

Two centuries ago, up and down Derbyshire Lane, donkeys daily carried milk in pannier churns from the farms of Norton parish to the expanding population of the industrial town beside the Rivers Sheaf and Don. One of these donkey-driving lads was Francis Legatt Chantrey, who became one of Britain's best-known and best-loved sculptors.

ABOVE *Sir Francis Legatt Chantrey (pictured here with an example of his work) rose from humble beginnings to become one of England's most sought-after portrait sculptors.*

Norton village—literally 'north farm', in relation to Dronfield a couple of miles to the south, but now a southern suburb of Sheffield—is the focal point for all pilgrims seeking traces of this great artist.

The Chantreys had been a fairly well-to-do family—some of them had been to university and one had been a rector—but their prosperity seems to have waned some little time before Francis was born in a small cottage at Jordanthorpe (just south of Norton) on April 7, 1781. His father was a carpenter and small farmer. Harold Armitage's local history, entitled *Chantrey Land*, records that young Francis attended Norton village school 'very irregularly, for no doubt there was much for him to do on the farm or in the workshop'. From infancy he drew pictures and was allowed, every Saturday, to cover the stone floor of the kitchen with drawings before his mother washed it.

Francis began work as an apprentice to a Sheffield grocer, but soon afterwards managed to transfer to the shop of Robert Ramsay, woodcarver and dealer in prints and plaster models, in the High Street, Sheffield. He spent his spare time modelling and drawing in a rented room in Hutton's Yard. Later he tried his fortune in Dublin and Edinburgh; in 1802 he finally moved to London, where he worked as a woodcarver. What really brought Chantrey to public notice was his bust of the radical English politician John Horne Tooke, exhibited at the Royal Academy in 1811.

Today Chantrey is perhaps best known for his statues of George IV in Trafalgar Square and at Windsor Castle, but Chantrey himself considered his finest works to be the figure of Lady Frederica Stanhope at Chevening and the bust of Sir Walter Scott at Abbotsford.

I remember going to Chantrey Land one remarkably hot summer: down into Owler Bar Wood from the Coal Aston side and following the old bridle road northwards to Povey Farm. This is a typical Elizabethan farmhouse, from which one looks out southwards to the woods and fields about Troway and Sicklebrook. Francis Chantrey must have known this pastoral landscape well; he would recognise it still. From there I went on to Norton village with its several important mansions, the most significant of which is The Oakes, or Oakes-in-Norton. The name is taken from the great wealth of oak trees found in this area—John Evelyn's

THE GLORIOUS OAK

WITH ITS EMERALD DOME of leaves, hard-wearing wood and life expectancy of up to 500 years, the oak has long been a symbol of English pride and vigour. The 18th-century actor David Garrick famously wrote 'Heart of oak are our ships/Heart of oak are our men', linking English naval power with traditional virtues of strength and endurance. The oak also features in history and folklore. Oak Apple Day (May 29) commemorates Charles II's restoration to the throne in 1660 and derives its name from an alleged incident in which the fugitive King hid in an oak tree to escape Parliamentarian forces. This event is still celebrated in various parts of England and in the common pub name The Royal Oak.

The remnants of ancient oak woods can still be found in various parts of the country, including Padley Gorge in the Dark Peak. Britain has two native species: the common oak, *Quercus robur*, whose acorns grow on long stalks; and the sessile oak, *Quercus petraea*, whose acorns are 'sessile', or stalkless. Apart from the acorns, which are a ready food for squirrels, oaks produce growths called galls, or oak apples, in response to invasion by the gall wasp. They are also host to a range of wildlife, from plants such as ivy, mosses and ferns to birds such as wood warblers, tree-creepers and nuthatches which feast on the 300 or so types of insect that inhabit these miniature ecosystems.

ABOVE *A mature oak tree is a mini-nature reserve, providing food or a home for a huge variety of plants and animals.*

LEFT *Oak apples are caused by the gall wasp* Biorhiza pallida, *which lays its eggs in the leaf buds.*

BELOW *Grey squirrels nest high in the oak's branches and feed on acorns, bark and birds' eggs.*

Sylva and Hunter's *Hallamshire* refer to Sheffield's fine oaks—and gnarled specimens still dot the park here.

The Oakes was built in the 17th century but was completely remodelled in 1827, resulting in a plain, nine-bay, two-and-a-half-storey building complete with Tuscan porch. It is open to the public in summertime. The terrace on the south front of the house was designed by Chantrey for Sir William Bagshawe, and the large urns there were a gift from the artist. The beautiful iron gates were made from metal obtained from Delves Wood on the estate and are thought to have been cast here.

School Lane bounds the western perimeter of Oakes Park, and here, until recently, stood the old school which Chantrey attended spasmodically. A while ago the school was demolished, and suburban villas now occupy the site. On the other side of School Lane, adjoining the main gates to The Oakes, I was pleased to see the old Post Office, which was illustrated on the frontispiece of *Chantrey Land*.

ABOVE *Linley Sambourne entertained readers of* Punch *magazine for 43 years with his satirical cartoons.*

School Lane leads to Cinderhill Lane and Jordanthorpe. The *Punch* artist Linley Sambourne was brought up at Jordanthorpe Hall. Across the drive stands the farm that was Chantrey's birthplace. In those days it was a small cottage, but when Chantrey became wealthy he had it enlarged for his mother, who lived there until her death in 1826. A school has been built in front of this farmhouse—spoiling the outlook from it—but the structure remains much as it did after Chantrey had finished with it. Even the original northeast-facing window of the bedroom in which he was born can still be seen.

The heart of Norton village lies a quarter of a mile to the north of Jordanthorpe, and is centred upon the parish church of St James. It is known that there was a church here when Robert FitzRanulph, lord of Norton and Alfreton, founded the abbey at Beauchief, not far away, because he bestowed the church upon that abbey; until the Dissolution of the Monasteries, a regular canon of Beauchief officiated and resided here. In the chancel is a memorial tablet to Sir Francis Legatt Chantrey, the work of his former assistant James Heffernan, and in more recent times a full-length plaster cast of Chantrey by John Bell has been erected there.

After his sudden death at his London home in November 1841, Chantrey lay 'in a gallery surrounded by the models of his works'. It is recorded that his old friend J. M. W. Turner visited on the day after his death 'but could not speak'. He would have had a particular affection for Chantrey, knowing the latter's homeland from those early forays with a pencil and sketchpad when he was seeking his fortune and Chantrey was a boy of twelve, long before their paths had crossed—though it is not beyond the bounds of possibility that the young Francis could have seen the older artist at work at Meersbrook as he himself drove the milk donkey down Derbyshire Lane from Jordanthorpe.

Chantrey had always intended to be buried in Norton churchyard, and years before had chosen the spot under the south face of the tower. It took the undertaker and his team six days to reach the village with the corpse, and the burial took place in driving rain on the afternoon of December 6. The granite tomb is plain to the point of severity because Chantrey disliked ornamentation for its own sake. The inscription is extremely deeply cut (he knew well enough the effects of weathering on shallow inscriptions and on soft stone).

Immediately to the west of the church stands Norton Hall, which was for a long period the home of the Shores (who also lived at Meersbrook House). When the mansion was rebuilt in 1815 Chantrey poured scorn on the new design, and described it as a 'packing-box with windows'.

On the remains of Norton Green, close to the church, stands the great obelisk of Cornish granite designed by Philip Hardwick and erected in 1854 as a memorial to Chantrey. Another tangible memorial is the Chantrey Bequest to the Royal Academy. The artist left his fortune to his wife, and upon her death income from it was to be spent on the most valuable works of sculpture and painting executed by artists of any nationality who were resident in Great Britain when the work was carried out. The purchases of the Chantrey Bequest are housed in the Tate Gallery.

Chantrey Land remains remarkably intact, despite the red-brick housing estates encroaching from the north and west, plans for a sewerage works in Hazlebarrow's fields, and a bypass road through Oakes Park, near the south front of the house. Standing on a quiet summer day in Lightwood Lane, or in the woods above the Moss, we can appreciate Harold Armitage's sentiments all those years ago—Chantrey's name will never be forgotten in the region of 'the church, the halls and the cottages that stand in the midst of the Norton's quiet fields'.

THE CIVIL WAR

Derbyshire and its close environs had none of those great encounters between the forces of Cromwell and the King's men that live on in national history and link a region with 17th-century strife on the grand scale. That is not to say that the troubles of the Civil War left the sleeping countryside unscathed. The following, I trust, will be of some interest, though it is not intended as an exhaustive study of the progress of the Civil War in these parts.

There are the well-known, perhaps partly traditional stories, such as that of the Royalist Sir Christopher Fulwood who rallied over 1,000 men from the lead mines of the limestone plateau to fight the Roundheads. He lived at Middleton, near Youlgreave, and when Parliamentary forces came upon the scene unexpectedly he was forced to hide in a cave in nearby Bradford dale. Here he was discovered and killed; the cave—known as Cromwell's Cave—remains. In the roof of a house now known as Royal Cottage, beside the road crossing Axe Edge between Buxton and Leek, tradition has it that Charles I lay in hiding while his Roundhead enemies passed by.

During 1644 a skirmish took place near Ashbourne. The Parliamentarians shot cannonballs at the west front of the parish church of St Oswald. Three of these cannonballs are preserved in the church. In August 1645 King Charles came through Ashbourne from Ludlow en route for Doncaster, and as it was Sunday

LEFT AND BELOW
St Oswald's Church in Ashbourne, a fine example of the Early English style of architecture, was the target of cannonball fire during the Civil War. Three cannonballs shot during an engagement between Royalists and Parliamentarians in 1644 are on display in the church.

he worshipped in the church. It is interesting to note in passing that King Charles's great-grandson, Charles Edward Stuart (Bonnie Prince Charlie), marched here from Cheshire, occupying Ashbourne Hall before moving on to Derby as part of his proposed march on London. Three days later he was back in Ashbourne, having been turned back by his opponents at Swarkestone Bridge on the River Trent. This proved to be the farthest south the Young Pretender ever reached in his bid to gain the throne.

The greatest story of this troubled time within Peakland and its fringes relates to the events connected with beautiful and sad South Wingfield Manor. This large and finely sited building was erected in about 1440 by Ralph, Lord Cromwell, who was Lord Treasurer to King Henry VI. Later it came into the hands of the Earls of Shrewsbury, and because of this connection we find that Mary, Queen of Scots spent some years in confinement there prior to 1585, when she moved to Tutbury Castle. At the commencement of the Civil War the manor was taken and garrisoned by the Parliamentarians. Then, in 1643, the Royalists successfully retook it under the command of the Marquis of Newcastle. Soon a storming party of Roundheads attacked again. They 'shattered the walls with artillery from the neighbouring heights'. The Royalist governor of the manor, a Colonel Dalby, attempted to conceal his identity by dressing as a member of the ranks, but a deserter from his garrison recognised him and shot him in the face.

RIGHT *South Wingfield Manor—a casualty of the Civil War. Years before it was ransacked by Parliamentarians the manor had served as a luxurious prison to Mary, Queen of Scots.*

After the Battle of Naseby in 1645 King Charles retreated northwards with about 3,000 horses—the remnant of his army—and met and defeated the chief Parliamentarian of the region, Sir John Gell, at Sudbury and Ashbourne. Though now a Roundhead stronghold, South Wingfield Manor was the scene of frequent skirmishes until the middle of 1646. Then, on June 23, 1646, the Parliamentarians gave the order for its destruction.

The wrecking of this massive building is the worst piece of 'knocking about' done by Cromwell in this part of England. When this mission had been accomplished and the manor lay in ruins on its hilly knoll above the River Amber, instructions were given for the destruction of Eastwood Hall, Ashover, six miles to the north of the Amber valley.

Eastwood Hall had been in the possession of the Reresby family from 1282 until 1623, when the rector of Ashover, the Reverend Emanuel Bourne, bought it. An old employee of the Reverend Bourne overheard the order for the march to Eastwood being given close by the smouldering walls at South Wingfield. Word was immediately sent, and the Reverend Bourne got together several horses and carts and removed as much furniture as possible before a company of dragoons in the charge of a Muster Master Smedley arrived the next day.

Possession was demanded in the name of Parliament. The owner agreed but said that he had 'never done any mischief' against Parliament and would report the outrage. That the whole affair passed off in a relatively cordial atmosphere is apparent when we read a contemporary account of how the troops offered to help remove the remainder of the hall's contents before demolition commenced.

A barrel of gunpowder was soon set in the centrally placed tower, and a violent report rocked the whole Ashover district. When the dust had cleared it was seen that half the hall had been destroyed and the remainder lay in ruins.

The troops assembled and sang a psalm. After this they marched the half-mile to Ashover church and listened to a sermon by Muster Master Smedley on the evils of popery and kingcraft. When the sermon was finished the Parliamentarians mounted their waiting horses and were not seen again in the Amber valley.

Eastwood Hall was never repaired. Today it is a picturesque ruin, partly covered by ivy, and the haunt of jackdaws. It is one of those small but attractive ruins that add an element to the atmosphere of our countryside, something almost permanent and perhaps best described as typically English.

These last encounters of any real significance in or near Peakland occurred in 1646, a matter of two and a half years before the execution of Charles I, when the Roundheads overcame all obstacles to ruling England as they saw fit. Away from the midsummer greens of the Amber valley they rode, over the hills and far away, leaving the inhabitants of Peakland to their age-old devices of farming, trading and squabbling in peace.

THE VALE OF AMBER

My own first encounters with the vale of Amber, long ago, have left few happy memories. It seemed a miserable sort of place, with Victorian houses of dull and massive gritstone, and the sun never shone. But explorations at a later period showed the valley to be full of promise.

The River Amber rises near Roach House Farm at 1,000 feet above sea level, close by the long, straight lane leading from Chesterfield to Two Dales in the Derwent Valley. All about are stone quarries; it is an area long exploited for its good-quality gritstone. The river finally joins the Derwent at Ambergate, approximately fifteen miles below Roach House Farm.

RIGHT *The vale of Amber's upper basin seems to embody the notion of England as a 'green and pleasant land'.*

All about the Amber's upper basin are scattered holdings and isolated cottages, relics of an ancient settlement pattern. Many of them are far from any public road and retain an air of remoteness beneath a wide, upland sky.

The most noteworthy house of the upper basin is Eddlestow Hall Farm, which looks out from 860 feet above sea level near the crest of Amber Hill, along and down the side of the Amber valley. It is the home of the Hole family and their well-known Amber herd of dairy shorthorn cattle, successful in the show rings of this part of England. The house is a dream of Elizabethan architecture, something of a jumble of styles but all the more attractive for that. Behind the house stands a building of probably greater antiquity, with two fireplaces. It is possible that with increasing wealth the Elizabethan yeoman farmers moved out of this ancient homestead to a new and larger dwelling and relegated the former to service as a cowshed or barn, which is what it has remained.

A long and almost straight lane follows the western watershed of the Amber's upper basin from near Gladwin's Mark, past the coniferous plantations on Upper Moor, Middle Moor and Bottom Moor (names given to relatively small divisions of Matlock Moor), and so over Amber Hill and southwards above Holloway to the hill end at Crich. It is the route of a very old ridgeway or packhorse track, which kept to the open country and so avoided the dense scrub and woodlands of the surrounding valleys in the Middle Ages and before. The demand for good stone led to the development of small quarries along the ridge, and this ridgeway remained in use, to be improved with limestone chippings and, latterly, tarmac.

Another old lane swings down from Eddlestow Hall Farm into the valley of the Amber, leading to Overton Hall. The Right Honourable Sir Joseph Banks inherited Overton Hall in 1792 and spent some time there every autumn in the quiet of a typical Derbyshire valley. Banks was one of the greatest botanists of Georgian times and had been elected a Fellow of the Royal Society at the age of twenty-three in 1766. In the same year he had undertaken a botanical survey of Newfoundland. Two years later he went round the world with Captain Cook, and went on to become the first botanical director of Kew Gardens. From 1778 until his death in 1820 Banks held the responsible position of President of the Royal Society.

Swinging round above Overton Hall, forming a western rampart for the middle basin of the Amber, is a fine, though broken, scarp of exposed gritstone. Along its bold, east-facing profile are several notable 'heads' or 'noses' of higher rock. The boldest brow is known as Gladstone's Nose as from certain situations the rock profile resembles an aquiline masculine face. Nearby is the site of the ancient Turning Stone and from this scarp-top viewpoint one looks out northwards over the width of the valley to Ashover itself. This is, of course, the real heart of the whole valley, the township of a large and scattered parish. Indeed, this is one of the largest parishes in England. The settlement was called Essovr at the Domesday survey in 1086, a name derived from Old English words meaning 'ash-tree slope'.

ABOVE *Joseph Banks was just 25 when he joined Cook's pioneering expedition to the southern hemisphere in 1768.*

RIGHT *Banks discovered many exotic plants on his trip to Australia, including the shrub* Banksia serrata, *which took his name.*

SIR JOSEPH BANKS

JOSEPH BANKS was a man of the Enlightenment. Born in 1743, he lived through a period of ground-breaking advances in science, technology, agriculture, industry and exploration, and he made contributions in all these fields.

The only son of wealthy parents with estates in both Lincolnshire and Derbyshire, Banks was educated at Harrow, Eton and Oxford. But the young Joseph was a reluctant scholar: instead he developed a passion for botany and the outdoors, and decided to pursue a career in natural history.

In 1768 Banks embarked on a great adventure—a three-year voyage round the world. At his own expense he and his party of assistants joined the *Endeavour*, captained by James Cook, on a voyage of exploration. The expedition was a great success: Cook discovered New Zealand and New South Wales, and Banks collected a massive haul of natural history specimens. Indeed, it was Banks's plant collecting that led Cook to name their first Australian landing site Botany Bay.

Back in London Banks was fêted as a great explorer: he was elected President of the Royal Society in 1778, made a baronet in 1781 and became an unofficial scientific adviser to the government and supervisor of the Royal Botanic Gardens, Kew. It was to Banks that the government turned when faced with the pressing problem of the country's overflowing gaols. His recommendation that felons be transported to Botany Bay led directly to the founding of Australia's first convict colony in 1788, and thus to his enduring epithet, the 'Father of Australia'.

The oldest part of the present Church of All Saints, consisting of the south doorway inside the porch, dates from about 1270. It is one of the loveliest churches in Peakland, and its crowning glories are the tower and spire, erected in 1419.

Of all the features of Ashover church's interior there is room here to mention but two, both unique and well worth examination. The first is the old lead font set upon a more recent base. The font measures twenty-five inches in width and is one foot high. On the outside are twenty upright figures, each holding a book in its left hand. As far as was known by the early-20th-century writer J. Charles Cox, only twenty other lead fonts were extant in England in Victorian times, and none farther north than the example at Ashover. Had it not been for the Reverend Emanuel Bourne, rector of Ashover at the time of the Civil War, the font might well have been defaced or, worse, taken and melted down by the Roundhead troops who destroyed Eastwood Hall, Bourne's residence, in 1646.

ABOVE *The medieval Church of All Saints serves the Domesday village of Ashover and its surrounding area.*

The other feature is one of the five bells hanging in the tower. No other English church bell possesses an inscription including the name Bonaparte. The inscription states: 'The old bell rung the downfall of Bonaparte, and broke April 1814.'

The Amber valley has long been renowned for its mineral waters. Few of its reputed 'eighty springs' of crystal water are marked on the two-and-a-half-inch Ordnance Survey map, but one stands out for special mention. Close by the winding valley road between Kelstedge and Ashover is a chalybeate well draining into the Marsh Brook. Chalybeate waters get their name from the Latin word *chalyps* meaning 'steel'. Such water contains iron salts, usually as a carbonate or sulphate but occasionally as a chloride. A worn, paved path leads to a substantial slab footbridge by the well, pointing to the fact that this was once an important place for general utilitarian use in addition to 'the curing of several distempers'.

ABOVE *The intricately engraved lead font at Ashover is a rare antique that has stood the test of time.*

The gritstone outcrop at Farhill, to the northwest of Ashover, has long been known as the Fabrick, probably referring to the tradition that stone used in repairs to the fabric of the parish church was taken from small quarries hereabouts. From the Fabrick, the southward view down the narrowing ridge gives only a hint of the position of Stubben Edge Hall, one mile distant. This ancient place was once the home of the Crich family. In Elizabethan times William Crich's widow married a member of the Dakeyne family. Later this Dakeyne married the favourite maid of honour of Mary, Queen of Scots. It is recorded that this woman, later the mistress of Stubben Edge Hall, faithfully attended Mary to the scaffold in 1587.

A last look out from the Fabrick reveals the contrast between the steep gritstone slopes overlooking the valley on east and west and the flattish fields around the village of Ashover, bounded by whitish walls of limestone. The middle basin of the Amber valley is, in fact, a geological curiosity representing a break in the surface uniformity of the rocks of Peakland: the overlying gritstone has been cut through by erosion to reveal the underlying, and older, limestone. This

PRINCE OF THIEVES

OUTLAW, SCOURGE of the rich and defender of peasants' rights—Robin Hood, England's greatest folk hero, has featured in ballads, plays, poems and films from the 14th century to the present, but has never been firmly identified with a historical person. Indeed, some scholars believe he is simply a figure of folklore who was associated with nature and fertility.

The Robin Hood legend is first fleshed out in medieval ballads. Tales such as *The Little Gest of Robin Hood* depict him as a cunning forest outlaw who pits his wits against the Sheriff of Nottingham, greedy clerics and royal officials. He excels at archery, poaches deer and is a master of disguise. At the same time, Robin respects the social order and is loyal to the King. What the ballads do not say is that Robin championed the poor against the rich, or the Saxons against the Normans—these themes appeared after the 15th century. Also, while the ballads number the brawny giant Little John and Will Scarlet among Robin's band of 'merry men', the jovial Friar Tuck and Maid Marian, Robin's supposed wife, are later additions, and there is no consensus about how Robin died. In the *Gest*, he is bled to death by the wicked prioress of Kirklees Abbey. In other versions, Robin has enough strength left to fire an arrow through a window to mark the place where he is to be buried.

BELOW *A 17th-century woodcut in a book of ballads dating from 1867 shows a rather well-dressed Robin Hood, Friar Tuck and Maid Marian.*

LEFT The Adventures of Robin Hood *(1938) cast Errol Flynn as the outlaw; others have followed in his footsteps but, for many, Flynn is the quintessential Robin.*

BELOW *The first literary mention of Robin Hood was in Langland's* Piers Plowman *in the 14th century. This extract is from one of the earliest manuscripts.*

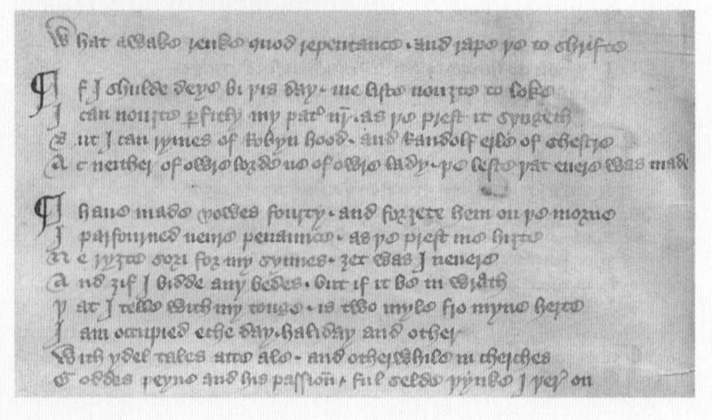

Despite a lack of conclusive evidence, it is possible that there was once a historical Robin Hood. In 1225, for example, it is known that a man of this name was outlawed in Yorkshire; and an exchequer record of 1261 lists an outlaw nicknamed Robehod; the adoption of the name by several later outlaws may explain why the legend kept evolving. There is also controversy over when and where the tales are set. Some scholars place them during the reign of Richard I or John, others in the reign of Henry III or Edward II. And while the ballads seem to have their roots in Yorkshire, other stories occur in the famous Sherwood Forest in Nottinghamshire.

LEFT *Robin Hood and his merry men entertain King Richard I at a banquet in Sherwood Forest in this painting by the 19th-century artist Daniel Maclise.*

phenomenon has been exploited here and there for both the pure limestone and for the associated fluorspar. There are still fluorspar mines being worked here. The Clay Cross Coal and Iron Company built the Ashover Light Railway for the purpose of carrying this quarried limestone from its own workings near Fallgate and Hate Wood, Ashover, to the blast furnaces at Clay Cross. Between the wars the little railway also carried passengers.

One last feature of the Amber valley, where it turns southwards out of its middle basin, is a great expanse of water where sails dip before every wind: Ogston Reservoir. Waterfowl have come here and may best be observed close to the banks, particularly among the reedy waters of the inlet under Woolley Moor. From the hill slopes about Ogston the smooth journeyings of the wind-driven vessels below are a thing of infinite variety and considerable interest. Lying upon the waving sward on South Hill of a June evening, watching the passing of the sailing boats below, is a pleasure not at once associated with Peakland, but all the more memorable for that.

ROBIN HOOD IN PEAKLAND

Robin Hood—fable or fact? Yeoman of the greenwood or last of the Saxons? There certainly was a character roaming the North Midland country who made a tremendous impact upon the life and law of his and subsequent times. Possibly he was the last of the Saxons, holding out against the Norman invaders as late as the 12th century.

What literary justification have we to support the legend? The oldest existing record of him is in the second edition of Langland's *Piers Plowman*, dating from 1377, where Sloth coupled him with Randle, Earl of Chester. Whoever this Robin was he would seem to have been contemporary with the earl who 'flourished in the reigns of Richard I, John and Henry III', and his tradition was fully grown by the first half of the 14th century.

The doings of the gallant greenwood band are located between Doncaster and Nottingham, especially in Barnsdale and Sherwood, but it is pretty certain that Robin and his followers spread further afield from time to time. Take the Peak District for instance, a wild and sparsely peopled region in the Middle Ages, and consider the number of places that are married to the myth, in name and by tradition.

Under the gritstone shadows of Gibbet Moor is the hamlet of Robin Hood, on the road from Chesterfield to Baslow, which takes its name from the gaudy hero on the signpost of the rebuilt inn. Then, of course, there is Robin Hood's Stride on Harthill Moor, near Birchover. As you approach this tumbled gritstone tor from the east it is easy to see why it was called Mock Beggar's Hall long ago. It resembles nothing less than a poor man's palace, a draughty hall of hard rock shared with magpie and carrion crow and tawny owl. Its two tallest pillars, called Inaccessible and Weasel, stand all of fifty feet apart. Tradition states that Robin made a single stride from one to the other!

Twenty-two miles to the northwest, two miles southwest of Glossop, are Robin Hood's Picking Rods. Here, on the rough grazings of Ludworth Intakes, stand two upright gritstone pillars set in stone sockets. Conjecture has been the historians' tool here too, though a current theory would seem to provide the answer to the origin of the Picking Rods: that they are, in fact, a pair of stones erected by medieval archers for the purpose of leverage, so that the bow could be bent in order to fasten the bowstring—like the Bow Stones on a similar hilltop to the south. Whatever their origin and purpose, the Picking Rods are now officially linked with Robin Hood, as evidenced by the Ordnance Survey tourist map of the Peak District.

If the village simply takes its name from an inn sign, if the stride story is pure fantasy and the Picking Rods merely coincidental with the legend, the environs of Hathersage, in the Derwent Valley, bear evidence more weighty, evidence believed to be authentic by great historians and local inhabitants alike. Stand by the four-foot-tall stone pillar called Robin Hood's Stoop on Offerton Moor and look a mile and a quarter to the northeast, to Hathersage church: Robin is said to have shot an arrow from this spot into the churchyard. And down there in the graveyard is a similar stone pillar; does this mark the spot where the arrow landed?

ABOVE *Robin Hood's Stride on Harthill Moor is one of several Peakland locations with supposed links to the rustic hero.*

A few yards away, beneath two yews, is the grave of none other than Little John. In 1776 a Walter Stanhope of Cannon Hall, near Barnsley, investigated the site, and this Stanhope's cousin, one Captain Shuttleworth, opened the ten-foot-long grave under the yews. Six feet down, a thighbone thirty inches long was found and taken away to Cannon Hall. Obviously, this was the grave of some giant of a man! The great 17th-century Oxford historian Ashmole records having seen John's longbow hanging inside the church in 1625. About six feet long, it was fashioned from spliced yew and tipped with horn, and needed an effort of 160 pounds to draw it.

A. M. W. Stirling, writing of Stanhope's inquiries, stated that:

> this famous companion of Robin Hood, who had been a native of Hathersage, was brought up in the local industry of nail making, till his wonderful strength and prowess made him try his fortunes elsewhere. Little is known of his career, however, till the Battle of Evesham in 1265, when he fought with the rebels under Simon de Montford, who was defeated. Little John with Robin Hood and many of the Earl's followers were outlawed. They forthwith retired to the woods and, escaping the arm of justice, lived a jolly, free life till old age overtook them. Robin Hood died at the age of fourscore and was buried by Little John in Kirklees Park, after which Little John sought out his native village, where he wished to lay his own bones. As he approached the Vale of Hathersage, it is said he remarked that

his career would soon be ended, and shortly after he breathed his last. From that time his great bow with some arrows and some chain mail were hanging in Hathersage church, together, it is said, with a green cap suspended by a chain; but when William Spenser became possessed of Hathersage he caused the bow and armour to be removed to Cannon Hall for safe keeping.

This bow can still be seen at Cannon Hall. And as far as the grave is concerned, the old rhyme is still sometimes heard in wooded corners of the village:

His bow was in the chancel hung,
His last good bolt they drave
Down to the notch, its measured length
Westward from the grave.
And root and bud this shaft put forth,
When Spring returned anon,
It grew a tree and threw a shade
Where slept staunch Little John.

J. Charles Cox investigated the Little John tale too, and reported that:

On the whole the evidence warrants us in assuming that a portion of the weapons and accoutrements peculiar to a forester were hung up in the church, that the said forester (both from the bow and the grave) was of exceptional stature, that both weapons and grave were popularly assigned to Little John more than two hundred years ago, and that the said weapons must have belonged to a man of extra-ordinary fame, or they would not have found such a resting place.

What of watering places? Well, there are wells of course. Three miles eastwards from Hathersage church, up on the moors of the Longshaw Estate, is Robin Hood's Well—a dripping spring in the heart of a dark greenwood, while half a mile to the south is Little John's Well, complete with a metal cup on a chain attached to the rock.

Finally, four miles to the north of Hathersage, the high gritstone ramparts of Stanage Edge stand out sternly above the dale, haunt of climber, walker and grouse. Near the Black Hawk end of this edge is the dark recess of Robin Hood's Cave. It is high up on the cliff face and difficult to access. Lots of climbing routes pass this way—Robin Hood's Chockstone Chimney, Robin Hood's Staircase, Robin Hood's Cave Gully, Robin Hood's Balcony Cave Direct—and yes, balcony is a fitting word, for behind a balcony of rock the recess opens into a natural hiding place; an inconspicuous place for an outlaw to retreat to—whether Robin came this way or not.

King Arthur's equivalent in the yeoman world certainly left his mark in Peakland. It would be hard to explain away all the place names and other associations as fables. Dr Cox accurately summed up the subject by stating that 'the opponents of the accuracy of the tradition seem to us to have far more difficulties with which to contend than those who accept it.'

ABOVE *The grave of Robin Hood's right-hand man, Little John, in Hathersage churchyard is cared for by the Ancient Order of Foresters. Legend has it that Little John was born in Hathersage, where he worked as a nailer before joining Robin's band of merry men.*

CHAPTER SIX

I KNOW A VALLEY

I CLIMBED A GORSE BANK, buttery with bloom, and lay in a cowslip meadow. A lark called distantly, away behind me. And as I lay the sun came from behind a small and passing cloud. My previous chapters' cavalcade of other years slid vaguely out of sight, down a long, green avenue of trees which melted into a distant wisp of cloud vapour, burnished by the summer sun.

The valley that opened at my feet and stretched away from the slope below me was revealed once more in all its astonishing loveliness. Cloud-led shadows caressed the steep fields and woods on either side, which clasped at their heart the jewel of still waters. My viewpoint was near the ancient bridleway that curls between Grange Hill and Wigley; my valley far below, wherein dwelt those curving woods and silent, summery waters, was Linacre.

I had first heard of this hollow in the hills after a friend visited it while camping with the Scouts, but I never knew, or bothered to find out, its exact location. Then, one day in early April 1960, I walked with friends along the footpath from Dronfield, by way of Barlow Grange, and came down that ancient bridleway that winds across the head of the vale of Linacre. Children were gathering wild daffodils in Nutterall Wood, through which the Birley Brook tumbles towards the valley. The memorable features of that day were the loose, brown rocks that rear above the headwaters of the brook and are surrounded by thickets of almost impregnable gorse; also memorable were the glimpses of water as we traversed down into the valley, glimpses through the slim and graceful sycamore trunks of Birley Wood to the surface of Linacre's upper reservoir. The floor of the wood was bright green with sprouting bluebells, and all around us in the sky were towering peaks of cumulus, white in the sunlight and blue-grey where they fell into shadow. We crossed the fields and passed through the fresh-budding larches of Kitchenflat Wood on our way northwards towards home.

Since that time the vale of Linacre has become a place well known to me, a valley of quiet woods and winter gales and spectacular atmospheric clarity on midsummer evenings, when the whole eastern world has been revealed in detail by the westerly sun. I am lucky to know many of the secrets of this valley of few men.

The complete length of the valley is four miles, running approximately from west to east. The stream draining it rises as Birley Brook at 850 feet beneath the smooth southern side of Grange Hill, and in less than two miles becomes the Linacre Brook. The name Birley can clearly be traced to the Old English terms *byre* and *leah*—'byre, or cow shed, in a clearing'. Linacre is likewise derived from Old English *lin* and *aecer*—'flax land', an area of cultivated land where flax grew, a not-unlikely crop in the moist soils of the valley bottom.

Birley Grange is the most important place in the upper vale. It is a long, ivy-clad farmhouse with substantial buildings, forming a sheltered quadrangle on a level terrace of land at 850 feet above sea level on the northern slope of the valley. The Grange belonged originally to the monastery of Louth and was an outlying farm with space for the storage of grain, as at other granges belonging to monastic foundations (Barlow, Harewood and the like). The abbot and convent of Rufford in Nottinghamshire had lands hereabouts in Brampton parish, granted by Henry VIII to the Earl of Shrewsbury, and Birley Grange had passed with the manor. A short distance up the slope from the Grange is Bluster Castle, a farm that catches all the winds that blow. It probably got its designation by way of humour, several examples of which remain in this part of Peakland.

A field in Bradley parish is Vols (Vole's) Croft, which illustrates the sense of humour of long-dead yeomen in naming tiny fields appropriately. We find 'Wren Park' occurring no less than thirty times within the county of Derbyshire alone, again used humorously to describe a small area of land. Likewise Hen Park, here in the parish of Brampton, and Mouse Park, Threepenny Piece and Napkin Piece elsewhere. There is also a considerable list of uncomplimentary names which usually refer to the infertility of the land. Cheat-all Patch, Clam Park, Hungry Bank, Vinegar Hill and Wilderness are some of these, while Treacle Nook occurs where a field's topsoil is largely clay and poorly drained.

Close in front of Birley Grange stands a cottage where a labourer and his family lived when the farm employed more men. Today it stands empty—empty, that is, of human inhabitants. It is filled with families of rabbits which were once fed daily by one of the old bachelor brothers who farmed the Grange. The first time I went round the cottage was at dusk, when the brothers and I went from room to room in the failing light, careful to close each door behind us so that the

ABOVE *A wooded walk beside one of the Linacre Reservoirs offers picturesque views of the author's beloved vale.*

ABOVE *Linen, linseed oil and even paper are all produced from the flax plant. Before It was superseded by imported cotton, flax was grown in vast quantities in Britain. Today its pretty blue flowers are once again a common sight, with farmers being subsidised to grow the crop.*

ABOVE *The author used to visit these two aged bachelor brothers when they were farming Birley Grange in the 1970s.*

families did not become mixed and so upset the breeding plan. White rabbits bobbed in the shadows and darker animals melted imperceptibly behind the scant furniture still in place in several rooms.

Just across the valley of the Birley Brook, across the steep angles of Nutterall Wood, stands little Birley Farm. It has always seemed to me that this is the original 'crooked house' of the nursery rhyme, for not only is it narrow when viewed from front or back but it seems perched, ready to topple, at the edge of a steep pasture field which drops through a row of lime trees to the brook below. In the field in front of the little farm is a deep well which is kiln-shaped, opening out below ground to twice the diameter at ground level. In the scattered trees above the farm are the ruins of an older farm and another well.

Since 1909 the farm has slowly fallen into a ruinous state, though part has been repaired and used as outbuildings for the newer Birley Farm across the bridle road. This newer place is remarkable for so small a holding, in that the south front of the house is faced with excellent dressed stone and there is a considerable weather stone above the front door. For very many years up to the 1930s it was the home of the Misses Botham, countrywomen of the old school, who lived almost entirely from what they produced. They took butter and eggs down the length of the valley to sell in Chesterfield, and returned with their baskets laden with those provisions that they could not produce at home—tea, salt, sugar and flour. A longer walk took them across country for six hilly miles to Dronfield station, where they caught a train to Sheffield to sell butter and eggs. In later life, and especially in winter, their laden return must have been hard work. Despite their simple, rugged life they both lived to a good age.

Mr Hasman of Hare Edge Farm remembers that one summer the sisters asked him to mow their hay and cart it to the stack when they had 'made' it. He agreed, and mowed the meadows on several fine evenings after doing his own work. For a few days the sisters turned the swaths with hay forks and raked the 'made' hay into heaps. Two or three labourers helped Mr Hasman thereafter to transport the hay with horses and cart and make the stack. When all was finished he told the old ladies that thirty shillings would cover the cost, being rather sorry for them.

'That is a lot of money for such a small task,' one of the sisters snapped. It was not that they were really without money but that they did not realise the value of time and labour in their lives, which were governed more by the season and the position of the sun than by the clock.

From the environs of Birley Farm there is an unspoilt view down the valley towards Chesterfield—unspoilt, that is, except for the red-brick expanse of recent developments on that town's western perimeter. On very clear days, notably after rain, one can tell the time by looking down the valley with binoculars at the clock on Chesterfield's parish church, topped by its famous crooked spire. From the lane above Birley Grange it is possible, in similar conditions, to see Lincoln Cathedral, no less than forty-two miles to the east.

The steep fields below the farm are a habitat for a wide range of spring and early-summer flora, especially lady's-smock in the damp outflows of field drains and cowslips in drier sites. Beyond, the gables of the very old and very well-preserved Birley Barn, belonging to Birley Grange, stand out of the trees—groves of deciduous giants ranging up the valley sides into Birley Wood and Copy Wood.

Cradled by the steeps of distant Linacre and Priestfield Woods, the waters of the Linacre Reservoirs are a surprise to the stranger and lead the eye on eastwards, beyond Chesterfield to the magnesian limestone escarpment at Bolsover. Over to the southeast Old Brampton church spire pokes above the tree tops, blunt and wide, and a corner of Hardwick Wood near Wingerworth crowns a conspicuous hillock to the south. On a sunny summer day...

When cuckoos call from Copy Wood
And bluebell haze fills Birley-side,
When larks rise over Linacre
And cloud-isles cross a deep, blue sea
Towards the eastern world so flat and wide...

...this is the atmosphere of the place, and even in winter there is tranquillity.

ABOVE *Legend has it that St Peter once dropped the keys to Heaven and, on the spot where they dropped, the first cowslip sprang to life, its flower heads resembling bunches of keys. Less romantic is the notion that 'cowslip' is a polite form of cowslop, as the flower is often found in fields used for grazing cattle.*

MEN OF STONE

The bridle road that passes Birley Grange and Birley Farm descends to the main tributary of the Birley Brook below Freebirch Quarry and continues up the far hillside as High Lane. This lane is the remnant of a very ancient, probably Saxon, route leading southwards out of the Barlow vale towards mid-Derbyshire. High Lane leads up to Wigley, the original home of the Wigley family. The Hall Farm looks out southwards with a face unusual in this district: a tall graceful front and windows on three storeys.

In the year 1254 this hamlet was called 'Wyggeley', a name that could have originated from *wigga* and *leah*—meaning 'the clearing where beetles were abundant' (*wigga* is still used in this context to refer to the family of insects we call 'earwigs'). Beyond the crossroads at Wigley Green is the hamlet of Wadshelf. It is known locally as Watchell, a name claimed by some to be derived from Watch Hill—a vantage point from which the advancing Scots could be seen. However, a more likely origin can be deduced if we consider that at the Domesday survey the hamlet was called 'Wadescel'; the man Wada is known to have held lands here according to the Domesday Book; and the Old English term *scelf* describes 'a shelf of sloping land'. So this was 'Wada's sloping land'.

From Wigley in the early part of the 20th century, one could have looked out to the northwest upon a scene of great industry, when steam cranes, horses, carts and many men toiled in the extraction of the useful coal-measure sandstone from Freebirch Quarry. The Margerison brothers of Ingmanthorpe were the last to work the quarry, and Mr Hasman recalls that one brother was the quarry foreman while the other one travelled about the countryside to get orders for this useful building stone. There were two traction engines working in the quarry, and they worked loud and long to win the stone.

A traction engine carrying stone from Freebirch Quarry towards Chesterfield once breasted the top of Puddingpie Hill above Wigley Green, when the driver attempted to change gear while still moving, as was his habit, but the engine gained momentum on the long, straight descent. He was unable to engage the gear and his mate jumped for his life as the engine and load gathered speed.

ROLLING BACK THE YEARS

GLEAMING PAINTWORK, the hiss of steam and the heady smell of coal smoke...this potent appeal to the senses captures the imagination of traction engine enthusiasts countrywide.

Traction engines were a product of the Industrial Revolution, using steam to power the new machinery of industry and later to pull heavy loads as well. By the last quarter of the 19th century they were in widespread use, easing the lives of, among others, those who worked in the fields, on the roads and in the fairground.

On the farm traction engines gradually replaced the heavy horse, where they could not only drive but also transport heavy threshers and balers. Road workers no longer had to push and pull heavy rollers, as converted traction engines effortlessly steamrolled hot tar and chippings into a smooth, even road surface. Travelling fairs used the engines to haul heavy equipment from village to village, where they would then power the musical organs and merry-go-rounds.

By the Second World War, however, traction engines soon became outmoded. Those that escaped the fate of the scrapyard were abandoned, left to gather more grime on top of the layers of dust, soot and oil that had been part and parcel of their working life. Paradoxically this very neglect ended up protecting the vehicles from the elements, and many have been lovingly restored. Summer once again echoes to the sound of them hooting and clattering their way down our country lanes.

LEFT *Traction engines, with their tall chimneys, were once essential to a busy fairground.*

BELOW *Steam enthusiasts proudly parade their restored traction engines at summer rallies.*

The driver attempted to slow the runaway by steering into the verge, but a deep drainage ditch running at right angles to the road locked the wheels on that side and the engine turned over, killing the driver. This accident is still remembered and talked about by older inhabitants of the district.

Kerb stones in particular were made from Freebirch stone, though farms, cottages and other buildings over a large area are also constructed from this material. Its only weakness is that some strata are liable to erode quickly when exposed to the elements, leading to a broken face of stone in old buildings. Such erosion can be seen in many places within several miles of Freebirch. Trade fell off with the increasing use of bricks, so that by the beginning of the First World War work in the quarry had virtually ceased. Today the quarries are covered by quaking grass, and tawny owls and hares live with foxes among the tumbled stones.

The name for all this level district is Freebirch, a corruption of the original name, 'Three Birch'. Lying comfortably in the trees between Wigley and Freebirch is Moorhay Farm. In a terrier (a book or roll in which the lands of private persons are described in detail) dated 1698 the place has its modern name, but by 1712 it had been corrupted in the local dialect to 'Morrey', and to this day it is so pronounced by the majority of local inhabitants. Moorhay Farm belonged to the Sitwell Estate, and during the second half of the 19th century was farmed by a John Furniss.

Furniss was something of a romantic and social reformer, regularly standing in the marketplace at Chesterfield to address the crowds on the evils of class and creed. About his land he piled heaps of large stones roughly hewn from Freebirch Quarry, to give focal points of interest to the scene. When his wife died in childbirth in 1888 he made known his intention to bury her in a corner of one of his fields. The vicar of Old Brampton pleaded with Furniss to have her buried in consecrated ground within the churchyard and even offered to pay for a church funeral, but the widower would have none of it and buried his wife at the edge of his field, where a group of deciduous trees stands and whence there is a fine view across to Birley and down the Linacre valley. The stone slab marking the grave is carved with a heart, upon which is cut the memorial to the young wife.

Subsequently, John Furniss had a large block of Freebirch stone moved to the very top of Puddingpie Hill, just beside the road, for it came out of the ground just as it stands today—in the shape of a useful chair where countless labourers, ramblers and cyclists have rested over the years. Furniss was something of an inventor, and about this period he put forward the idea of an aircraft, but few people took him seriously and his aircraft scheme never came to fruition.

Half a mile away to the northwest stands the little farm at Hare Edge where my friend Mr Hasman was born. He is one of that breed of hardy countrymen who seem to go on forever without the slightest change.

In his youth he was made to work long and hard. It was a regular thing in the first years of the 20th century for haymaking to continue until eleven o'clock at night in order to make the best of the fine

BELOW *This stone, naturally shaped like a chair, was discovered over 100 years ago by philanthropic farmer John Furniss. Furniss placed the stone at the top of Puddingpie Hill as a place for weary travellers to rest—a purpose it serves to this day.*

weather. One night, after haymaking on a neighbouring farm with the team of horses, he stayed for supper and arrived home at midnight. He had been up since before five o'clock that morning. His father asked why he was so late coming home, then added, 'Don't go to bed, lad, I want you out with the mowing machine in a couple of hours.' So young Ernest simply watered and fed the horses and lay down on the kitchen sofa until two o'clock. He went out again to the horses—he hadn't bothered removing their collars—and fastened them to the mowing machine; soon he was off in the cold darkness to start cutting the next field of hay. This occurred day in and day out while the fine weather lasted. In the haymaking season the odd day's rain was praised by many an exhausted farm boy and labourer for the rare break that it offered from the backbreaking hard work.

BRAMPTON'S PAST

A mile and a half eastwards down a smooth-topped ridge brings us to Old Brampton, 'Brantune' at the time of the Domesday survey. The village's most notable building is the blunt-spired parish church. In 1846 this church was aptly described as being 'an ancient embattled structure on a bold elevation on the north side of the village; it has nave, chancel, side aisles, lower tower, from which rises a short contracted spire'.

There were originally three manors in Old Brampton, two of which were joined soon after the Domesday survey and given by Henry II to Peter de Brampton, supposedly a son of Matilda le Caus. She died in 1224 and her effigy is on the west wall inside the church, having been discovered under turf in the churchyard in 1739. Though the le Caus family became extinct in the male line in about 1460, Caushouse Farm, built on the foundations of medieval Caus Hall, still remains near the Chesterfield to Old Brampton road at Ashgate.

BELOW *A stone lion is one of several carvings on Old Brampton church that date back to Norman times.*

In about the year 1100 the Dean of Lincoln received the parish of Chesterfield, including the two dependent chapelries of Brampton and Wingerworth, from William II. After rebuilding was completed early in the 13th century, Brampton chapel was consecrated by Bishop Brendan in the summer of 1253. Eleven years later a chantry with thirty-five acres was founded and 'given to God and the Chapel of the Apostles Peter and Paul, Brampton'. There are early carvings of both apostles high upon the outside of the church's south wall, together with numerous others, one of which is a curious face with a man in its mouth. Relics of late-Norman work include part of the outside wall of the south doorway, and upon the west wall of the porch is an enigmatic lion carved in the carboniferous stone of which the church is constructed.

The spire, battlements and porch were added in the middle of the 14th century, probably at the time of Thomas Ball, a priest remembered by an alabaster slab which has been much mutilated and now stands at the foot of the west wall of the north aisle, utilised in the 18th century as a memorial to another family. Near this, leaning on the west wall of the nave, was the effigy of one Hiskanda, Domina de Brampton. The effigy has gone but it has been suggested that the carved head at the spring of the arch at the west end of the nave may be part of it. Next to the arch is a large wooden cross made from the timber of Ypres Cathedral and brought from the grave in Flanders of Major Lord Borrell, a member of a local family.

The church and its environs upon the rounded ridge top are mellowed with great age, and from the fields that fall northwards towards the Linacre valley one can look back upon the quiet settlement and recall the busier days of previous centuries. In winter weather, and particularly after snowfall, the village takes on an air of former times: the peace increases and the silhouettes of church and ridge-top cottages stand framed by old and naked trees. At such times one is reminded of the medieval custom that the people of Brampton were bound to take the corpse of the first person who died in Brampton, Loades, Pocknedge, Wadshelf or Wigley after New Year's Day to be buried in Chesterfield, at the parish church of St Mary and All Saints. The vicar of Chesterfield received all the fees and mortuary offerings that would normally have been paid if the body had been buried at Brampton.

One of the Mower family of Barlow, who resided at Barlow Woodseats Hall, had in his possession an ancient book in which was recorded the quick burial of

THE DOMESDAY BOOK

TWENTY YEARS after the Norman Conquest of 1066 William the Conqueror ordered the compilation of an inventory that would provide him with detailed information on his subjects' lands and property. This mammoth task—evidence of William's determination to exact maximum revenues—came to be known as the Domesday survey, for its results were said to be as set in stone as the decisions made on Judgment Day.

Teams of government men visited towns and villages across England to assess the value of each landowner's property, down to every last cow or sheep. The census was very unpopular among the ordinary people, who were already suffering the burden of heavy taxation and the added hardships of pillage, famine and disease. Nevertheless, William ran an efficient administration, and his clerks speedily gathered thorough results from most of England, with only a few omissions: the far north of England and several cities, including London and the then capital, Winchester.

William employed monks to transcribe the results into two volumes: Great Domesday, which summarises the information received from all the investigated areas except for Essex, Norfolk and Suffolk, and Little Domesday, which records in full the details of the three outstanding counties. Since its creation the Domesday Book (as the volumes are collectively known) has been invaluable: in medieval times it was a standard government document which travelled with the King around the country; right up until the early 1900s it was used to settle legal disputes over land; and today it is a unique primary source for historians of Norman England.

ABOVE AND RIGHT *The original hand-written vellum manuscripts of Great Domesday and Little Domesday* (right) *are still legible some 900 years after their compilation. In Great Domesday, the entry for Derbyshire* (above) *mentions, among others, the village of Ashbourne.*

LEFT AND BELOW *The top of the spire of Old Brampton's church* (left) *collapsed during a storm in 1911. The spire received a new top, and the old one was imaginatively converted into a unique birdbath* (below).

Godfrey Foljambe of Moorhall, the son of Sir Godfrey Foljambe. He died 'on Monday at morn, about first cock-crowing' November 15, 1591, and was buried with all speed in Brampton church. His body had this hasty burial 'in the chancel under the high altar, where it stood the same day towards night, for it could not be kept'. No tablet or memorial exists to record this burial or to mark the exact spot.

To the west of the graveyard, close to the thatched lich gate, stands the school, erected in 1830 together with the original master's residence. It is recorded that the National School Society gave £100 towards the endowment of this little school. There had been a school here for a remarkably long period, at least from the latter quarter of the 17th century, when Peter Calton left ten shillings per year, along with six other benefactors who left sums ranging up to two pounds per year and the interest on forty pounds. In 1846 it was recorded that 'in consideration of these sums the master instructs sixteen children free'. The school no longer provides free education, the nearest primary school being at Wigley Green.

Across the road stands ancient Brampton Hall, until recently the home of the Peak pack of bloodhounds. Now the pack has been disbanded and no longer does the romantic baying echo across fields and woods; no longer do the brown coats flash with tails erect from hedge to hedge.

A short distance west of the church and old school stands the cottage row where Old Brampton's Post Office used to be. Here lived Jack Collis, who was a collier at Grassmoor Colliery, and it was he who dug a well sixty-three feet deep at Hare Edge for Ernest Hasman's father when work in the pit was scarce. The post office was retained in the old part of his cottage, where another deep well still stands in the front garden close beside a most unusual birdbath. It is a small gritstone bath supported upon an elaborately carved stone pedestal which was the original top of Old Brampton church steeple, erected over 600 years ago. It was torn down by a great thunderstorm in the summer of 1911 and a new spire top was incorporated in the reconstruction.

LINACRE'S LAKES AND LANES

From the village two footpaths lead down northwards into Linacre vale and the three wooded reservoirs there. Linacre vale slopes up due westwards from Chesterfield and, when in 1825 fifty-eight citizens of that town successfully pressed for a proper water supply, this valley was the obvious choice for the water's collection and storage. In those early days of civic utilities a masonry weir was erected across the stream, not far from Holme Hall, and 51,000 gallons daily were taken into a pipe and fell by gravity to a reservoir in West Street. Pipes from this tank fed street taps.

The lowest reservoir was built after an Act of 1855, two-thirds of a mile above the original 1825 weir, and has a surface area of eight and a half acres. Strangely enough, and for reasons best known to the Chesterfield Waterworks and Gas Light Company, the next reservoir to be constructed was the uppermost—Linacre Upper—in 1863. Its construction resulted in a boom for the Gate Inn at Pratthall, for the navvies went there to drink. This probably accounts for the inn's rebuilding in an ugly Victorian style. The Upper is the largest reservoir, having a surface area of eighteen acres and reaching a depth of sixty-one feet.

ABOVE *Thomas Linacre was physician to Kings Henry VII and Henry VIII; in 1518 he founded the Royal College of Physicians, the first official body to regulate the practice of medicine in England.*

Finally, in 1904, the middle reservoir was built, filling the valley floor between the Upper and Lower dams, where previously had been rough woodland and grass. By 1909 the undertaking was completed, with filter beds standing on the northern slope below the conifers of Kitchenflat Wood. For the first eighty years of its existence (until 1905), the Linacre Reservoirs supplied Chesterfield with all its water needs.

It is a happy thought that no old house, farm or cottage was flooded when the reservoirs were made. However, in 1938 ancient Linacre House—which stood on the northern slope, almost in line with the middle reservoir's impounding wall—was vacated by the Riggott family, who had farmed there for several generations. It was believed that drainage from the farm was polluting the waters of the lower reservoir. The Riggotts moved to Upper Newbold Farm beyond Cutthorpe village, and their old home fell into decay.

Linacre House was rather ugly, with three storeys, but stood upon the site of medieval Linacre Hall (called 'Lynacure Hall' in 1519), the ancestral home of Doctor Thomas Linacre, who became the first president of the Royal College of Physicians. He rose to favour with royalty, becoming a tutor to Prince Arthur and Princess Mary (brother and sister of Henry VIII). He also taught Sir Thomas More and Erasmus. In 1938 new choir stalls in Old Brampton church were dedicated to his memory, and a bronze tablet is set in the north wall of the chancel behind them. The ruins of Linacre House have finally all but disappeared, and with them the ancient mason's marks in the vaulted cellars, which indicated that monks passed this way en route between Beauchief Abbey and its penitentiary at Harewood Grange.

Half a mile away, towards the northeast, stands the straggling village of Cutthorpe. The Cutt family were resident hereabouts from the 14th century. Literally, then, this was 'Cutt's outlying farm'. Today it is in the parish of Brampton, but Cutthorpe has some claim to independence as a historic settlement in its own right for it contains several notable farms and private residences. Probably the most interesting is the Old Hall, a very fine Elizabethan yeoman farmer's house, remarkable in this area for the fact that the eastern portion consists of three main storeys with the stairway in an attached wing. Viewed across the fields from the south this looks most impressive, giving the appearance of a tower or turret, with just a suggestion of fortification. To my mind it represents the height of an

THE POWER OF PLANTS

ABOVE *An assortment of plants used in herbalism, and a copy of Nicholas Culpeper's influential* Herbal *(1653).*

UNTIL PHARMACEUTICAL drugs became readily available in the mid-20th century, the only remedies available to the common people were those they could obtain from the woods and hedgerows or from their own gardens.

Flowers, fruits, leaves and roots have been gathered for their medicinal properties for many thousands of years, since ancient peoples discovered that plants could treat all manner of illnesses. The use of plant medicine was widespread in the Far and Middle East from very early times, and the first herbal—a book listing herbs and their uses—appeared in China around 3000 BC. The Western tradition of herbal medicine began with the Greeks, who had a sophisticated health service supported by a citizens' tax. In the 4th century AD the Greeks set up medical schools which attracted botanists and herbalists from far and wide, and many herbals were written during this period.

Mediterranean herbs were introduced to Britain by the Romans, who carried

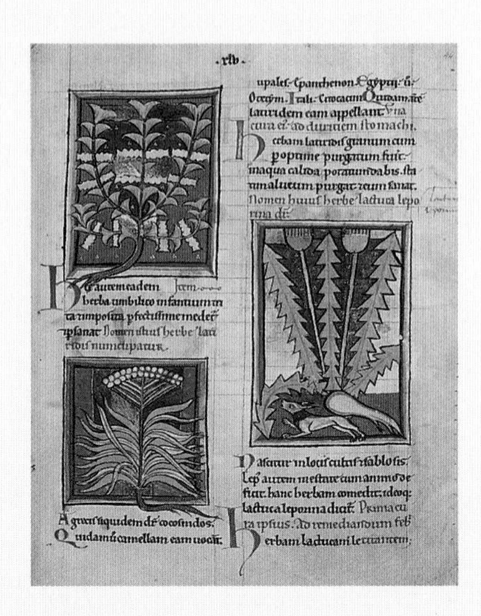

ABOVE *A medieval illuminated copy of a Greek herbal depicts medicinal plants and describes their properties and uses.*

plants such as rosemary and lavender with them on their military campaigns. The Anglo-Saxons also used herbs widely, and worshipped nature as a goddess; but the Saxon concept of a female creator of the natural world contradicted Christian teachings about an omnipotent male god and, in an attempt architectural style that has never been bettered in the three centuries or more since it was contrived and executed.

Almost opposite Cutthorpe Old Hall a lane leads directly down beneath an avenue of trees to the wooded slopes about Cutthorpe New Hall. This is a lovely old place, too, but is the result of several additions during the 17th and 18th centuries. On a warm summer evening it is pleasant to explore the field paths in this part of the vale of Linacre. Daffodils bloom in a copse close by the New Hall in spring, and it was from this colony that a local man called Heathcote prepared a concoction to cure 'the distempers' of Queen Anne when she visited the district in the early years of the 18th century.

Quite close to the site of Linacre House there is an uphill path through the fields of Linacre Wood to the hamlet of Pratthall. From this high ridge the trees below hide the faces of the man-made lakes but the views on every hand from close beside the ancient Hall Farm are extensive and, in clear conditions, remarkable. The name 'pratt' is derived from Old English meaning 'trick', and this, in turn, became the name of a local family—perhaps a name earned through sly

to stamp out paganism, the new Christian Church banned unauthorised herbalists. In the 14th century the Church prohibited women from practising medicine and midwifery; this persecution culminated in the horrific witchcraft trials of the 15th to 18th centuries.

But the traditional knowledge lived on, and while the Church taught that the pains of childbirth were punishment for the sins of Eve, the village 'wise woman' would use raspberry-leaf tea to ease labour. Healers had extensive knowledge of such natural drugs. One wise woman in Shropshire was famous for a herbal concoction she prescribed for heart conditions; this is known to have contained foxglove, and it is no coincidence that the same ingredient is used in modern 'digitalis' drugs to treat heart failure.

With the drift of people to the towns during the Industrial Revolution, much traditional country knowledge became lost, but in modern times, as patients tire of the side effects of synthetic drugs, there has been a renewal of interest in herbal medicine. As the knowledge of our ancestors is revived, modern research into the properties of plants is proving that they do indeed have valid medical uses.

BELOW *In the Middle Ages, the common people gathered wild herbs, but richer households and monasteries cultivated physic gardens where they grew such plants as fennel, sage, rue and mint for making medicines.*

LEFT *Daffodil juice was once taken internally as a purge, while the crushed bulbs were used on bruises.*

BELOW *A modern-day herbalist dispenses dried marigold flowers to be made into an infusion.*

dealings or by way of a joke. So Pratthall was 'the hall of a man called Pratt', though there is no trace now of a local family of this name. Here at Pratthall is a small Methodist chapel, identical with one at Hollins, one mile west of Old Brampton. At Hollins—the Old English for 'hollies', so called on account of the abundance of holly trees in the district—lived the Drabble family, well known throughout the district as good farmers, who had a little chapel built close to their large holding. Today it is an outhouse.

From Pratthall, paths lead down into the vale of Linacre and one slants across the level fields by Birley Grange to the very head of the valley. Where the old bridle road crosses the headwaters of the Birley Brook there is a glimpse between the towering gorse bushes towards the lower reaches of the vale, to the vista of woods and field slopes which has its successful culmination in the blunt, far-off spire of Old Brampton church. A further walk of a few hundred yards brings one out, quite suddenly, onto the flat sward at the crest where the vale of Linacre breaks away towards the east.

BELOW *Clouds pass shadows over the vale of Linacre, but they fail to detract from the burgeoning beauty of this little corner of England.*

In any season, at any time of day or night, this is a fine viewpoint. With the advancing year the mood of the prospect changes. The daffodils bloom in secret Nutterall Wood—these are true wild bulbs, but the quantity of flowers has decreased in recent years, due, it is thought, to the heavy demands made by pickers who came here each Easter on an annual expedition from Pratthall Methodist Chapel. Later the cowslips and bluebells come into flower and brighten the view once more. After sundown the distance of the valley is reduced, it seems, by the coming of darkness. I have seen wonderful sights in the shades of autumn nights and at the depths of winter evenings.

My particular guide—whoever he may have been, I do not know—brought me to this grassy crest, and I began an exploration of this and every countryside which will never be completed:

I walked this valley long ago
On a lovely, lonely summer's day.
This was a peaceful, unknown land;
If anywhere this was where God showed his hand.
For lovely, lonely summer days,
For widest eastward views above our fields
To distant ridges under clearing skies,
To watch the farthest smoke-screen rise.

ABOVE *Highgate Lane lies between the towns of Dronfield and Chesterfield, and is part of the rural landscape that the author has known and loved since childhood.*

It came to pass that, as I lay upon the high vantage point where, in a semi-dream, all that has gone before was clearly seen between the very edges of the clouds, the last vision occurred. There is an overwhelming feeling of sadness or pleasure—perhaps a combination of both—in a landscape. That feeling must ever remain within the individual, within the bounds of the flesh wherein it was created, for no other living creature can enter into and experience exactly the same interplay of the senses and related associations. Words can hardly convey the magic and living reality that is my vale of Linacre, with its hanging woods of secret memory and long history.

And, as I lay, I saw that far, green hilltop which in actuality is hidden behind the Pratthall ridge from this place. It was that green hilltop of early memory, and I could see Highgate Lane stretching close to the fields where larks were singing overhead. The soft, brown dust was blowing along the lane, driven by a breeze that has blown intermittently through all those intervening years. That, at least, has not changed. ■

TRAX

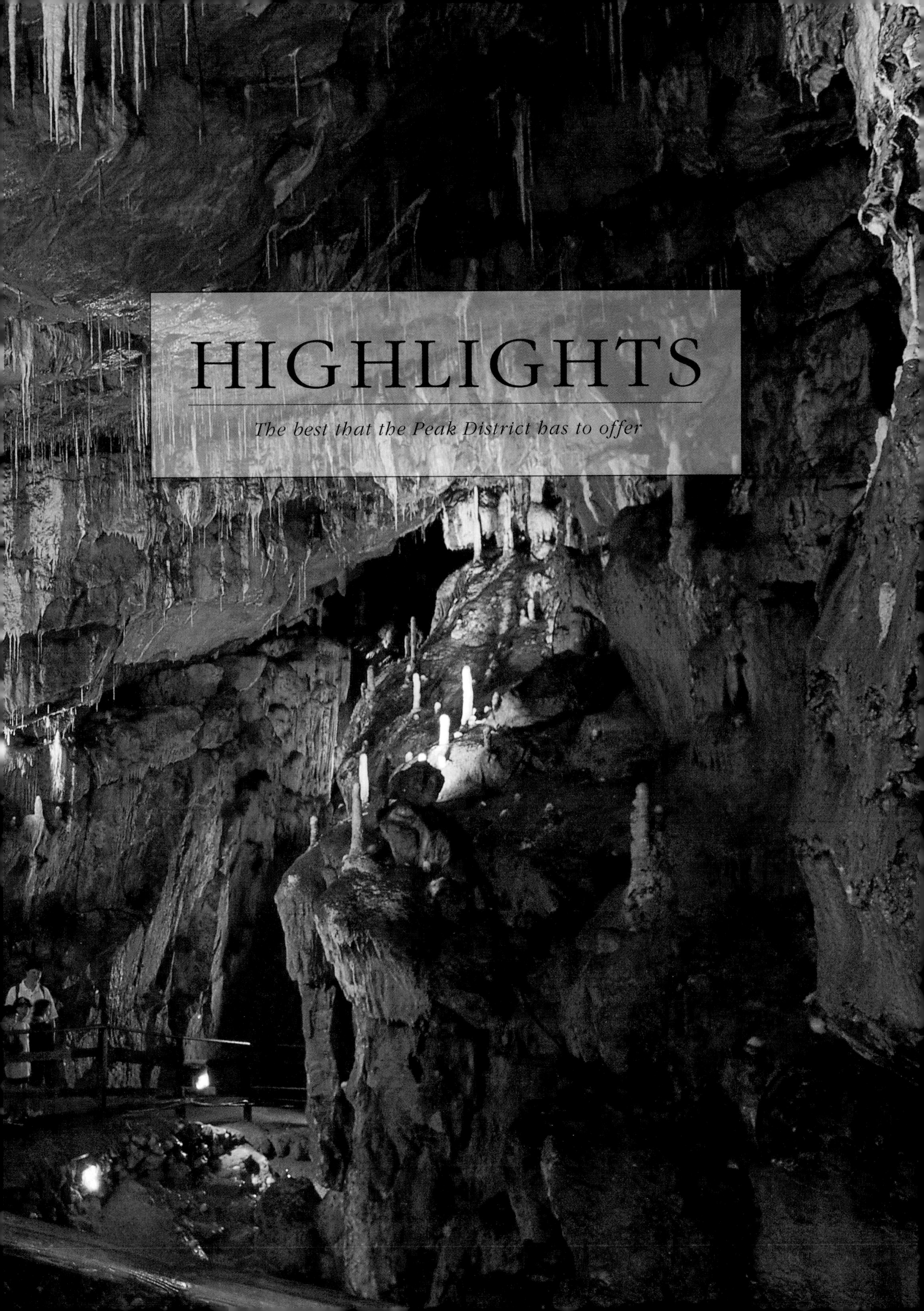

HIGHLIGHTS

The best that the Peak District has to offer

ABOVE *Time has stood still at Haddon Hall* (see page 157), *whose wood-panelled banqueting hall remains as it was in medieval times.*

BELOW *Reynard's Cave in Dove Dale* (see page 161), *with its impressive natural arch, was used as a dwelling in Roman times.*

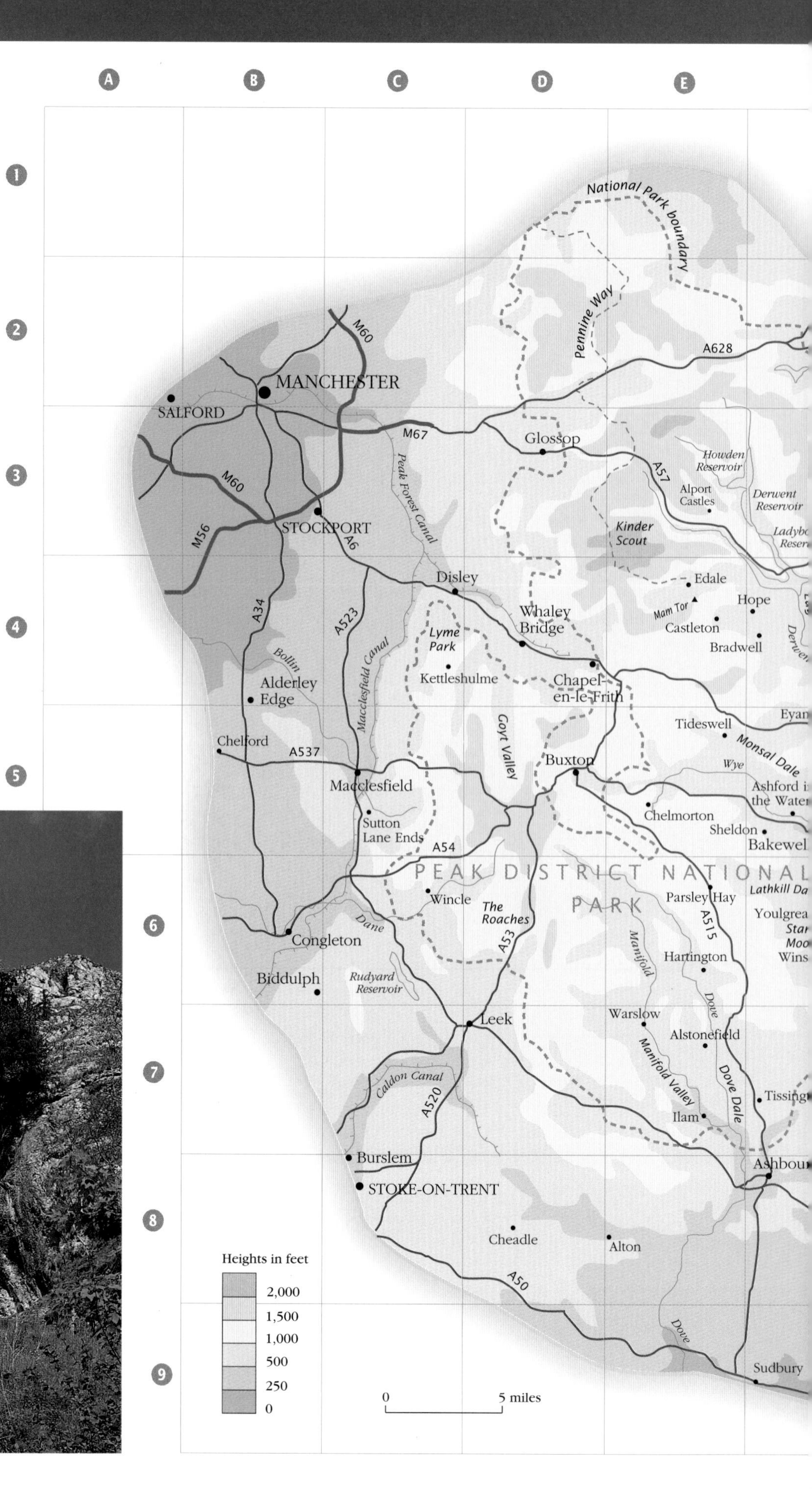

LEFT *A toy boat with a crew of teddy bears is on show at the Museum of Childhood at Sudbury Hall* (see page 158).

BELOW *The strangely twisted spire of the Church of St Mary and All Saints in Chesterfield* (see page 153) *is a famous landmark in the area.*

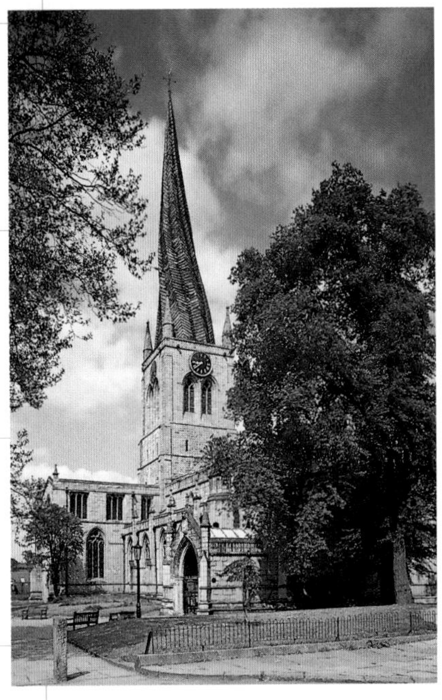

RIGHT *The Peak District custom of well dressing* (see page 155) *dates from pre-Christian times, but displays often depict Christian themes.*

BELOW *This vase, which stands in the Great Dining Room at Chatsworth House, is made from Blue John* (see page 164), *a colourful local mineral.*

CONTENTS

ABOUT THIS SECTION

If *Peakland Days* has left you wishing to visit some of Roger Redfern's haunts or roam further afield in the Peak District, the section that follows presents a distillation of the best that the area has to offer. Walkers, climbers or even those who wish to venture underground can find challenges galore on pages 161–5; culture lovers (and night owls) should head for Manchester, just on the area's borders, and described on page 156. Meet famous Peaklanders past and present on pages 165–7, and revel in a range of entertaining local festivals and events, listed on page 169.

For further information on these events and on the sites listed, such as specific dates and opening times, readers should consult local tourist offices or websites, whose details can be found on page 169.

To help you find your way around, entries contain grid references, where appropriate, for the map opposite.

CITIES, TOWNS AND VILLAGES

Alstonefield E7

On the plateau high above Dove Dale lies this quietly attractive stone village with a tree-shaded green. St Peter's Church is mostly of the Decorated and Perpendicular styles, but has some earlier work, notably a Norman chancel arch and remains of Saxon crosses in the porch; its chief glories are the 17th-century furnishings, with a set of box pews and a fine two-decker pulpit.

Ashbourne F8

Almshouses and the Old Queen Elizabeth Grammar School of 1585 contrast with the predominantly Georgian brick of the main street. Near the triangular marketplace, an unusual 'gallows' inn sign running right across the street links the Green Man with the former Black's Head Royal Hotel, with which it amalgamated in 1825. Within St Oswald's Church, with its prominent 212-foot spire, are 15th- and 16th-century monuments to the Cockayne and Bradbourne families, as well as a remarkably lifelike sleeping child carved in Carrara marble in memory of a five-year-old who died in 1793. Ashbourne is renowned for its bottled water, its Shrovetide football match, and its locally sold gingerbread—reputedly made to a recipe given by French prisoners held here in the Napoleonic Wars.

Ashford in the Water F5

The 'Water' is the River Wye, crossed by the low-arched Sheepwash Bridge, where sheep are still occasionally brought into the special enclosure alongside prior to being tossed in the river for washing. Comprising mostly 17th- and 18th-century cottages, the village retains a hexagonal marketplace. Holy Trinity Church has several memorials made from 'black marble', the term given to a highly polished grey limestone quarried locally.

Bakewell F5

An important crossing place over the River Wye from AD 924 or earlier, and home to a bustling Monday cattle and general market, Bakewell is the largest town within the Peak District National Park boundary. The park information centre occupies the Old Market Hall, a 16th- or 17th-century sandstone structure. The Rutland Arms, formerly the White Horse Inn, was the birthplace of Bakewell pudding (never known as Bakewell tart in the town): around 1860 a cook's assistant was attempting to make strawberry tart, but erroneously placed the egg- and butter-based flaky pastry over the jam; the dish was a great success with the guests, and more than one bakery in town claims to have the original recipe. Lanes and stepped paths lead to an attractive area beyond the parish church, which contains imposing monuments

ABOVE *Bakewell puddings and other local produce make an attractive window display.*

to the Vernons and Manners of nearby Haddon Hall; the building itself was restored in the 19th century but has traces of its Saxon origins as well as Norman arches. Bakewell's oldest house is the aptly named Old House Museum, dating from Tudor times, which contains a collection of local bygones, including costumes and toys.

Buxton D5

The Romans based the spa of Aquae Arnemetiae beside the lukewarm waters that gush from St Ann's Well. During medieval times the spring was credited with miraculous curative powers and became a place of pilgrimage until its closure under Henry VIII. In the 1780s William Cavendish, the fifth Duke of Devonshire, used the profits from his lucrative Ecton Hill Mines to fund the revival of the spa. Employing the architect John Carr, he created the magnificent Crescent that was to rival that of Bath, and Buxton soon became a fashionable place to take the waters. The town's fortunes were further boosted by the arrival of the railway in 1863, and the Pavilion and adjacent Pavilion Gardens were developed. Another survival of this heyday is the Devonshire Royal Hospital (now closed) which originated in 1790 as a stable for the use of people staying in the Crescent; in 1880 it was roofed with a spectacular unsupported dome measuring 154 feet across. The final grand gesture to the spa was the Opera House of 1903 which today stages concerts, operas, rock music and theatre, and is the focus of the Buxton Festival. The past fortunes of the town and story of the Peak District from prehistoric times are recorded in the Museum and Art Gallery. On the edge of town, working limestone quarries scar the landscape, but more attractive views are had from Solomon's Tower, a folly built in 1896 near Poole's Cavern in Buxton Country Park.

Castleton E4

Laid out to a grid plan in medieval times and standing on the divide between the Dark and White Peaks, Castleton is at the hub of some of the most spectacular geological features in the National Park and throngs with visitors at weekends. Just outside the village are Mam Tor, Winnats Pass and the Blue John, Treak Cliff and Speedwell show caves, while in Castleton itself the huge mouth of Peak Cavern rises to some 50 feet. Perching on a hill high above Castleton and the gorge of Cave Dale, Peveril Castle was built by William Peverel, a favourite knight or illegitimate son of William the Conqueror. Henry II built the keep, which stands almost to its original height. St Edmund's Church is believed to have been the garrison church for the castle, and the zigzag-decorated chancel arch is a Norman feature; the 17th-century box pews survived a thorough restoration in 1837.

Chapel-en-le-Frith D4

The church that gives the small market town on the northwest side of the Peak its name originated as a chapel dedicated to St Thomas à Becket. It was built in the 13th century by men who worked in the Peak Forest, or 'en le frith'. Outside town is the Chestnut Centre, an animal conservation centre where visitors can see otters, owls and other endangered species that breed on site.

Cheadle D8

This market town's major landmark is the Roman Catholic church, with its 200-foot spire and extravagantly decorated interior. Built in 1846 for the Earl of Shrewsbury, it is one of the masterpieces of the 19th-century architect Augustus Pugin.

Chelmorton E5

This quiet one-street village beneath the towering grassy heights of Chelmorton Low retained its medieval open-field system (where land was farmed in strips) until 1809, when the land was enclosed by dry-stone walls, creating a remarkable 'fossilisation' of agricultural practice in times past. The strips run at right angles to the street, and can best be seen from higher ground by following the lane rising from near the church and the pub.

Chesterfield H5

Derbyshire's largest town is a busy industrial and commercial centre with a lively market, but it is best known for the crooked spire of St Mary and All Saints. Originally this structure was as straight as any other, but the wooden frame supporting the lead tiles warped—probably owing to a combination of the weight of the lead, the use of unseasoned timber and fluctuations in temperature. The church contains a Norman font, screens dating from the early 1500s and some striking 16th-century monuments to the Foljambe family. The Museum and Art Gallery houses displays on Chesterfield's heritage as well as temporary exhibitions.

Derby G9

The largely 18th-century cathedral church of All Saints, boasting the second-highest tower (212 feet) in England, is an impressive monument and contains the world's oldest peal of seven bells. Most of the city's growth occurred after the Industrial Revolution, and two popular attractions are the Derby Industrial Museum and the Royal Crown Derby Visitor Centre, which offers factory tours as well as a museum and demonstration area. The Derby Museum and Art Gallery boasts a fine array of Derby porcelain and has an unrivalled collection of paintings by the local 18th-century artist Joseph Wright, including his masterly *A Philosopher Lecturing on the Orrery*. Pickford's House, built in 1770, exhibits costumes and looks back on domestic life in the 18th century, while the Derbyshire Constabulary Memorabilia Museum has a huge array of police badges, truncheons, handcuffs and uniforms.

ABOVE *The 'pattern book' village of Edensor; the Duke of Devonshire, who commissioned it, could not decide which architectural style to choose, so ordered one house of each type from the pattern book.*

Edensor F5

The sixth Duke of Devonshire, owner of Chatsworth House, felt that Chatsworth estate village spoiled the view from his house, so he employed the architect John Robertson to replace it with a new one. Pronounced 'Ensor', the more discreetly situated village was built from 1838–42 in collaboration with the duke's head gardener, Joseph Paxton. Robertson's creation was an engaging medley of styles, said to have been inspired by an architectural pattern book the duke had perused. No two cottages are alike—one is based on a Swiss chalet, another resembles a Tudor cottage, and there is even a scaled-down Italianate villa.

Eyam F5

(*See feature below*)

EYAM: THE PLAGUE VILLAGE

TRAGEDY BEFELL the peaceful little village of Eyam in September 1665 when a bale of cloth infested with plague-carrying fleas arrived at the local tailor's from London, where thousands were dying of bubonic plague. Within days the tailor's hapless assistant had succumbed to a raging fever and purulent sores, the symptoms of plague. Over the next 14 months Eyam lost a third of its population, some 260 people.

By early summer 1666 the epidemic had become almost uncontrollable, and the local rector, William Mompesson, realised that drastic action was needed to try and contain it. Mompesson asked his parishioners to follow three rules: each family was to bury its own dead; church services were to be held outside so that individuals could keep a safe distance from each other; and, most seriously, Eyam was to cut itself off from the outside world.

The self-imposed quarantine was the most courageous action the small community could have taken. Stones and troughs were placed on the village boundaries to demarcate the plague territory and to allow people to collect supplies of food and medicine. The benevolent Earl of Devonshire of nearby Chatsworth Estate donated many goods to the stricken village. Eventually, the plague ran its course, and by November 1, 1666 it had claimed its last victim. Today, an annual gathering is held in Cucklet Delf, the spot where Mompesson held what he hoped were life-preserving church services, in remembrance of those who gave their lives to save others.

ABOVE *In 1951 a local man compiled this register of plague deaths using information gathered from Eyam's original parish register.*

CITIES, TOWNS AND VILLAGES (CONTINUED)

Glossop D3

After the bleak, empty moors beside the Snake Pass, the descent into Glossop presents a pleasing change of scene, with former textile mills and compact terraces of cottages which were laid out in the 19th century. Old Glossop, with its 13th-century market cross and parish church, has several 17th-century houses. Local history is recorded in the Heritage Centre.

Hartington E6

Situated close to the River Dove, and a popular starting point for walks into Beresford and Wolfscote Dales, Hartington has a spacious triangular marketplace presided over by the old town hall and two inns, recalling the town's former status as a major commercial centre. A variety of Stilton cheeses, as well as Sage Derby and Hartington Blue, are made at Hartington's Dairy Crest dairy and sold in a shop in the village. The limestone houses and cottages are typical of the area, with gritstone used for such features as quoins and mullions. Tucked away from the village centre is Hartington Hall, a handsome Jacobean manor house (now a youth hostel) where Bonnie Prince Charlie once stayed.

ABOVE *Matlock Bath has been a spa town since the late 17th century, when the sides of the gorge were accessible only on foot; today's tourists can ride to the top by cable car, visible in the far distance.*

Hathersage F4

Set beside the A625 as it drops towards to the floor of the Hope Valley, Hathersage has become something of a commuter satellite town and has changed greatly since the 19th century when it was a mill town for the needle and pin industries. In the churchyard lies what is supposedly the grave of Little John, friend and lieutenant of legendary hero Robin Hood (*see feature on page 130*).

Leek D7

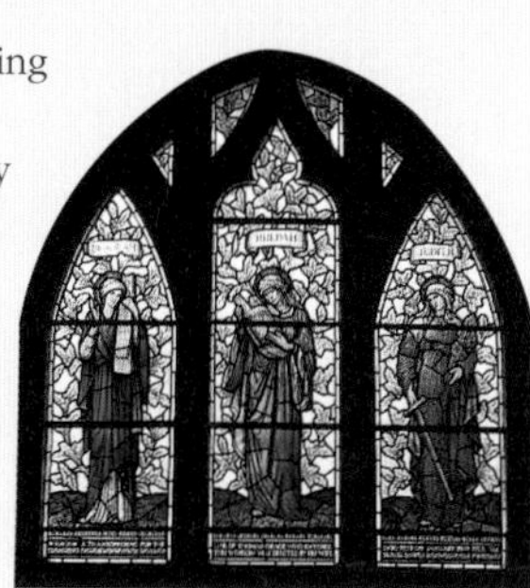

Silk manufacturing was for many years a mainstay of Leek's economy, and the town still possesses old mills—now serving other purposes—and terraces of red-brick houses built for mill workers. In the heart of the town are the cheerful, cobbled marketplace and the parish church of St Edward the Confessor, with stained glass by William Morris's company (*above*) and remains of Saxon crosses in the churchyard.

Macclesfield C5

Although Macclesfield is a long-established market town, what survives of it is mostly of the industrial age, when the town was the centre of the silk trade (*see also page 159*). This era is recalled in the Silk Museum and Paradise Mill. The Macclesfield Canal cuts round the east side of town, beneath the western buttresses of the Peak, where Tegg's Nose Country Park offers sweeping vistas across the Cheshire Plain.

Matlock G6

Rows of bay-windowed Victorian houses and the municipal Hall Leys Park are legacies of Matlock's former spa days. Industrialist John Smedley built the citadel-like hydro which in its day offered water, or hydropathy, cures, but which now houses the offices of Derbyshire County Council.

Matlock Bath G6

Set in the crag-girt Derwent Gorge, Matlock Bath is an erstwhile spa endowed with stately 19th-century villas, the old spa pavilion (now housing the Peak District Mining Museum) and a cable car linking High Tor with the Heights of Abraham, where there are caves to visit and a prospect tower overlooking the gorge. Other family attractions include the Aquarium and Hologram Gallery, Gulliver's Kingdom adventure park, and (in the former station) the Whistlestop Wildlife Centre, run by the Derbyshire Wildlife Trust. To the east, in the grounds of Riber Castle—an eerie 19th-century ruin—is Riber Castle Wildlife Park, which has a collection of species from around the world; lynx have been bred here for reintroduction into the Vosges Mountains in France.

Rowsley F6

The old village clusters round Caudwell's Mill, built in 1874, a water-powered, turbine-driven roller mill open to the public. Rowsley South is the terminus for Peak Rail steam trains running via Darley Dale to Matlock. At Darley Dale, the Red House Working Carriage Museum has a fine collection of horse-drawn vehicles, which are used for pleasure trips and for the film industry; carriage-driving lessons are on offer for the adventurous.

Stoke-on-Trent C8

Six towns—Burslem, Fenton, Hanley, Longton, Stoke-upon-Trent and Tunstall—make up the conurbation that is Stoke-on-Trent (also known as the Potteries), one of the largest ceramics-producing areas in the world. In addition to the factory shops, many potteries are open to the public (*see pages 160–61*), while the Potteries Museum and Art Gallery displays some 5,000 pieces as well as local archaeological finds, recreated Victorian shops and a Spitfire plane, the celebrated Second World War fighter designed by Stoke-born engineer R. J. Mitchell. Some of the novels of Arnold Bennett (*see page 165*), such as *Clayhanger*, were based in the area, albeit with altered place names.

Tideswell E5

Lead mining and the wool trade accounted for the prosperity of this small town during medieval times. In the 14th century much money was lavished on the building of the Church of St John the Baptist, whose grandeur has earned it the epithet 'the Cathedral of the Peak'. Certainly no other Peak church is as impressive, with an airy chancel typical of the Late Decorated style and the later pinnacled tower, a fine example of Perpendicular style. There are memorial brasses to Sir John Foljambe (1383) and Bishop Robert Pursglove (1579), founder of the local grammar school, and a wealth of 19th-century woodcarving.

Tissington F7

Since the Elizabethan era the FitzHerbert family have owned Tissington Hall (not open to the public), which was extended in Georgian times. Little has changed since those days in this most attractive of estate villages, with its broad verges, duck-populated pond and restored Norman Church of St Mary, with many FitzHerbert memorials. It was at Tissington that the tradition of well dressing is believed to have started (*see feature, above right*). The village also gives its name to the Tissington Trail, which passes nearby.

Winster F6

This former lead-mining town has many fine 18th-century houses, as well as alleys lined with humbler cottages. At the heart of the village is the 16th-century Market House, which was acquired by the National Trust in 1906 as its first Derbyshire property. It now serves as an (unstaffed) information centre.

Wirksworth G7

Limestone quarries and spoil heaps form an unattractive backdrop to this historic town, which has nevertheless managed to retain much of its early character as a lead-mining centre with its narrow alleys, or jitties, set in an irregular web known locally as the 'puzzle gardens'. Stained glass by Edward Burne-Jones adorns the interior of the medieval Church of St Mary, but the building's most famous artefact is an 8th-century Saxon coffin lid carved with scenes from the life of Christ, and which has become known as the Wirksworth Stone. The church stands in an attractive close, flanked by a group of Elizabethan almshouses and the 19th-century former grammar school. Mining disputes have been settled by the Barmote Court since 1266 or earlier: it meets in April in the Moot Hall, and the public are welcome to attend. The Heritage Centre in Crown Yard chronicles the development of Wirksworth and has a town trail. Just outside the town is Carsington Water, a huge reservoir opened in 1992 and popular for water sports. Also nearby, the National Stone Centre tells the story of stone, covering its origins and use from prehistoric to modern times; visitors can take trails across fossilised tropical reefs, visit a working quarry (by arrangement), or take part in gem panning and fossil rubbing. East of Wirksworth, Crich Stand has views as far as Lincoln Cathedral, and is topped by the Regimental War Memorial of the Sherwood Foresters.

Youlgreave F6

This former lead-mining centre occupies a hillside above the River Bradford just east of Lathkill Dale. Its circular water tank, known as the Conduit Head or the Fountain, supplied the first piped water to the village in 1829. The pinnacled and gargoyle-embellished 15th-century church tower rises to 96 feet, and the church interior, dating from Norman times, is similarly grand in scale. Its 13th-century font is rare in having two bowls, and there is a tiny effigy of Thomas Cockayne, who died as a child in 1488, as well as 19th-century stained glass by Edward Burne-Jones and William Morris. To the west, Arbor Low is the most striking prehistoric monument in the Peak District, with 47 stones, all lying flat, within a circular bank; it probably dates from around 2000 BC. In the next field is Gib Hill, an earlier henge dating back to the early Bronze Age.

WELL-DRESSED WELLS

THE PEAK DISTRICT is blessed with many rich veins of water, from tumbling rivers such as the Derwent and the Dove to a plethora of springs, streams and wells. Every year villagers celebrate this gift of water by decorating their wells with tableaux made from flowers and other natural materials.

The tradition is thought to derive from pre-Christian times, when wells and springs were believed to be the haunts of nymphs, whose favour was courted by means of offerings. In time the practice was Christianised, and wells were festooned with flowers on saints' days. The modern-day custom of well dressing may have started in Tissington in 1615, when the village's wells survived a severe drought, or perhaps as far back as 1348–9, when they continued to supply pure water during the Black Death.

The floral tableau is usually created on a large wooden board covered with a layer of smooth, white clay. The designs, which often feature biblical scenes, are first pricked out and then filled with alder cones, seeds, mosses, lichens, pebbles and berries. Finally, colourful flower petals are pressed on—a task delayed until the last minute so that the picture stays fresh for as long as possible.

ABOVE *Biblical stories often provide the inspiration for the colourful tableaux that are created on Peak District wells on saints' days.*

MANCHESTER

A BUSY PORT AND *thriving commercial centre, Manchester is the industrial capital of the northwest. A thriving arts scene, too, has in recent years made it one of the most vibrant cities in Britain. And when you have had your fill of culture, the moors of the Peak District are right on the doorstep.*

It was cotton that brought fame and fortune to the city, but its origins are Roman, dating from AD 79 when Agricola established a fort above the confluence of the Rivers Medlock and Irwell. By medieval times Manchester was a small but flourishing town. In the 18th century trade with the American colonies expanded, and the population mushroomed as Manchester became the main commercial centre for the prospering Lancashire cotton industry.

The smoking factory chimneys have disappeared, but many imposing civic buildings survive from the city's Industrial Revolution heyday. Widespread damage to the Arndale Centre and nearby buildings by an IRA bomb in 1996 sparked off an ambitious redevelopment of the city centre, due for completion in 2001. The scheme will include landscaping and pedestrianising the area close to the cathedral, together with construction of a new cathedral visitor centre and a cultural centre.

CENTRAL MANCHESTER

The centre has migrated southwards from the medieval town—a compact area around Shambles Square and the cathedral, a broad 15th-century church that was enlarged after attaining cathedral status in 1847.

Laid out in the 18th century, Exchange Street and St Ann's Square form an attractive traffic-free promenade, flanked by the Royal Exchange, where business transactions for the textile industry and its offshoots were carried out; today a circular steel structure inside houses a theatre and crafts centre. Close by, Barton Arcade is a fanciful Victorian shopping arcade of curved glass and ornamental ironwork. In Deansgate the highly ornate John Rylands University Library of Manchester (1890) houses the Althorp Library, which holds changing exhibitions of printed books, manuscripts and archives.

Albert Square, with its canopied Albert Memorial of 1861, is dominated by the 286-foot clock tower of the exuberantly Gothic Revival Town Hall. To the east, spanned by the gold leaf and ceramic Imperial Archway, Faulkner Street marks the hub of Chinatown. Bridgewater Hall has since 1996 been the home of the world-famous Hallé Orchestra; guided tours can be booked through the box office.

CASTLEFIELD

A walk from Deansgate along St John Street, Manchester's finest Georgian street, leads into Castlefield Urban Heritage Park, where a replica of the Roman stone fort stands close to the huge railway viaduct of 1830. The viaduct itself is castellated in memory of the fort, the last vestiges of which were destroyed during construction of the railway. The Castlefield Centre has self-guided trails around the area. Walks extend along the towpath of the Rochdale Canal from the basin at the meeting with the Bridgewater Canal. Partly housed in the former Liverpool Road rail warehouse and railway station of 1830 (the world's first passenger station), the huge Museum of Science and Industry includes a gallery on the city's textile industry, and the Air and Space Gallery (*below*), where visitors can have a go

in a flight simulator. Nearby, another popular attraction is Granada Studios, whose tours take a look at the production of television programmes and include the set of *Coronation Street* and replica sets of *Blind Date* and *Emmerdale*.

OUT OF THE CENTRE

In the suburb of Rusholme, Platt Hall contains the Gallery of English Costume, with a display ranging from the 17th century to the present. To the north of the centre, the Manchester Jewish Museum charts the story of the city's Jewish population from 1740, while in Cheetham the Museum of Transport looks at the city's public transport from the era of the horse-drawn bus to the city's modern Metrolink tram. Old Trafford, the soccer stadium of Manchester United—the most popular football team in the world—offers tours of the dressing room and a walk through the tunnel onto the pitch, and there is a museum of trophies and memorabilia. On the waterfront in Salford stands The Lowry, a major cultural and entertainment complex including a gallery of paintings by L. S. Lowry (*see feature on page 97*). At the University of Manchester, the Whitworth Art Gallery exhibits British watercolours and modern works in other media. Stockport has Britain's only museum devoted to millinery, as well as a Second World War air-raid shelter offering tours.

LEFT *Manchester's industrial buildings are being given a new lease of life with their conversion into cafés and bars, as seen on Canal Street.*

HOUSES AND GARDENS

Adlington Hall Macclesfield **C5**
Owned by the Legh family since the 14th century, Adlington Hall is by no means the only English country house displaying features from very different building periods. What is impressive, however, is the quality of its diverse architecture, and how gracefully it all hangs together. The great hall dates from the late 1400s; a century later, the dazzling black and white wing was added. The porticoed south front of mellow brickwork (1757) is in classic Georgian style, and the landscaped gardens were heavily influenced by Capability Brown. The house is open to groups of visitors by prior arrangement only.

Alton Towers
Alton **E8**

The 500-acre theme park at Alton Towers is one of Britain's foremost family attractions. Stomach-churning rides (*right*) are constantly being added to its repertoire. Older visitors are pleasantly surprised by Alton's fine grounds, always immaculately kept, with vistas, lakes and fountains just as spectacular as the Nemesis or Ripsaw rides. Spring is a good time to visit, when the rock garden and rhododendrons are at their best. An aerial cable car gives marvellous panoramas. Only the shell survives of the huge, once-splendid neo-Gothic mansion.

Biddulph Grange Biddulph **B6**
Surprise is the overriding sensation in this extraordinary garden north of Stoke-on-Trent. After a decade of painstaking restoration by the National Trust, this long-neglected oddity can now be enjoyed as intended in its Victorian heyday. A sequence of imaginatively themed gardens linked by rock tunnels and hidden corridors accommodates rare specimens from many parts of the world, including China and Japan, the Middle East and the Americas. Flowering periods have been orchestrated to last almost all year round, from colourful bulbs in early spring to a fiery display in late autumn from the garden's huge range of trees.

Capesthorne Hall Chelford **B5**
A disastrous fire in 1861 wrecked much of the 18th-century red-brick hall which stood on an estate dating back to Domesday times. The long-established incumbents are the Bromley-Davenport family, and the present squire is the Lord Lieutenant of Cheshire. The house, flamboyantly remodelled in turreted Gothic by Anthony Salvin, has an immensely long façade. Inside is a fine collection of antiques from around the world. There is also a Georgian chapel and ice house.

Chatsworth House Bakewell **F5**
(*see feature on pages 66–7*)

Dunge Valley Hidden Gardens
Kettleshulme **C4**
These beautiful gardens on the western fringes of the National Park consist of over five acres of woodland and rhododendron plantations, bog gardens and water features. The rose gardens, containing many old-fashioned varieties, perfume the summer air. Keen gardeners will enjoy visiting the plant nursery, which offers many unusual species of shrubs and perennials for sale. Blue poppies, rhododendrons and ornamental trees are among Dunge Valley's specialities.

Eyam Hall Eyam **F5**
This small but charming manor house in the famous plague village (*see feature on page 153*) has been the home of the Wright family for over 300 years. The stone-built house has only recently opened to the public, and it retains the intimate atmosphere of a much-loved private home. A Jacobean staircase, fine tapestries and an impressive tester bed are among its interior treasures. A craft centre is housed in the stableyard.

Gawsworth Hall Macclesfield **C5**
The earliest parts of Gawsworth date from 1480, though much of the structure became unsafe and was remodelled during the early 18th century. A low-slung, rambling black and white building, Gawsworth has had a number of notable occupants, including Mary Fitton, possibly Shakespeare's Dark Lady (*see entry on page 166*). Still a private home, this delightful house contains many fine artefacts and Pre-Raphaelite stained glass.

Haddon Hall Bakewell **F5**
This medieval manor house revels in a romantic setting of magnificent terraced gardens and woodland overlooking the River Wye. Haddon was unoccupied during Georgian and Victorian times and thus escaped the fashionable improvements of the time. Its castellations provide a backdrop for many films and costume dramas. Inside, the timbered banqueting hall (*pictured on page 150*), painted chapel and 14th-century kitchens are among the most memorable rooms. The 16th-century rose gardens were the alleged setting for the 18-year-old Haddon heiress Dorothy Vernon's elopement with John Manners, the youngest son of a local earl, in 1563.

ABOVE *Steps lead from the Italian Garden to the Rhododendron Ground at Biddulph Grange, where the gardens were laid out in Victorian days as a series of outdoor 'rooms', each capturing the feel of a different corner of the globe. A walk around the grounds is like a miniature tour of the world.*

HOUSES AND GARDENS (CONTINUED)

Hardwick Hall Doe Lea I6
This splendid Elizabethan mansion represents the apogee of its first owner's worldly ambitions. Bess of Hardwick (*see entry on page 165*) built the existing house soon after the death of her fourth and most powerful husband, the Earl of Shrewsbury, and stamped her indelible mark on its six towers in monograms and coronets. The structure was innovative in its time, departing from the classic Elizabethan 'E' shape in favour of an 'H'. The building progressed extremely quickly during the 1590s, and much of its excellent craftsmanship was local work, though the high ratio of windows to load-bearing walls ('Hardwick Hall, more glass than wall', the saying goes) disconcerts present-day surveyors. Inside, the High Great Chamber makes a sumptuous setting for a series of Brussels tapestries depicting the life of Ulysses, and has a wonderful plaster frieze of classical scenes.

The Herb Garden Hardstoft I6
Opened in 1983, this is one of the country's foremost herb gardens. Sheltered by beech hedges, the Main Garden contains culinary, medicinal and perfumery herbs in beautifully arranged parterres. Posters describe the history and use of the herbs on display. The Physic Garden contains a sinister array of pharmacological plants, many of which are poisonous; the Pot Pourri Garden features scented species that dry well; and the Lavender Garden has over 40 different varieties. Naturally, there's a retail outlet with over 300 types of herb on sale.

Kedleston Hall near Derby G9
Ancestral home of the Curzon family for over 850 years, Kedleston is now in the care of the National Trust. The present mansion dates from the late 18th century, and is one of the foremost examples of Robert Adam's classical interior design (*right*). It was built primarily as an art gallery for the first baron's collection, which can still be seen amid exotic mirrors and rich furnishings. On the ground floor is a museum of artefacts assembled by the Marquess Curzon while he was Viceroy of India. The hall is set in extensive parkland, and the parish church contains a family memorial.

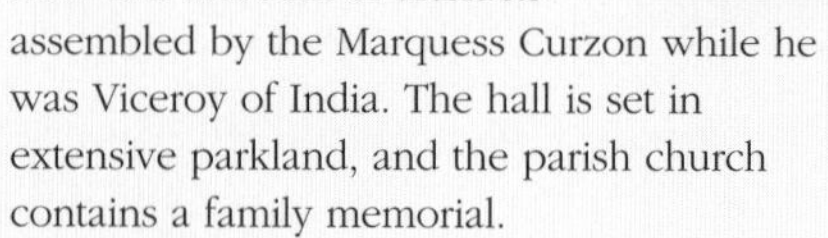

Lea Gardens Lea G7
These beautifully landscaped woodland gardens cover about four acres of hillside in an old millstone quarry. Its main strengths are rhododendrons and azaleas (some 650 varieties), exotic shrubs, alpines and spring bulbs. Woodland walks through the grounds reveal many birds, which are encouraged with nesting boxes. Best seen in May.

ABOVE *Building work began on Little Moreton Hall in the late 15th century and continued for about 100 years. This beautiful house boasts some of the finest half-timbering in the country.*

Little Moreton Hall Congleton B6
The unforgettable 'magpie' architecture of this marvellous house singles it out as one of the most perfect specimens of half-timbering in Britain. There is nothing very 'little' about it. Rambling around courtyards in a series of Chinese boxes, it dates from about 1480, and took a century to build. Fortunately for posterity, its Royalist owners had no money for refurbishing after the Civil War, and so it passed down to the present century substantially intact. The elaborate embellishments of the exterior reveal an age that no longer had to spend all its energies in defending dwellings from potential attack: the moat and bridged gatehouse are largely decorative rather than functional. Painted panelling in the parlour was discovered during electrical work in the 1970s.

Lyme Park Disley C4
Keen location spotters may recognise this seemly mansion—a marvellous amalgam of Elizabethan, Georgian and Regency architecture—as 'Pemberley' in the BBC production of *Pride and Prejudice*. The mainly Palladian exterior virtually engulfs the Elizabethan features which can still be seen in the drawing room and long gallery. Grinling Gibbons's superlative limewood carvings in the saloon are a major talking point. The grounds encompass a deer park.

The Revolution House Whittington H5
Just over 300 years ago, three local aristocrats (the Earls of Devonshire and Danby, and Mr John D'Arcy) met in this quaint thatched cottage, then an alehouse called the Cock and Pynot, to plot the overthrow of King James II in favour of William and Mary. The upper floor houses a changing programme of exhibitions and a video show recounting the story of the 1688 Revolution (*see page 60 for photograph*).

Sudbury Hall Sudbury F9
This imposing house (*below*) on the Derbyshire/Staffordshire border was the home of the Vernon family until it passed to the National Trust in 1967. Its main influences date from the reign of Charles II, and it is one of the finest examples of the Stuart style in the country. In 1840 it was leased to Queen Adelaide, widow of William IV, whose funeral instructions are displayed in the Queen's Room. A magnificent carved staircase and a splendid long gallery are other notable features. In the servants' wing, the National Trust Museum of Childhood contrasts the nannied and nurseried lifestyle of privileged children with the poor child's lot of chimneys and coal mines.

INDUSTRIAL HERITAGE

THE PEAK DISTRICT *is littered with relics of its manufacturing past, and although there are plenty of ruined mills and mines to be seen, many of these skeletons of former industries have found a new lease of life as informative museums explaining the region's industrial heritage. Previously abandoned canals, too, now teem with pleasure craft, and lovingly restored steam trains puff along old railway lines.*

CANALS

The canals that ring the Peak (*see also feature on pages 108–9*) retain much of the atmosphere of the early Industrial Revolution, and their towpaths can be explored on foot. The **Cromford Canal** crosses an aqueduct near the Leawood Pumphouse of 1849, which used to top up water supplies by pumping from the River Derwent. Narrow-boat cruises from Whaley Bridge and Furness Vale Marina explore the **Peak Forest Canal**, which at Marple crosses an aqueduct and climbs a flight of 16 locks. A picture of dereliction awaits along the **Chesterfield Canal** at the Norwood locks, with thirteen locks in four 'staircases', but there is a livelier scene with narrow boats near the old lime kilns at the wharf at Froghall on the **Caldon Canal**. In Trafford Park, Manchester, the **Barton Swing Aqueduct** is a remarkable construction which rotates 800 tons of water to allow clearance for vessels on the Manchester Ship Canal.

RAILWAYS

The **Manchester to Sheffield line** is the only surviving cross-Peak route (there were once three). It leads through New Mills, Edale and Hathersage before taking the three-and-a-half-mile Totley Tunnel—England's second longest—to emerge in the Sheffield suburbs. Other lines have been closed and are now walking and cycling routes, such as the Tissington Trail and the Monsal Trail, which was part of a line linking Matlock to Manchester via Bakewell. Steam trains operated by **Peak Rail**, however, run along the four-and-a-half-mile section from Matlock to Rowsley South. The **High Peak Trail** takes in a section of the former Cromford and High Peak Railway, which included the 708-yard Middleton Incline, where the Middleton Top Engine House provided steam haulage to enable trains to climb the gradient of more than one in nine. The engine house now has a visitor centre, and the winding engine is operated on occasion. Two miles to the east is the Sheep Pasture Incline, with remains of another engine house, and a 'catchpit' introduced in 1888 to avoid a repeat of an incident in which two wagons ran away down the slope, cleared the canal and main line railway at the bottom and ended up in a field.

Just outside Ripley, the **Midland Railway Centre** has an extensive railway museum with a variety of locomotives, as well as a Victorian Railwayman's Church and a demonstration signal box; steam trains run along narrow-gauge and standard-gauge tracks. **Chesterfield Museum** recalls the days of the railway pioneer George Stephenson (*see feature on page 62*), who settled in the area in 1838 to work on the building of the North Midland Railway.

TRAMS

Manchester has a modern tram system, the Metrolink, but for the originals, the **National Tramway Museum, Crich**, is the largest

collection of its kind in Britain. There are vehicles of all ages from all over the world, some as static displays and others taking visitors along a scenic stretch of track (*above*).

MILLS AND MILL TOWNS

The great textile mills of the 18th and 19th centuries in and around the Peak are among the most striking legacies of the Industrial Revolution. Many are very much part of the landscape—for example, **Litton Mill**, notorious for the treatment of its child labourers (*see feature on page 160*)—and nearby **Cressbrook Mill**, both in Monsal Dale. One of the most dramatic sites is **New Mills**, where the eerie ruins of the old water-powered mills occupy the Torrs—the gorge of the Rivers Sett and Goyt that splits the town of New Mills in two; the Heritage Centre records the town's industrial past.

Cromford Mill is now a museum paying tribute to the work of Richard Arkwright (*see feature on page 31*), who established the world's first water-powered cotton-spinning mill here in 1771. **Cromford** itself retains many houses of the period, notably in North Street, and at the edge of the village is Arkwright's massive red-brick Masson Mill.

In 1784 Samuel Greg harnessed the waters of the River Bollin to power **Quarry Bank Mill**, a cotton-spinning mill which now gives hand-spinning and weaving demonstrations, and shows power looms in action. The nearby **Apprentice House** evokes the living conditions of pauper children, explained by interpreters in Victorian costume. In Belper, **North Mill** (1804) was constructed with brick arches and an iron frame to avoid a repeat of the fire that had destroyed the previous building. State-of-the-art in its day, it now houses the Derwent Valley Visitor Centre.

Of several silk-producing towns around the Peak, **Macclesfield** was foremost. It is not known how silk first came to the town, but by the 18th century it was renowned for the manufacture of silk buttons. The industry was initially based in weavers' garrets, some of which were in use until the 1930s, but in 1744 the first of the mills appeared. Power looms began to take over from hand looms in the 19th century, but **Paradise Mill** kept its hand looms until closure in 1981, and has been preserved as a working museum. Housed in a former Sunday school, the **Silk Museum** tells of Macclesfield's trade with the Far East and how the silk industry developed. The **Silk Trail** is a self-guided walk through town, passing former weavers' garrets and mills. Silk is still woven and printed in the town, mainly for the production of ties and scarves, although the bulk of local textile production is now polyesters. An early 18th-century silk mill houses the **Derby Industrial Museum**, which has displays on Derbyshire's industry and railways, as well as the Power Gallery with interactive exhibits showing how power is used in industry; also here is the world's biggest collection of Rolls Royce aeroplane engines, which are made in Derby.

A range of corn-grinding water mills has also survived. The National Trust grinds flour on Victorian machinery at the 15th-century **Nether Alderley Mill**, which is powered by wheels fed by a lake. **Brindley Mill**, in Leek, was built by canal engineer James Brindley in 1752 and houses a museum about his life. **Stainsby Mill**, on the National Trust's Hardwick Estate, dating from 1849 to 1850, evokes the workplace of a Victorian miller; its design enabled it to be operated by one man. More advanced still was **Caudwell's Mill**, Rowsley, which was fully automated and is the only extant flour mill of its type in the country. It essentially uses the same process

INDUSTRIAL HERITAGE (CONTINUED)

as present-day electrically driven flour mills, but here the Wye powers two turbines that activate the mostly pre-1914 machinery. Flour is sold in the mill shop, and the site also houses craft workshops.

MINING

Evidence of lead mining, an industry dating from Roman times, is a feature of the Peak landscape. The **Peak District Mining Museum** at Matlock Bath has a full-size mock-up of the inside of a mine shaft, as well as pumping engines and social history and mineral displays. The entrance fee covers a visit to nearby **Temple Mine**, and the museum can also arrange trips to **Magpie Mine**, near Sheldon, the most extensive surface remains in the Peak. Dating from about 1740 and now a field centre, it includes an engine house, spoil heaps, winding gear and a smithy.

Lathkill Dale abounds in evidence of the lead industry, especially around the former Mandale and Lathkill Dale mines near Over Haddon. The workings often suffered from flooding, so an aqueduct and watercourse were constructed, together with engine houses, for pumping water out of the mine.

Other minerals were also excavated in the area. In the Manifold Valley, the **Ecton Hill copper mines** near Warslow are thought to have made the Dukes of Devonshire richer by over £1,000,000 during the 18th century—and the profits are said to have funded building work at both Chatsworth and the Crescent in Buxton; today, waste tips in the otherwise beautiful dale are the main reminders of the busy days of the 1780s.

STAFFORDSHIRE POTTERY

The Stoke-on-Trent conurbation, also known as the Potteries, is one of the greatest concentrations of ceramics factories in the world. Before the Industrial Revolution the Potteries began in a modest way on smallholdings where red clay and coal (to fire the kilns) were readily available; this activity mushroomed in the 18th century, and from then until the 1950s the air was thick with coal smoke belching from some 2,000 bottle kilns. In 1956 the Clean Air Act forced a change to cleaner ovens, and bottle kilns became redundant.

The ceramics industry continues to be the main employer in Stoke-on-Trent, where dozens of factory shops offer cut-price pieces, and it is possible to tour many of the smaller potteries without booking ahead. The major factories are very popular and have visitor centres as well as tours; workers show their skill in painting vases and figures, throwing pots, creating clay flowers and other objects, and there are opportunities to try these

LOST CHILDHOODS

LEFT *A 19th-century book depicts the cruel working conditions of children in the mills.*

RIGHT *Litton Mill, now a ruin, was once notorious for the way its child workers were treated.*

THE FIRST WATER-POWERED cotton mill in the world was opened by Robert Arkwright at Cromford in 1771, heralding the arrival of the Industrial Revolution. The revolution had a profound effect on the lives of the local people, who sought employment in the many textile mills that sprang up in the area. Child labour—still legal in those days—was particularly in demand because it was cheap, and their good eyesight and supple hands made children useful workers. Boys and girls as young as five worked in the mills; some were so small they had to use stools to reach the machinery. Standing for long hours could cause bow legs and crooked backs, and tiredness often led to accidents and even deaths.

Litton Mill, in Miller's Dale, earned a reputation for being the worst of its day after sensational disclosures about its treatment of children appeared in a radical periodical called *The Lion* in 1828. The story was based on the life of Robert Blincoe from London, who worked at Litton from the age of 10. He accused Ellis Needham, the mill's owner, of wilful cruelty towards his apprentices, claiming that Needham and his sons frequently chastised 'idle' children with a stick.

Later investigations have thrown doubt on the authenticity of this account, but even the most benevolent mill owner imposed fines for breaches of discipline and had children working 12-hour days as well as night shifts. It was not until 1880 that an Education Act decreed that children should be in school, not slaving in the mills.

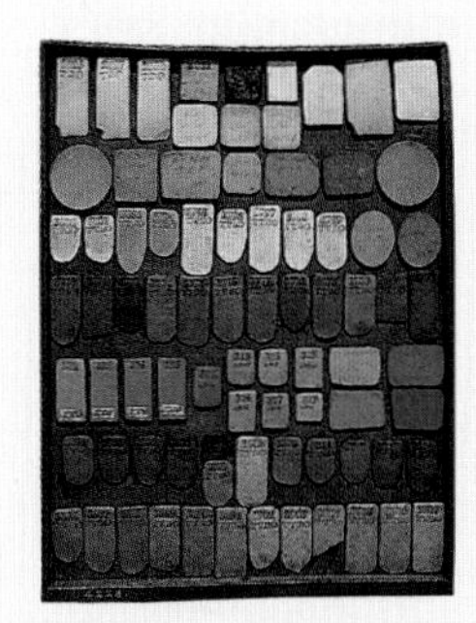

RIGHT *A tray of Wedgwood jasper ware samples of different colours.*

activities yourself—under an expert eye—and take home what you make.

The three main potteries have distinctive features of their own. **Wedgwood** is best known for blue and white jasper ware. The visitor centre has a sumptuous collection of rarities, including two 'First Day Vases' made on June 13, 1769 by the great Josiah Wedgwood (*see entry on page 167*) when he established his factory, Etruria.

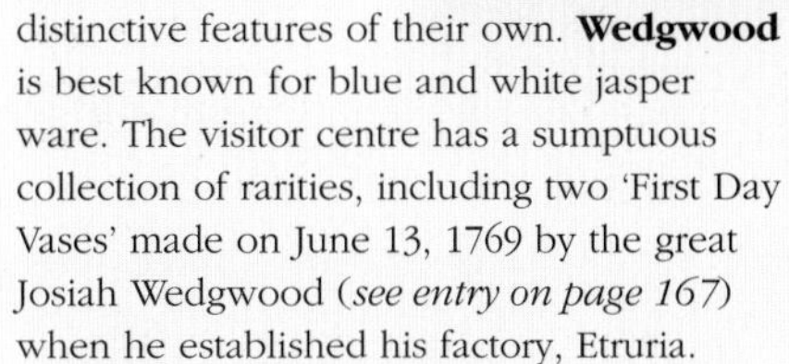

Royal Doulton prides itself on hand-assembled, painted figurines (*left*), of which its visitor centre exhibits the world's largest collection. **Spode** occupies its original 1770 factory, where it produces distinctive blue and white bone china.

The **Gladstone Pottery Museum** is Staffordshire's last complete coal-fired Victorian pottery. This unique working museum where bottle kilns surround a cobbled yard, shows how 19th-century potters worked. There are crafts demonstrations and hands-on activities including pot-throwing. Visitors can walk into the bottle ovens and learn about factory conditions in Victorian times. There is also an eye-catching display of lavatory bowls with names such as the Deluge.

The **Ceramica Experience** in Burslem's Old Town Hall is an interactive learning centre based on the pottery industry, featuring a factory production line, a kiln and an archaeological dig, while the pride of the **Potteries Museum and Art Gallery** is its magnificent Staffordshire ceramics collection. Sandwiched between two canals, the **Etruria Industrial Museum**, Britain's last surviving steam-powered potters' mill, shows how a beam engine was used to power gear-driven grinding pans to crush bone and flint for use in the pottery and agricultural industries. The crushing process is now carried out in the adjacent modern, family-run mill, but the old mill is in perfect working order and the beam engine is in steam once a month from April to December.

WALKS AND WILD PLACES

WHILE THE PENNINE WAY *offers one of Britain's most challenging hikes, starting with a daunting, virtually unsheltered traverse across the Dark Peak, the limestone country to the south has gentler walks through the dales and the dry-stone-walled pastures that rise above them. Several old railway tracks in the area have become long-distance pedestrian and cycle routes, and there are many canal towpaths that can be followed. Some landscaped estates—including Shipley Country Park near Heanor, and parts of Lyme Park and the Chatsworth estate—have generous access for walkers. Climbers flock to the gritstone edges and limestone cliffs, in search of ever greater challenges.*

Alderley Edge B4

Geological faulting has produced this sandstone escarpment, which rises abruptly above the Cheshire Plain just east of the town of Alderley Edge. Cloaked with planted woodlands and designated a Site of Special Scientific Interest for its geology and biology, the edge retains remnants of an ancient heath and attracts a variety of moths and butterflies, as well as birds such as tawny and little owls. From the car park near the Wizard Inn paths lead past abandoned cobalt, lead and copper mines, worked in ancient times and again from the 18th century until the First World War. The summit beacon was used as a signalling point when the Spanish Armada was sighted off the coast of Cornwall in 1588.

Derwent Gorge G6

'I can assure you there are things in Derbyshire as noble as Greece or Switzerland,' enthused Lord Byron of this dramatic limestone gorge. High Tor soars above woodlands on the east side, where a path climbs above the gorge before dropping southwards through limestone caves and a fernery. A cable car ascends from a point near Matlock Bath station to a prospect tower on the Heights of Abraham on the west side of the gorge. The heights are said to have been named by one of the officers who fought at the Battle of Quebec, which took place in a gorge of the same name in Canada in 1759. To the north is St John's Chapel, which was built into the cliff in 1897.

Derwent Valley Reservoirs E3, F3 & F4

The Howden, Derwent and Ladybower Reservoirs form a scenic chain spreading some 10 miles from north to south and serve Nottingham, Leicester, Sheffield and Derby. The construction of Ladybower Reservoir from 1943–5 entailed drowning two villages and 13 farms, although the spire of Derwent church protruded above the surface until 1947. Level tracks and roads through forests and along the water's edge provide easy walking and cycling. Higher paths along the edges of the valley give wonderful views, including the pinnacle of Win Hill.

Dove Dale E7

Forming part of the National Trust's South Peak Estate, this most magical of dales displays a host of classic karst features—including spires, caves, crags and pinnacles—many with fanciful names: Lover's Leap (a 130-foot-high spur), the Twelve Apostles (a series of eroded spurs forming pinnacles), Reynard's Cave (a 40-foot-tall natural arch), and the unmistakable Lion's Head Rock. The tiny hamlet of Milldale was a favourite haunt of Izaak Walton who used to stay here while contemplating the delights of angling with his friend Charles Cotton (*see feature on page 167*). The limestone grassland harbours varied plant life, and grey wagtails and dippers are often seen near the river.

Edale and Kinder Scout E3 & E4

At weekends Edale's small railway station becomes busy with backpackers venturing along the opening stages of the Pennine Way. The Way trails through pastures to Kinder Downfall, a rock escarpment that forms a magnificent show of icicles in the depths of winter. Kinder Scout dominates the landscape of peat hags that constitute the remnants of a vast blanket bog; the National Trust is attempting to restore it after centuries of damage by air pollution and overgrazing. To avoid further erosion walkers are asked to keep to marked paths.

Froggatt Edge G5

This windswept moorland rim high above the leafy Derwent Valley is dotted with abandoned quarries which once provided many of England's millstones. Just off the main path along the edge is a small Bronze Age stone circle, while southwards, above Curbar, a walk along Baslow Edge can be combined with visits to monuments dedicated to Nelson and Wellington.

Goyt Valley D5

Rhododendrons brighten the eerie ruins of Errwood Hall, built by the Grimshawe family in the 1830s but abandoned when the valley

WALKS AND WILD PLACES (CONTINUED)

was evacuated for the construction of Fernilee and Errwood Reservoirs in 1938 and 1967 by the Stockport Corporation. Regimented spruce and larch plantations create a sombre mood around the waters, but paths climb by way of Goyt's Moss to Shining Tor, the high point on an exhilarating moorland-ridge walk that extends northwards to Pym Chair.

Gritstone Trail C4

Starting from the landscaped elegance of Lyme Park, this 18-mile route heads along the western gritstone edges of the Peak District. The trail climbs Kerridge Hill, a narrow ridge that, like Tegg's Nose Country Park through which it passes farther south, has been quarried and gives spectacular panoramas across Cheshire and into North Wales. Near Rushton Spencer the Gritstone Trail joins the Staffordshire Way, which can be followed for a few miles to the Cloud, a piece of moorland perching above Congleton and the Macclesfield Canal.

High Peak Trail E6

Popular with cyclists as well as walkers, this 17½-mile trail (*below*) follows an abandoned railway track from Parsley Hay to High Peak Junction. In its final section it descends a slope past two engine houses, which used to provide haulage for engines ascending the steep gradient, and reaches a former station by the Cromford Canal, where the towpath can be followed to Cromford Wharf.

ABOVE *Ash trees flank the River Lathkill near Over Haddon. The river is inset with a sequence of weirs which dam the water and encourage trout to spawn.*

Ilam Park Ilam E7

Kingfishers and grey wagtails inhabit the river banks of the Manifold and Hamps rivers, which resurface here in 'boil holes' after travelling deep underground. Rare lime trees can be seen in Hinkley Wood. At the heart of the estate, which is owned by the National Trust, is Ilam Hall (now a youth hostel), and nearby is the tiny village of Ilam.

Lathkill Dale F6

The most spectacular section of the valley can be followed from just below Over Haddon, passing relics of old lead mines. The north bank was planted in the 19th century with ash, beech, elm, sycamore and Scots pine, and the dale has a wealth of limestone flora. It is also a noted site for the orange-tip butterfly (*right*).

Longshaw Estate and Stanage Edge Grindleford F4

From the former shooting estate of Longshaw, now a National Trust country park, walks can be taken to Burbage Rocks, a high moorland edge above Carl Wark hill-fort, and on to Stanage Edge. Southwest of Longshaw Lodge the land slopes down above the ancient, lichen-encrusted oak woods of Padley Gorge, a haunt of the pied flycatcher (*left*), which nests in tree holes.

Mam Tor E4

The ramparts of an Iron Age hill-fort and two Bronze Age burial mounds cap this breezy summit at the end of a spectacular two-mile ridge. The slopes shelve down either side to Edale and the Hope Valley. Comprising unstable layers of gritstone and shale, Mam Tor has suffered so many landslips that it has come to be known as the Shivering Mountain; in 1977 a severe slip caused the closure of the old A625 beneath its southern side. To the south, in the heart of Castleton's cave district, westward-bound traffic now travels through Winnats Pass, a limestone gorge formed after the last Ice Age.

Manifold Valley E7
Running along the floor of the valley, where the River Manifold flows underground beneath a dry, stony riverbed, the track of the former Leek and Manifold Light Railway is now surfaced and suitable for cyclists and wheelchair users. Above the gorge, a path leads up to Thor's Cave, where there is evidence of settlement from Iron Age to Roman times.

Monsal Trail D5
The former Buxton to Rowsley railway line now provides much of the route for this nine-mile footpath, which leads from Blackwell Mill Junction, east of Buxton, to Coombs Road viaduct, southeast of Bakewell. From the car park beside the old station at Miller's Dale, the trail leads eastwards past Litton and Cressbrook mills to cross the River Wye by the spectacular Monsal viaduct. Meanwhile the trail west from Miller's Dale leaves the railway at a tunnel entrance and follows the river, eventually passing along it by stepping stones close to the bank, beneath the sheer cliff of Chee Tor; this section can be treacherous, and the stepping stones sometimes become submerged when the river is in full spate.

The Roaches D6
This lofty moorland ridge provides superb upland walking. Beneath Roach End and hidden away in the forest, Lud's Church is a tiny, landslipped gorge (*see picture on page 91*). A secret place of worship for the Lollard sect, it may have taken its name from their leader, Walter de Lud-auk. Some maintain that Lud's Church was the Green Chapel mentioned in the anonymous medieval poem *Sir Gawain and the Green Knight*.

Rudyard Reservoir C6
Built in 1799 to feed the Caldon Canal, the reservoir and village of Rudyard were purchased by the North Staffordshire Railway Company in 1845 and developed as a resort. John Lockwood Kipling and his wife Alice became engaged while holidaying there and later named their son after the village.

Stanton Moor F6
Overlooking Darley Dale, this gritstone outlier in predominantly limestone country is dotted with prehistoric burial mounds. Here too is the Nine Ladies stone circle, erected for some mystical purpose during the Bronze Age and said to represent maidens turned to stone for dancing on the Sabbath. Paths lead on to the Cork Stone, one of a number of weathered outcrops, which is covered with centuries of graffiti (one dated 1613); metal rungs give access to the top.

Tissington Trail E8
Well-endowed with picnic sites and level for its entire length from Ashbourne to the High Peak Trail at Parsley Hay, this 13-mile trail gives easy walking or cycling, passing close to the villages of Tissington and Hartington.

THE PENNINE WAY

ABOVE *The Pennine Way passes across Bleaklow, whose peat bogs present one of the toughest challenges on the 270-mile walk across the Pennines and the Cheviot Hills.*

WHEN TOM STEPHENSON first proposed 'a long green trail ... a Pennine Way from the Peak to the Cheviots' in a newspaper article in 1935, he could scarcely have envisaged how popular such a trail would prove to be.

A committed access campaigner, Stephenson wanted to open up the moors of the Peak and Pennines, then barred to walkers by landowners and their gamekeepers. It took him 30 years of battling to set up the Pennine Way, Britain's first and toughest National Trail, which winds up the Pennines and Cheviots for 270 miles.

The route starts from the Nag's Head pub in Edale, before ascending the 2,000-foot Kinder Scout plateau. From there it crosses Bleaklow and Black Hill and over the South Pennine moors to enter the Yorkshire Dales. The Way then heads across Pen-y-Ghent, Wensleydale and Swaledale to Teesdale, reaching its highest point at 2,930-foot Cross Fell. The Tyne Gap and Hadrian's Wall are the next objectives, then the route passes through the conifers of Wark and Redesdale Forests to the Cheviot Hills before the final descent to Kirk Yetholm, just across the Scottish border.

Stephenson's 'faint line ... engraved on the face of the land' is now a veritable motorway for walkers, with many thousands of people every year attempting the mountain marathon. And nearly 20 miles of the 'long green trail' are now paved, using recycled slabs from defunct textile mills, to combat the erosion of the soft peat moors by the tread of thousands of pairs of boots.

CAVES

BEAUTIFUL AS *its hills and dales are, the Peak District is equally impressive below the surface. Stalactite and stalagmite formations and rich veins of the Blue John mineral provide the decorations in an underground wonderland through which visitors can travel by boat or on foot—or, if they are feeling particularly energetic, by abseil on a caving adventure.*

Bagshawe Cavern Bradwell F4
Fit visitors with no caving experience can get a taste of the sport with an adventure trip of some two hours in this cave system, discovered by miners in 1806. Participants should be prepared to crawl 60 feet in sweat-inducing conditions, and then encounter ice-cold water.

Blue John and Treak Cliff Caverns Castleton E4
Both of these caverns are mined for a blue and yellow crystalline fluorite known as Blue John, which is unique to the Castleton area.

BELOW *An intrepid potholer abseils down into the dark, underground depths of Blue John Cavern in Castleton.*

MAGICAL TRANSFORMATIONS

ABOVE *The impressive stalactite known as The Stork in Treak Cliff Cavern shows the magical changes wrought over millennia.*

ABOVE LEFT *Spires of limestone, such as Jacob's Ladder, are visible remnants of the coral reef that was ancient Derbyshire.*

UNIMAGINABLE AS it may seem today, 330 million years ago Derbyshire was a coral reef beneath a warm, shallow sea, and a thriving home for myriad sea creatures. These animals used calcium carbonate in the water to form their shells and skeletons, and, when they died, the debris slowly built up into thick layers of sediment. During the millions of years that followed, the sediment gradually transformed into rock, and the sea withdrew. Movements of the earth's crust, coupled with erosion, left parts of the ancient reef system exposed across much of northern England, including the Peak District, in the form of limestone outcrops and escarpments.

Limestone is soluble in slightly acid water, and over thousands of years ground water passing through natural cracks in the limestone has dissolved it, producing a landscape of hollows, ridges and caves well-loved by potholers. As the ground water drips and evaporates, its calcium carbonate content is left behind, slowly forming spectacular stalagmites and stalactites in caves such as the Treak Cliff and Peak Caverns of Castleton.

Circulating waters have also deposited valuable minerals in the cracks in the limestone: a form of fluorite known as Blue John—unique to Castleton—and metal ores of lead, copper, zinc and silver are the most common and have been mined since Roman times. Magpie Mine near Sheldon, for instance, has been a lucrative source of lead, as has Castleton's famous Speedwell Cavern—a subterranean canal—which was excavated by lead miners over 200 years ago.

ABOVE *The mineral known as Blue John, composed of bands of blue and yellow fluorite, has only ever been found in Castleton.*

The product is made into vases, jewellery and trinkets. Within Blue John Cavern are the colourful Grand Crystallised Cavern and the stalagmite-embellished Waterfall Cavern. The cave system has dramatic narrow depths. Treak Cliff Cavern is smaller but has a magnificent display of formations, including The Stork stalactite in the Dream Cave, and the Peak's richest vein of Blue John.

Heights of Abraham Matlock Bath **G6**
Within the wooded country park above the Derwent Gorge are two show caves reached from the valley by cable car. The tour of Great Rutland Cavern–Nestus Mine recalls the era of lead mining, while the natural cave of Great Masson Cavern has also been worked for lead.

Peak Cavern Castleton **E4**
A short walk from Castleton village centre leads to Britain's largest cave entrance. Until 1830 there was a community of rope makers living in the cave mouth (ropes were used in mining); one of their cottages survives and others have been excavated. Using a reconstructed ropewalk (a terrace cut into the stone), costumed guides show how rope was made. In times past, the local gentry were brought into the cave to enjoy banquets in the chamber known as Pluto's Dining Room, and were entertained by choral concerts in the Orchestral Chamber.

Poole's Cavern near Buxton **D5**
Situated just outside Buxton, the cave is believed to take its name from an outlaw who hid here in the 1440s. Earlier traces of occupancy, from Neolithic and Roman times, have been found, and are exhibited in a small museum. Concretions include delicate stalactites and unique 'poached egg' stalagmites, where water seeping through the overlying iron oxide has stained the rock orange. No other show cave in Britain has such a long horizontal view, extending fully 500 feet. In 1999, using ground-penetrating radar, it was discovered that the system extends for around one and a half miles beyond the show cave.

Speedwell Cavern near Castleton **E4**
Visitors are taken by boat through the underground canal (over 200 years old) of a former lead mine. The guides point out safety holes where miners sought shelter when dynamite was used to blast the rock. At the end of the tunnel is a soaring natural cavern, its roof out of sight, and a pit that the guides wryly claim to be 'bottomless'.

THE FAME OF THE PEAKS

***DANIEL DEFOE** described the Peak District as a 'howling wilderness', but many have gained inspiration from this land of contrasts. Its industrial towns have appeared in the fiction of Arnold Bennett and the paintings of Joseph Wright; and the delights of village life and the local birds and animals have been enchantingly evoked in the books of Alison Uttley and the drawings of Charles Tunnicliffe. The cities on the fringes of the Peaks have produced modern heroes in sport and politics, but the area is also rich in historical echoes: ladies of the court, mysterious muses and dealers in intrigue have all lived here.*

Richard Arkwright *(See feature on page 31)*

Anthony Babington
Catholic plotter
(1561–86, born in Dethick) A Catholic by birth, Anthony Babington served Mary, Queen of Scots during her captivity in Sheffield and fell in love with her, even though she was more than twice his age. He became involved in a plot—which now bears his name—to murder Mary's captor Elizabeth I and put his beloved on the English throne in her place. But letters between Babington and Mary were intercepted by a double agent, and Babington was condemned to death. Despite begging Elizabeth for mercy and offering £1,000 for his life, he was savagely executed for his part in the conspiracy.

Alan Bates
Actor

(Born 1934 in Allestree) Bates made his stage debut in 1955 in Coventry, and over a long career has appeared in numerous plays, including *Look Back in Anger* (1956) and *The Caretaker* (1960). His first film role was in *The Entertainer* (1960), and he went on to feature in many of the most popular and important films of the decade, most notably *A Kind of Loving* (1962), *Georgy Girl* (1966) and *Far From the Madding Crowd* (1967). He remains a popular actor today.

Arnold Bennett
Writer
(1867–1931, born in Hanley) Trained as a solicitor, Bennett came to journalism after winning a writing competition; he then moved to London and became assistant editor of *Woman* magazine. Bennett published his first novel, *A Man from the North*, in 1898 and in 1902 wrote *Anna of the Five Towns*, the first of his books about the Potteries (from which he omitted Fenton, the sixth of the Potteries towns). Although he spent much of his life in Paris and London, the area of his birth appears as the setting of almost all his major novels.

Bess of Hardwick
Lady in waiting

(?1520–1608, born at Hardwick Hall) From relatively humble beginnings, Bess of Hardwick managed to amass huge wealth and influence through four tactical marriages. First widowed at around the age of 15, Bess went on to marry Sir William Cavendish; together they built the first house on the Chatsworth Estate and had six children. After his death, Bess became lady in waiting to Elizabeth I. On the death of husband number four—the powerful sixth Earl of Shrewsbury—Bess became the second-richest woman in England after the Queen. She lived out her days at her childhood home of Hardwick, where she built the magnificent New Hardwick Hall.

Vera Brittain
Writer
(1893–1970, born in Newcastle-under-Lyme) Vera Brittain spent her formative years in Edwardian Buxton, but found it a stifling place. She escaped to Oxford University in 1914, but with the outbreak of the First World War temporarily abandoned her studies to work as a nurse. Brittain wrote of her wartime experiences in her autobiographical book *Testament of Youth* (1933), an indictment of war in which she tells hauntingly of losing the men she cared about most—her beloved brother and her fiancé. A pacifist and feminist, she was renowned for her outspoken views. Her daughter is the Liberal politician Shirley Williams.

Sir Francis Legatt Chantrey
(See pages 119–22)

THE FAME OF THE PEAKS (CONTINUED)

Charles Cotton *(See feature on page 167)*

Mary Fitton
Maid of honour
(*c.* 1578–1647, born in Gawsworth) Mary Fitton was a member of Elizabeth I's entourage but has achieved fame through her alleged association with William Shakespeare. She has been identified by some historians as the mysterious Dark Lady of Shakespeare's sonnets, whose fickleness was responsible for a darkening of his mood in the early years of the 17th century. Although Mary appears as a sultry beauty on a family portrait in Gawsworth Church, there is no conclusive evidence that she actually knew Shakespeare. But if she was the woman who spurned his love, then she is perhaps to be thanked for inspiring the playwright's greatest tragedies.

Georgiana, Duchess of Devonshire
Socialite and politician
(1757–1806, born at Althorp) Three days before her 17th birthday, Georgiana Spencer awoke and was told that she was to be married to the Duke of Devonshire that day. Like her descendant Diana, Princess of Wales, the new duchess soon became the most fashionable woman of her day, attracting the cream of society to her homes at Chatsworth and Devonshire House. Her dearest friend, Lady Elizabeth Foster, became a permanent member of the Devonshire household. The public glitter, however, concealed an unhappy personal life—Georgiana's extravagant lifestyle led her into serious debt; and the duke seemed to be the only man who was not totally charmed by her. Soon he, Georgiana and Elizabeth were living in a ménage à trois, with both women bearing the duke's children. In 1792 Georgiana became pregnant by Charles Grey (later Prime Minister); Grey abandoned her, and the duke exiled her to France. The following year she was allowed to return to Chatsworth, from where she pursued a career in politics until her death.

Sir Stanley Matthews
Footballer
(Born 1915 in Hanley) Stanley Matthews began his professional football career playing for Stoke City at the age of 17. Two years later he was picked for the England team and went on to become one of the most popular players of all time. Sporting in both senses of the word, Matthews did not receive a yellow or red card in his entire 33-year career, and in 1965 he became the first footballer to receive a knighthood. In that same year he finally retired from the game—at the age of 50.

Florence Nightingale *(See feature below)*

Emmeline Pankhurst
Suffragette
(1858–1928, born in Manchester) For 40 years Emmeline Pankhurst and her daughters Christabel and Sylvia led the fight for female suffrage. Pankhurst was gaoled on three occasions between 1908 and 1909; and in 1913 was imprisoned no fewer than 12 times under the government's notorious 'Cat and Mouse Act' whereby hunger strikers were released until they had regained their health, then sent back to gaol. When the First World War broke out in 1914, Pankhurst called off the suffrage campaign and the government released all 'suffragette' prisoners. Women's active participation in the war effort persuaded the government to establish voting equality for men and women after the conflict,

THE LADY OF THE LAMP

NAMED AFTER the Italian town where she was born in 1820, Florence Nightingale grew up on her family's Derbyshire estate. Florence found her sheltered life stifling, however, and after observing the hardships endured by her father's estate workers, she became intent on improving social conditions. At this time hospitals were insanitary, overcrowded places, staffed mainly by prostitutes who carried on their trade in the wards. In 1845 Florence announced to her family that she wanted to become a nurse. They were horrified, and fought her decision until 1853 when they finally allowed her to become superintendent of an institution for sick gentlewomen.

A year later war broke out in the Crimea. Incredibly, more lives were lost through disease than combat, and the Secretary for War, a personal friend, asked Florence to take a group of nurses to the field.

Wearing a uniform of grey dress and cloak and white cap designed by Florence herself, 38 nurses arrived in 1854 to be greeted by scenes of appalling filth and suffering—and obstruction from the medical authorities. As conditions worsened, however, her help was sought, and within a few months her innovative sanitation schemes had dramatically reduced the death rate. Her practice of walking the wards at night carrying a lantern soon earned her the nickname the 'Lady of the Lamp'.

ABOVE *Although ill health made Florence Nightingale an invalid in her later years, her influence on public life did not abate.*

After returning to Derbyshire in 1856, Florence established nursing schools and continued campaigning for improvements to public health. In 1910 this angel of mercy died, having achieved an overhaul of army conditions; a revolution in health care; and acceptance of nursing as a respectable profession for women.

and the Representation of the People Act, giving universal suffrage, was passed a few weeks before Pankhurst's death in 1928.

Dame Edith Sitwell *(See feature on page 28)*

Charles Tunnicliffe
Artist

(1901–79, born in Langley) Tunnicliffe studied at Macclesfield School of Art before winning a scholarship to the Royal College of Art in London. While he was still a student, some of his etchings were bought by the Victoria and Albert Museum. Tunnicliffe provided the illustrations for Henry Williamson's *Tarka the Otter* (1932), and this marked the beginning of a long and successful career in book illustration. He published six books of his own and produced many works for the RSPB, and although it is as a bird artist that he is best remembered he drew and painted a variety of other natural history subjects.

Alison Uttley
Children's writer

(1884–1976, born in Cromford) At the age of 46, Alison Uttley was widowed and took up writing to support herself and her school-age son. Her first book, *The Country Child* (1931), was followed by a series of stories revealing her love of the countryside and introducing characters such as Little Grey Rabbit, Little Red Fox and Sam Pig, who soon became firm favourites with a generation of young readers.

Izaak Walton *(See feature below)*

Josiah Wedgwood
Potter and industrialist

(1730–95, born in Burslem) Wedgwood's innovative mass production and distribution techniques were instrumental in transforming Staffordshire pottery into a major industry. He pioneered a cream earthenware that was cheap enough to be bought by the masses, yet sufficiently sophisticated for the Queen herself to order a tea service—this line was subsequently called Queen's ware. Wedgwood is best known, however, for his jasper ware, which features white classical designs on a coloured (often blue) background. Despite losing a leg in his thirties, Wedgwood remained active: he campaigned for the abolition of slavery and was a successful scientist. He fathered five children and was the grandfather of no less a figure than Charles Darwin.

Joseph Wright (Wright of Derby)
Painter

(1734–97, born in Derby) Joseph Wright's home town was also one of the birthplaces of the Industrial Revolution, and, although the artist began his career as a portraitist, most of his paintings reflect a delight in the new machinery of industry and science and its applications. His most famous works are realistically observed industrial scenes, lit dramatically by the moon or by candlelight: Wright became known as the greatest painter of light effects of his time.

ABOVE *Joseph Wright's 1768 oil painting* Experiment with an Air Pump *shows the artist's masterly use of light to emphasise the drama of the new machinery of the Industrial Revolution.*

FISH TALES

LEFT *An illustration by Arthur Rackham in a 1931 edition of* The Compleat Angler *shows Izaak Walton fishing on the River Dove.*

FIRST PUBLISHED IN 1653, Izaak Walton's book *The Compleat Angler* has become a classic of English literature, both for its expertise on fishing and its evocation of country life. Walton's days of angling were spent with his friend Charles Cotton along the River Dove, one of his favourite haunts.

Born in Stafford in 1593, Walton spent most of his youth in London, eventually setting himself up as a milliner and draper. Yet despite his humble trade, Walton showed literary leanings and claimed as friends the poet John Donne and the ex-Provost of Eton, Sir Henry Wotton. His first publication, a biography of Donne, appeared in 1640. Two years later, when the English Civil War broke out, Walton returned to Staffordshire, finding solace from the nation's troubles in fishing. The result of these days 'viewing the silver streams gliding silently' was the *Angler*.

The book is written as a dialogue between Piscator, a fisherman, and Venator, a hunter, in which Piscator inducts his companion into the joys of fishing with a mixture of anecdotes, poems, songs and fishing lore. Two years after the book's publication, a second, enlarged edition was issued, and this in turn was revised in 1676, when a section on fly-fishing by Cotton was added.

Walton lived to the ripe old age of 90 and died in 1683. Although he wrote other biographies, including one of the poet George Herbert, it is the *Angler*—an 'excellent good book' as Cotton described it—that has continued to cast its timeless spell.

HISTORIC INNS AND PUBS

The Bull i' th' Thorn Buxton **D5**
Tudor panelling and a stone-flagged floor transport customers back in time when they step into the bar. Travellers along the old Roman road (now the A515) have slaked their thirsts here since 1472, and the Bull was an important coaching inn on the Derby to Manchester route during the 18th and 19th centuries. Its name is believed to be a combination of the original name, the Bull, and a later one of Hurdlow Thorn; among several carvings on the front of the building is a scene of a bull entangled in a thorn bush.

The Castle Castleton **E4**
Three hundred years ago, in the reign of Charles II, the landlord here was found guilty of brewing beer without a licence. Patrons today can relax and enjoy a drink safe in the knowledge that the inn is all above-board; any suspect goings-on can be blamed on the four ghosts said to haunt the Castle—look out for a jilted bride or a city gent in a pin-striped suit.

The Cheshire Cheese Inn Hope **F4**
This inn takes its name from the days when guests—predominantly those working the old salt route across the Pennines to Yorkshire—paid for their board and lodgings in Cheshire cheese. The inn's location near the Pennine Way makes it a popular base for walkers.

The Devonshire Arms Beeley **G5**
The Devonshire Arms is less than a mile from Chatsworth House, the Duke of Devonshire's estate. The inn first opened its doors in 1747, and in those days was in competition with three other hostelries in the village, but it is the only one to have survived the test of time. In the 19th century Charles Dickens often enjoyed the warm hospitality that is still offered here. It is rumoured that the inn played a part in the 20th century's first royal scandal by providing rooms for King Edward VII and his mistress Alice Keppel.

The Grouse and Claret Rowsley **F6**
The Grouse and Claret was known as the Station Hotel when neighbouring Rowsley railway station was in operation. Tradition has it that the good companions of J. B. Priestley's eponymous novel set off on their travels from this building. The inn's new name is that of a type of fishing fly made from a grouse feather and claret thread, and it is conveniently located near the River Derwent where good fishing can be had.

The Miners Arms Eyam **F5**
Lead miners who worked the seams of the surrounding district were once frequent patrons of this inn, which also served as a meeting place for the lead-mining industry's Barmote Court. Built in 1630, the inn predates the spread of bubonic plague to Eyam, as do the ghosts of two unfortunate girls who died in a fire on the site before the inn was built. In 1684 the Miners Arms was the scene of much drunken merriment when the local vicar became inebriated while celebrating a baptism and promptly married the landlord's daughter. In his drunken state, the vicar had forgotten that he was already engaged to someone else, who in turn sued him for his ungentlemanly behaviour.

Ye Olde Gate Inne Brassington **F7**
Ye Olde Gate Inne has been a popular watering hole since 1616. The former clientele of lead miners and travellers stopping at the London to Manchester turnpike, or the Gate, has since been replaced with walkers and tourists. Black-leaded ranges and scrub-top tables create a warm atmosphere in this stone building which is supported by timber beams salvaged from wrecks of the Spanish Armada. If the front door seems too conventional a way of leaving at closing time, there's always the option of the highwayman's secret escape tunnel.

ABOVE *The hand-painted sign of the Ship Inn depicts the* Nimrod, *which carried Shackleton on his expedition to the South Pole.*

The Ship Inn Wincle **C6**
In times past access to the grounds of the Swythamley Estate could be gained only with a pass obtained from the Ship. It is often wrongly assumed that the inn was named in honour of the *Nimrod*—the ship illustrated on its sign—which Sir Philip Brocklehurst of Swythamley Hall boarded in 1907 to accompany the great explorer Sir Ernest Shackleton on his expedition to the South Pole. In fact, its name dates back to the 19th century and is believed to have been a return compliment by the local squire to a friend who had named a ship *Swythamley*. The *Swythamley* was wrecked in 1862, but the *Nimrod* returned safely to England in 1909 with Brocklehurst on board.

Sutton Hall Sutton Lane Ends **C5**
In the 11th century Sutton Hall stood on monastic lands, but a century later it had become a baronial residence. It reverted once more to a religious centre, as a convent, in 1950, only taking on its present role as a pub, restaurant and hotel in the early 1980s. Sutton Hall, near the village of Sutton Lane Ends (which is known locally as Sutton), revels in its rich history: parts of the building have walls that are four feet thick, and the Sutton family's 16th-century coat of arms hangs proudly above the fireplace in the library.

CALENDAR OF FESTIVALS AND EVENTS A SELECTION

THE CALENDAR FOR *the Peak and surrounding areas features long-standing traditions such as well dressing and any number of country fairs and shows, sheepdog trials, carnivals, antique fairs, vehicle rallies and arts festivals. Tourist information centres have further details of these and numerous other events. Precise dates may vary.*

JANUARY

MANCHESTER CHINESE NEW YEAR FESTIVITIES Street celebrations in Chinatown (January or February).

FEBRUARY

ASHBOURNE SHROVETIDE FOOTBALL An unruly survival of the precursor to soccer, played between Up'ards and Down'ards, who live on opposite sides of Henmore Brook. Played on Shrove Tuesday and Ash Wednesday, this free-for-all features any number of players, with goalposts set three miles apart.
WINSTER PANCAKE RACES Following the bell-ringing on Shrove Tuesday.

MARCH

MANCHESTER IRISH FESTIVAL Celebrating Irish arts and culture in various locations across the city.

APRIL

CHESTERFIELD EASTER MARKET Open-air market and street entertainment.

MAY

CASTLETON GARLAND DAY Around May 29, known as Oak Apple Day, the Garland King rides through the village, leading his consort and a procession featuring children dressed in white. A wooden, beehive-shaped frame adorned with a garland of flowers and leaves covers the upper part of the King (*above*).

The ceremony is probably a pagan celebration of the coming of spring but also commemorates the return to the throne of King Charles II in 1660.
ELVASTON CASTLE COUNTRY PARK (NEAR DERBY) DERBYSHIRE COUNTY SHOW
LEEK ARTS FESTIVAL Music and arts throughout the month.
MANCHESTER STREETS AHEAD Street theatre and mime festival.
TISSINGTON WELL DRESSING The longest-standing venue of the Peak's best-known tradition, which takes place in various villages from May until September (*see feature on page 155*).

JUNE

ETRURIA INDUSTRIAL MUSEUM, STOKE-ON-TRENT ETRURIA CANAL FESTIVAL A gathering of boats (rides available) plus steam rally, jazz, crafts and children's activities.
STOKE-ON-TRENT POTTERIES MARATHON Twenty-six-mile race around the area.
TIDESWELL WAKES WEEK CARNIVAL and WELL DRESSING Wakes weeks date from Victorian times when factories closed for the local festival or 'wake'.
WINSTER WAKES FESTIVITIES

JULY

ALPORT CASTLES WOODLANDS LOVEFEAST Communion service dating from the 18th century when preachers converted farm workers and others through camp meetings.
BUXTON FESTIVAL AND FRINGE Opera, dance and jazz.
CHESTERFIELD MEDIEVAL MARKET
DERBY CAMRA BEER FESTIVAL Held by the Campaign for Real Ale.

AUGUST

BAKEWELL SHOW Horticultural exhibits and show jumping events.
EYAM PLAGUE SUNDAY SERVICE Held on the last Sunday of the month at the so-called Cucklet Delf, an outdoor site where the rector, William Mompesson, held church services during the plague (*see feature on page 153*).
MACCLESFIELD FOREST CHAPEL RUSHBEARING The Peak's only surviving example of the tradition of strewing rushes in the church.
MATLOCK BATH ILLUMINATIONS From late August to the end of October the riverside gardens are illuminated, and at weekends decorated boats make trips on the River Derwent.

SEPTEMBER

WIRKSWORTH CLYPPING THE CHURCH Parishioners hold hands round the churchyard in a symbolic embrace of the church.

OCTOBER

BOLSOVER CASTLE FIREWORKS AND LASER SHOW
MACCLESFIELD MUSIC FESTIVAL

NOVEMBER

BOLSOVER VICTORIAN FESTIVAL AND FIREWORKS

DECEMBER

MATLOCK–CROMFORD BOXING DAY RAFT RACE
STOKE-ON-TRENT GLADSTONE POTTERY MUSEUM VICTORIAN CHRISTMAS FESTIVAL

USEFUL INFORMATION

Listed below are the details of Tourist Information Centres for a selection of popular Peak District destinations. Please note that these details may be subject to change.

ASHBOURNE
13 Market Place
Ashbourne
Tel. (01335) 343666

BAKEWELL
Old Market Hall
Bridge Street
Bakewell
Tel. (01629) 813227

BUXTON
The Crescent
Buxton
Tel. (01298) 25106

CHESTERFIELD
The Peacock Centre
Low Pavement
Chesterfield
Tel. (01246) 345777

DERBY
Assembly Rooms
Market Place
Derby
Tel. (01332) 255802

GLOSSOP
The Gatehouse
Victoria Street
Glossop
Tel. (01457) 855920

MATLOCK
Crown Square
Matlock
Tel. (01629) 583388

The following websites may also be of interest (NB website addresses can change):

Peak on-line:
http://www.interfacedesign.co.uk/peakhome.htm

Peak District National Park Authority:
http://www.peakdistrict.org

High Peak Net Ltd:
http://www.highpeaknet.com

The-peaks.co.uk:
http://www.the-peaks.co.uk

INDEX

and acknowledgments

Note: page numbers in ***bold*** refer to captions for illustrations

D

E

F

N

O

P

ACKNOWLEDGMENTS

The editors gratefully acknowledge the use of information taken from the following publications during the preparation of this volume:

AA Focus on the Peak District, AA Publishing 1997
AA Ordnance Survey Leisure Guide: the Peak District, The Automobile Association/Ordnance Survey 1996
The Buildings of England: Cheshire by Nikolaus Pevsner and Edward Hubbard, Penguin 1978
The Buildings of England: Derbyshire by Nikolaus Pevsner, Penguin 1979
The Buildings of England: Staffordshire by Nikolaus Pevsner, Penguin 1975
Country Eye by Geoffrey Young, George Philip 1991
Down on the Farm, Reader's Digest Association Ltd 1986
Eyam and the Plague by Carolyn Fooks and Nick McCann, Derbyshire Countryside Ltd
The Forgotten Arts by John Seymour, Dorling Kindersley 1984
The Good Pub Guide edited by Alistair Aird, Ebury Press, 1998
The Great Artists edited by Clive Gregory, Marshall Cavendish Ltd, 1986
Industrial Archaeology of the Peak District by Helen Harris, David & Charles 1971
The Ordnance Survey Landranger Guidebook to the Peak District, Ordnance Survey and Jarrold, 1990
The Peak District by John Barnatt and Ken Smith, B. T. Batsford Ltd, 1997
The Peak District by K. C. Edwards, Fontana 1973
The Peak District by Lindsey Porter, David & Charles 1989
The Peak District by Rob Talbot and Robin Whiteman, Weidenfeld and Nicolson, 1997
Regional Wildlife: the Peak District by Paul Sterry, Dial House 1995
Stories of the Derbyshire Dales by John Agg Large, Footprint Press Ltd 1997
Sunday Times Book of the Countryside edited by Philip Clarke, Brian Jackman and Derrik Mercer, Macdonald General Books 1980
Town & Village Discovery Trails: the Peak District by Norman James and Abigail Bristow, Sigma Leisure 1997
Traction Engines in Focus by John Crawley, John Crawley Ltd, 1982
Traditional Folk Remedies by Michael Howard, Century 1987
Transformation of a Valley by Brian Cooper, Heinemann 1983
Visitor's Guide: Peak District by Lindsey Porter, Moorland Publishing Co. Ltd 1995
The Which? Guide to Country Pubs edited by Peter Haydon, Which? Ltd, 1999
Women of Derbyshire by Susan Watson, Footprint Press Ltd

PICTURE ACKNOWLEDGMENTS

T = top; *C* = centre; *B* = bottom; *L* = left; *R* = right

Front Cover Mike Williams Photo Library/Peak National Park/Ray Manley **Back Cover** *T* V. K. Guy Ltd/Mike Guy *B* Hedgerow Publishing Ltd **2** Rod Leach **4** Karen Frenkel Landscape Photography **6–7** The National Trust Photo Library/Joe Cornish **10** *T* Courtesy of Sheffield Galleries and Museums Trust *B* Private Collection **11** Mike Williams Photo Library **12** The National Trust Photo Library/Joe Cornish **13** Images Colour Library **14** Collections/Robin Weaver **15** *T* Woodfall Wild Images/Peter Moore *C* Woodfall Wild Images/Robert Dickson *B* Mike Williams Photo Library **16** David Broadbent **17** Mike Williams Photo Library **18** Images Colour Library **19** *C* Julian Cotton Photo Library *R* Collections/Gerry Gavigan **20** *T* Collections/Robin Weaver *B* Mike Williams Photo Library/The Bentley Collection **21** Derbyshire Dales District Council **22** Natural Image/Peter Wilson **23** Collections/Robin Weaver **24–5** Collections/Robin Weaver **26** Roger Redfern **27** Collections/Robin Weaver **28** *L* Jeremy Whitaker *R* Hamiltons Photographers Ltd/Horst P. Horst **29** Skyscan **30** *T* Collections/Robin Weaver *B* Pamela Kettle **31** *TR* Bridgeman Art Library, London/Philip Mould, Historical Portraits Ltd, London *BL* Bridgeman Art Library, London/Science Museum, London *BR* The Arkwright Society **32** *TL* NHPA/Stephen Dalton *TR* Woodfall Wild Images/John Robinson *C* Woodfall Wild Images/Robert Dickinson *B* The National Trust Photo Library/Andrew Cooper/BBC Natural History Unit Picture Library **34** Mike Williams Photo Library **35** Mike Williams Photo Library **37** Ann Ronan/Image Select **38** Karen Frenkel Landscape Photography **40–41** Mike Williams Photo Library **42** *L* David Broadbent *R* Woodfall Wild Images/Steve Austin **43** *L* Hulton Getty *R* Collections/Robin Weaver **44** Mike Williams Photo Library/Donald Berwick **45** Natural Image/Mike Lane **46** Geoscience Features **46–7** Mike Williams Photo Library **47** John Cleare/Mountain Camera **48** *T* Woodfall Wild Images/M. Hamblin *B* Mike Williams Photo Library **49** *T* John Cleare/Mountain Camera/Chris Craggs *B* Karen Frenkel Landscape Photography **50** Hedgerow Publishing Ltd **51** *L* Geoscience Features *TR* Collections/Robin Weaver *BR* Mike Williams Photo Library **52** Karen Frenkel Landscape Photography **53** Bayerische Staatbibliothek, Munich **54** Jim Rubery **55** Cliff Williams **56** Roger Redfern **57** *L* NHPA/David Woodfall *R* Woodfall Wild Images/Steve Austin **58** Roger Redfern **59** Chesterfield Museum and Art Gallery **60** *T* Chesterfield Museum and Art Gallery *B* Ann Ronan/Image Select **61** Jim Rubery **62** *T* Science & Society Picture Library/National Railway Museum *C* Science & Society Picture Library/National Railway Museum *CR* Science & Society Picture Library/Science Museum *BL* Bridgeman Art Library, London/Institute of Mechanical Engineers, London *BR* Science & Society Picture Library/National Railway Museum **63** Science & Society Picture Library/National Railway Museum **64** Science & Society Picture Library/National Railway Museum **66** By permission of the Trustees of the Chatsworth Settlement **67** *L* David Tarn *C* By permission of the Trustees of the Chatsworth Settlement *R* By permission of the Trustees of the Chatsworth Settlement **69** Karen Frenkel Landscape Photography **71** Hedgerow Publishing Ltd **72** Frank Lane Picture Agency/Bill Broadhurst **73** *L* Holt Studios International/Julia Chalmers *R* Compassion in World Farming/C. Beer **75** *L* Rare Breeds Survival Trust *R* Mike Williams Photo Library **76** Mary Evans Picture Library **77** Stephen J. G. Hall **78** *L* Rural History Centre, University of Reading *R* Bridgeman Art Library, London/Bibliothèque Centrale, Ghent, Belgium **79** *L* Collections/Robin Weaver *R* Rural History Centre, University of Reading **80** Holt Studios International/Nigel Cattlin **81** Roger Redfern/E. Hector Kyme **82** Derbyshire County Council: Derbyshire Record Office D505. Reproduced by permission of the County Archivist **83** Mary Evans Picture Library **84** *T* Karen Frenkel Landscape Photography *B* By permission of the British Library **85** David Broadbent **86** Ann Ronan/Image Select **88** Collections/Robin Weaver **89** *L* Bridgeman Art Library, London/British Library, London *R* Collections/Robin Weaver **91** *TL* Bridgeman Art Library, London/Bradford Art Galleries and Museums, West Yorkshire *TR* Collections/Robin Weaver *B* Bridgeman Art Library, London/Private Collection **92** *T* NHPA/Michael Leach *B* Woodfall Wild Images/M. Hamblin **93** Mike Williams Photo Library **94** Robin Weaver **95** *L* By permission of the British Library *R* Bridgeman Art Library, London/Private Collection **96** *L* Topham/Ray Green *R* Bridgeman Art Library, London/© Southampton City Art Gallery **99** *L* Hedgerow Publishing Ltd *R* Royal College of Arms **100** Hedgerow Publishing Ltd **100–101** Mike Williams Photo Library **101** *T* Hedgerow Publishing Ltd *B* Mike Williams Photo Library **103** Collections/Robin Weaver **104** The National Trust Photo Library/Joe Cornish **105** Woodfall Wild Images/M. Hamblin **106** Karen Frenkel Landscape Photography **107** *TL* Derby Local Studies Library *TR* Collections/Clive Shenton *B* Christine Richardson/John Lower **108** *L* The Boat Museum *R* British Waterways Photo Library **108–9** Trustees of the Wedgwood Museum, Barlaston, Staffordshire **109** Robert Harding Picture Library/Nelly Boyd **110** British Waterways Archive/National Railway Museum, York **111** Images Colour Library **112** *T* Derek Pratt/Waterways Photo Library *B* Adlington Hall/Steve Allen **113** Robin Weaver **114** Karen Frenkel Landscape Photography **115** Derek Pratt/Waterways Photo Library **116** Ruskin Gallery, Collection of the Guild of St George, Sheffield **117** Jim Rubery **118** Jim Rubery **119** The Royal Collection © Her Majesty The Queen **120** *L* Frank Lane Picture Agency/M. J. Thomas *TR* Natural Image/Peter Wilson *BR* NHPA/Alan Williams **121** By courtesy of the National Portrait Gallery, London/The Maas Gallery **123** *T* Derbyshire Countryside Ltd *R* Robin Weaver **124** English Heritage **126–7** Karen Frenkel Landscape Photography **128** *L* By courtesy of the National Portrait Gallery, London *R* Natural History Museum, London **129** *T* Karen Frenkel Landscape Photography *B* Jim Rubery **130** *TL* Mary Evans Picture Library *TR* Mary Evans Picture Library *C* The Bodleian Library, University of Oxford/MS.Laud.Misc.581, fol.22v *B* Bridgeman Art Library, London/Castle Museum and Art Gallery, Nottingham **132** Collections/Robin Weaver **133** Collections/Robin Weaver **135** *T* Robin Weaver *B* Holt Studios International/Nigel Cattlin **136** Roger Redfern **137** Natural Image/Bob Gibbons **138** *L* Bridgeman Art Library, London/Castle Museum and Art Gallery, Nottingham *R* Ann Ronan/Image Select **139** Robin Weaver **140** Natural Image/Peter Wilson **141** *T* Public Record Office/Alecto Editions *B* Public Record Office **142** Natural Image/Peter Wilson **143** Royal College of Physicians **144** *L* Science Photo Library/Erika Craddock *R* Bridgeman Art Library, London/British Library, London **145** *T* Natural Image/Bob Gibbons *BL* Reader's Digest/Plate from *Traditional Folk Remedies* by Michael Howard, 1987, Century Hutchinson *BR* Science Photo Library/Paul Biddle **146** Karen Frenkel Landscape Photography **147** Karen Frenkel Landscape Photography **148–9** Rod Leach **150** *T* Haddon Hall *B* Robert Harding Picture Library/Roy Rainford **151** *T* The National Trust Photo Library/Andreas von Einsiedel *CL* Derbyshire Countryside Ltd/Brian Lawrence *CR* Collections/John D. Beldom *B* By permission of the Trustees of the Chatsworth Settlement **152** David Broadbent **153** *T* Mike Williams Photo Library *B* Derbyshire Countryside Ltd/Nick McCann **154** *T* V. K. Guy Ltd/Mike Guy *B* Collections/Clive Shenton **155** Mike Williams Photo Library **156** *T* Reader's Digest *B* Marketing Manchester **157** *T* Raymonds Press Agency *B* The National Trust Photo Library/Nick Meers **158** *T* The National Trust Photo Library/Rupert Truman *BL* The National Trust Photo Library/Nadia MacKenzie *BR* The National Trust Photo Library/Andrew Butler **159** The National Tramway Museum **160** *L* Mary Evans Picture Library *R* Collections/Robin Weaver **161** *T* Trustees of the Wedgwood Museum, Barlaston, Staffordshire *B* Royal Doulton Ltd **162** *T* Collections/Robin Weaver *BL* Karen Frenkel Landscape Photography *BC* Woodfall Wild Images/Paul Hicks *BR* Woodfall Wild Images/John Robinson **163** Jim Rubery **164** *TL* Collections/Robin Weaver *TR* Derbyshire Countryside Ltd/Andy Williams *BL* Hedgerow Publishing Ltd *BR* Geoscience Features **165** *L* Topham *R* The National Trust Photo Library/John Bethell **166** *T* Hulton Getty *C* By courtesy of the National Portrait Gallery, London *B* Topham **167** *T* Bridgeman Art Library, London/National Gallery, London *B* Bridgeman Art Library, London/Victoria and Albert Museum, London **168** *T* Karen Frenkel Landscape Photography *C* Kaleidoscope Press/Vintage Inns *B* Network/Homer Sykes **169** Collections/Brian Shuel

SEPARATIONS Studio One Origination Ltd, London
PAPER Périgord-Condat, France
PRINTING AND BINDING Printer Industria Gráfica SA, Barcelona, Spain

615007/1